MASTERING THE ART

OF

PULLED THREAD EMBROIDERY

ACKNOWLEDGEMENTS

Once again I would like to thank my many friends and students for the encouragement I received during the long process of drafting this book. Special thanks go to my long time friend and advisor Dorothy Armstrong of Delanco, New Jersey, who once again devoted much love and time to the typing of the manuscript. I also wish to thank Alfred Studer and William Kurz for doing the photography for the frontispiece and back cover respectively; their expertise is greatly appreciated.

Ilse Altherr

No part of this book may be reproduced mechanically, electronically or by an other means including photo-copying, without written permission of the author.

Copyright 1989 Ilse Altherr,
P. O. Box 127 Lancaster, NH   03584
Printed in the United States of America

First printing September 1989

ISBN 0-9624090-0-6

TABLE OF CONTENTS

	Page
INTRODUCTION	1
THE MANY NAMES OF PULLED THREAD EMBROIDERY	2
THE MATERIALS	3
Fabric, threads, needles, frames, hoops	
COLOR	8
Shading, contrast in value	
WHAT YOU MUST KNOW BEFORE YOU BEGIN	9
Pulling..in which direction?	
Fastening ends. Direction and Method	
HOW TO BEGIN	12
The importance of the doodle cloth	
Transferring design to fabric	
Choosing the proper patterns	
IDEAS FOR PROJECTS	15
Design-Sketches	
THE STITCHES	19
Straight or Corded Stitches (Patterns A)	20
Double Back Stitches (Patterns B)	36
Crossed Stitches (Patterns C)	55
Faggot Stitches (Patterns D)	69
Wave Stitches (Patterns E)	85
Four-sided Stitches (Patterns F)	104
Eyelet Stitches (Patterns G)	119
Composite Patterns	132
REFERENCES	133

INTRODUCTION

The purpose of this book is to guide the Pulled Thread enthusiast towards excellence in embroidery technique as well as in understanding the principles of design for this charming and enjoyable form of stitchery.

As with most types of embroidery, Pulled Thread stitches and stitch patterns are divided into families, each family representing one particular type of stitch and its variations. The basic stitches must be learned first. One stitch can be varied in so many ways that it alone can form many patterns and elaborate combinations of these to suit the most discriminating taste and thus be used for an entire project. Tension, stitch length and stitch direction are the most important factors in Pulled Thread Embroidery.

The suitability of the ground fabric as well as of the threads is of utmost importance. Guidance for this is given in the following pages.

Please read all information before you begin so you will know where to look when in doubt.

Happy Pulling!

THE MANY NAMES OF PULLED THREAD EMBROIDERY

Also known in the embroidery world as Drawn Fabric, Dresden Work, Tondra Embroidery and lately as Deflected Element, the effect is to resemble lace-like, open work. The fabric threads are distorted in one direction or another, depending on the chosen pattern. The distortion occurs by the tension applied to the embroidering thread. A slight, medium or tight tension will thus determine the airiness of the pattern. Not all patterns can be worked in all three types of tension. Much depends on the ground fabric, the placement of the design as well as the adjacent patterns. I hope to cover most of these aspects in the next pages. However, I always recommend that you work a sample of the pattern first on the same material you have chosen for the project to see how the pattern behaves.

Pulled Thread patterns are often combined with other counted patterns. Straight or satin stitches for example will add texture and play of light as well as lustre to the overall pattern. Early Dresden work, so named after the city of Dresden, now East Germany, shows this combination frequently in its patterns.

In Germany during the early 18th century, Pulled Thread was often incorporated in Pique work. After the layered Pique work was completed, the bottom layer of fabric was trimmed away and the Pulled Thread pattern was then worked into the top layer only. Vests and men's coats were embroidered in this manner which due to its double layer and inserted stuffing added some weight and body to the garment.

Point de Saxe as well as Flemish point also translate into Pulled Thread embroidery as it was worked in Belgium and the Netherlands.

THE MATERIALS

Fabrics

Since we want to create an open, airy effect as in lace, the ground fabric should preferably be loosely woven; its warp and weft threads must not be interlocked.

I prefer to work on even weave linen, not only for its beautiful sheen, but also for its durability and high quality. It is important however that the linen be chosen with caution as to its number of threads per inch as well as to its weight or thickness of these threads. For example: A fabric with a 25 thread count per inch is suitable if the threads are thin and the space between the threads distant. One can also buy fabric with the same thread count which is totally unsuitable for Pulled Thread Embroidery, but would be suitable for Blackwork or cross stitch. The diagrams below will explain this more clearly. It is difficult to purchase the proper fabric just by its thread count, as listed in mail order catalogs, without seeing the actual example of the goods. If you must order, try to get a sample swatch before ordering quantity.

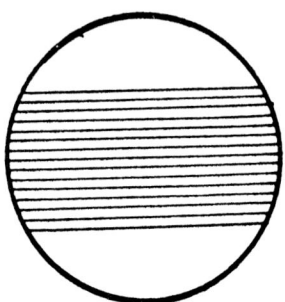   

Thin Threads, Large Spaces   Thick Threads, Small Spaces
Suitable   Not Suitable

The looser the weave, the better the pull! Here a word of caution is in order; a loosely woven fabric, while producing a lacier, more open effect, also distorts more readily. While we want distortion in the pattern itself, we must take care that the edges of the cloth are not warped to the point where framing or hemming becomes impossible. This distorting of the fabric can be avoided by choosing the proper stitches or stitch patterns for the item to be embroidered.

A piece which will be framed, i.e. a picture which will be mounted over a backing board, securely laced and subsequently framed, in most cases, can be pulled back into shape when laced firmly around the backing board. See "Overture & Finale to Linen Embroidery," Ilse Altherr, 1987.

A piece of table linen regardless of size must have a perfectly straight edge. The slightest distortion of the fabric will result in an unsightly hem. If the embroidery is worked close to the hemline, patterns with minimal distortion should be used. If the embroidery is placed towards the center of the cloth, the fabric between the embroidery and the hem will assure an even hemline.

A fabric with a high thread count, closely woven, is not suitable for this technique, as little room for distortion is available. The rule applies mainly to today's needlewomen, as time, patience, eyesight and determination, as well as the need and availability of fine lace is measured differently in today's times. Museums throughout the world show many fine pieces worked on batiste and lawns, counting as many as fifty-eight or even more threads per inch. The finest contemporary piece I have seen is a floral composition stitched by Mary Fry on fifty-eight count, loosely woven polyester fabric.

I have told you much about fabric, but helped you little in your selection. Suggested linens are as follows:

"Dublin" from Zweigart, 25 thread count, available in white ecru and many pastel tints.

Eva Rosenstand/Clara Weaver, 27 count and 30 count, available in ecru.

Danish Handcraft Guild linen, 27 count.

OOE linen, 25 count.

Surely there are many more suitable linens available in today's well stocked market; the ones listed are just a sampling and reflect those fabrics I have used widely.

For canvas workers I recommend the available Congress cloth or 18 count canvas. To distort the canvas threads more readily it helps if the canvas is moistened slightly in the area which is pulled. This makes the canvas more pliable. Beware however of water stains, especially when using Congress cloth. Dampen slightly the immediate and only area which is to be embroidered. A damp cotton swab works well as you can carefully moisten the canvas row by row.

Beware of colored linen fabric should this be our choice. Dyes do not penetrate the linen fibers easily which results in white or bleached spots in the areas where warp and weft cross. When the fabric threads are distorted, these white spots emerge giving the piece a spotty effect. Distort some threads in a corner of the bolt before buying!

Threads

Threads should be strong to withstand the pull. Use a fine thread for a small stitch pattern, i.e. a pattern worked over a small number of threads, Cotton Perle #12 works very well on a 27 count linen. A slightly heavier Perle #8 can be used for patterns with less pull and a heavier thread yet can be used for those patterns which are not pulled at all but are combined in composite patterns. Cordonnet cotton also works very well. It is strong, comes in different weights and is readily available. Since it is strongly twisted, it is a bit more difficult to handle and tends to curl and knot.

One can also pull with multiple strands of six-stranded cottons such as Mouline, commonly known as floss. A fine DMC Cebelia lacemaking or tatting cotton as well as linen threads are a good choice.

Should colored threads be used in Pulled Thread Embroidery? It is my personal opinion that one should not use a strongly contrasting thread for patterns that are pulled. As in lace, the pulled patterns are distinguishable for their lacy effect, the holes rather than the stitches. Stitches should be as invisible as possible so that the eye is never distracted from the lacy, airy effect of the embroidery. A minimal variation in value of that of the fabric can sometimes enhance the embroidery, but contrasting colors should be avoided. For example, a slightly darker thread color such as DMC #644 stitched on ecru linen can give the project a desirable antique look, while a white thread on ecru linen can lighten the overall effect considerably.

Composite patterns can confidently be enhanced with contrasting thread if the color is used for that part of the pattern which is not pulled. All flat or satin stitches fall under this category.

Flat stitches are best worked with a smooth, fluffy type of thread, not with a highly twisted one. Six-stranded cotton is my preferred choice as I can adjust the thickness by using two, three or more strands to suit the ground fabric best. Total coverage is desirable. A smooth, silky surface can easily be achieved by separating the individual strands one by one, dampening them at the same time as they are being stripped. This will remove any kinks left in the thread and will aid in laying the threads smoothly next to one another. To dampen the threads simply hold the six-strands firmly at one end having first wrapped a moist sponge, cotton ball, folded paper towel or any other soft object, around the strands and "stripping" the strands one by one through this moist aid. By the time the needle is threaded the strands should be dry, smooth and ready to be worked.

Needles

You need a supply of tapestry needles. A good size is #24 for fine threads and #22 for heavier ones. You also need a chenille needle of the same size for working outlines and other surface stitches which are frequently used in combination with pulled thread patterns. A chenille needle has a sharp point with which one can pierce the fabric threads, a **MUST** when outlining a shape. Tapestry needles have a blunt point and must be used for the stitch patterns as fabric threads must never be pierced.

Frames and Hoops

If you are working on a project which is small enough to be stapled or tacked firmly onto a stretcher frame I would recommend that you use this method to keep the fabric taut at all times and the design visible in its entirety. You will then be able to judge at a glance if the design maintains its proper balance with every new stitch pattern that is incorporated. A larger piece or a long narrow strip as for a ruffle or valance, must be worked on a hoop for comfort in stitching. The hoop must be wrapped before it can be used and only wooden hoops are recommended as they will retain their rigidity. Plastic hoops will be squeezed while stitching thus loosening the fabric considerably.

Never use the tight machine embroidery hoops, those which have the inner metal and outer flat, plastic ring. These hoops cannot be wrapped and will mar the fabric, leaving a shiny ring mark.

Some pulled patterns can be worked "in the hand" or rolled over a finger, but not too many patterns will benefit from this method. Tightly pulled straight or rope stitches as well as other small count stitches such as four-sided or wave stitch, can be effectively worked in this manner. I prefer to use a hoop in all cases although I sew rather than stab most tightly pulled stitches.

Instructions for Wrapping the Embroidery Hoop

Wrapping a wooden hoop serves several purposes. Since the linen material must be kept taut at all times, the tightly fitting hoop will flatten the linen fibers thus creating a shiny ring mark which is not removable. It is important that both rings of the hoop be wrapped in order to cushion the fabric the hoop holds. A wrapped hoop will also keep the fabric tighter as the material will no slip but cling to the wrapping. Furthermore it will keep the fabric clean.

Gauze bandage material from your drugstore works best to wrap a hoop. The bandage comes readily cut in a convenient strip and is rolled for added comfort. All you need to do is to fasten one end to the hoop, right under the screw, with a bit of adhesive tape, wrap around and around on a slight slant until you reach the screw again. Fasten both ends with a few stitches and remove the tape. Do the same with the inner ring starting anywhere. Do not wrap too thickly since there must be enough room between rings to accommodate the thickness of the fabric.

COLOR

Shading - Contrast in Value

As in all types of embroidery techniques, shading is of utmost importance in order to give a design the character it deserves. Pulled Thread Embroidery is no exception. Since we are not using colored threads, shading must be done by way of choosing the proper patterns for each area. The more open or lacy a pattern, the darker its value. Since we are working "holes" rather than stitches, these are of darker value as they get larger or more abundant, since it is the hole that lets the underlying object such as a table in the case of a tablecloth, a garment in case of a collar, show through. It is therefore important that the patterns be chosen carefully and be distributed in a balanced manner throughout the entire design.

A densely embroidered pattern or one with hardly any or no tension, would be of a light character while an open, lacy pattern, one to which tight tension has been applied, would be of darker value.

Again, the doodle cloth will direct you in choosing the appropriate patterns for your project.

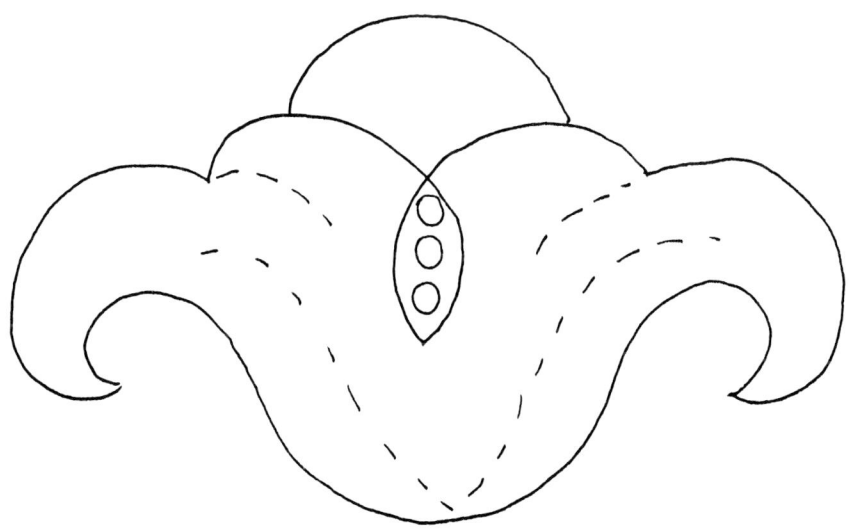

WHAT YOU MUST KNOW BEFORE YOU BEGIN

"Pull" can be referred to as the tension which is applied to the embroidering thread and/or to the direction in which the tension is applied.

Tension

The look of a pattern will change greatly with the tension applied to the thread. For an open, lacy look, more tension is desirable. A stitch pattern which needs a large number of threads, i.e. a large pattern, must not be pulled too tightly as the fabric would bunch up and buckle and the pattern would become unsightly. A flat stitch in a composite pattern in most cases requires no pull at all.

A doodle cloth is of utmost importance when determining the needed tension for a pattern. More about this in the next chapter.

Direction

Here we will explore the direction in which the tension is applied. To illustrate this further, directional pull can be applied by pulling up, down, to the right, to the left or away.

Pulling UP: Fabric threads are being picked up with the needle and the tension is applied with an upward motion, thus gathering the fabric threads together in the upper part of the work. Illustration A.

Pulling DOWN: Tension is applied in a downward motion. Illustration B.

Pulling to the RIGHT/LEFT: Tension is applied to the side. Illustration C.

Pulling AWAY: Tension is applied in a perpendicular direction to the work, i.e. at a right angle. Illustration D.

Illustrations

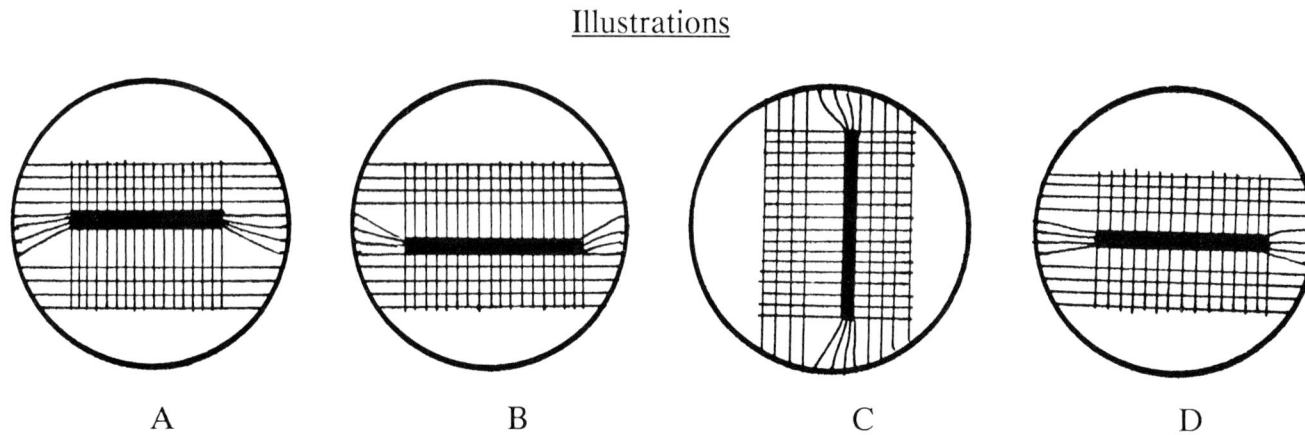

A B C D

General Rule

As in most counted thread techniques, Pulled Thread embroidery is worked in rows. These could be horizontal, vertical or diagonal. Since we want to produce a tidy hole for a lacy pattern effect, the directional pull must thus be applied in the opposite direction from the way the needle travels. For example; if the row is worked towards the right, the pull should be applied to the left and vice versa. The same is true if the direction of the pattern leads upward, the pull must be made downward and vice versa.

Example

The diagrams illustrated below are for the four-sided stitch. Diagram A shows a row worked from the right to the left while the row in Diagram B is worked from left to right. Lets first analyze the directional pull.

Diagram A. Vertical arrow 1 points down. By working arrow 2 next, stitch 1 is being pulled up, those a hole is formed as tension is applied. If we were to reverse the direction of arrow 4, stitch 4 would not have a clean hole. At the end of the row we want to place another row of stitches above the one already worked. If all arrows, i.e. stitches point down, clean holes with the correct pull are being created. If instead we were to place a row below the first one, the vertical arrows/stitches of the first row should point up. Diagram B. If you keep this rule in mind, you should have no problem traveling from one row to the next.

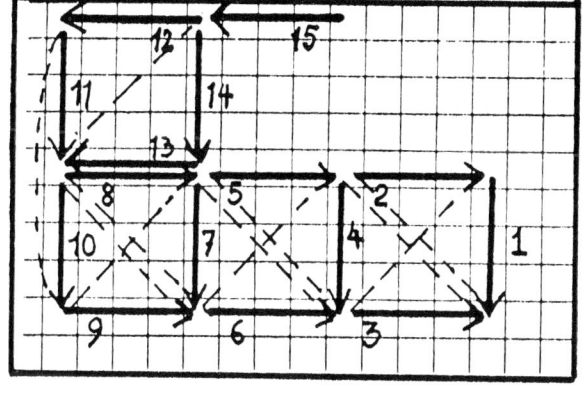

Diagram A

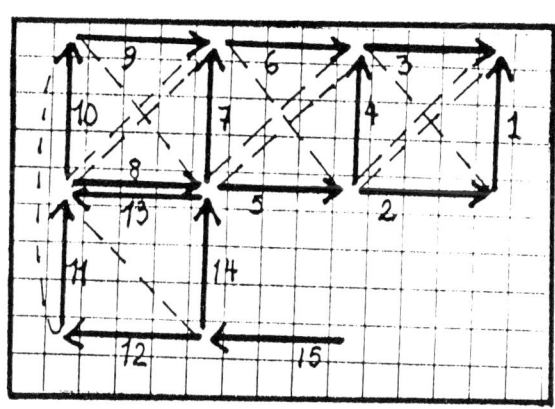

Diagram B

Fastening Ends

In Pulled Thread embroidery special care must be taken that the thread to be fastened, being the start of a thread or the end, be guided under the existing stitches in such a manner that it does not show through the holes and that the correct directional pull is maintained on the first and last stitch. It is recommended that the new thread be fastened after it has been used up rather then stitched over with the pattern stitches. The directional must also be observed. The same rules apply as stated in the previous chapter.

An exception to the above presents itself when working a row of tightly pulled satin stitches. These could be straight stitches, one stitch between each fabric thread, or slightly slanted stitches, one stitch in every other or every third hole of the fabric. For example: the very first thread being used in such a row of tight satin stitches may very well be stitched over, that is, the "tail" may be placed in such a position that the stitches to follow will cover it, thus securing it firmly under the row. See Diagram A. The end of the thread, however, must not be run under, i.e. fastened under the just completed row, but rather be placed ahead, that is, in the direction the row progresses and brought up through the fabric temporarily. The stitches of the new thread will then cover this tail which may then be cut off. The beginning of the new thread may be sewn under the last stitches taken. Diagram B.

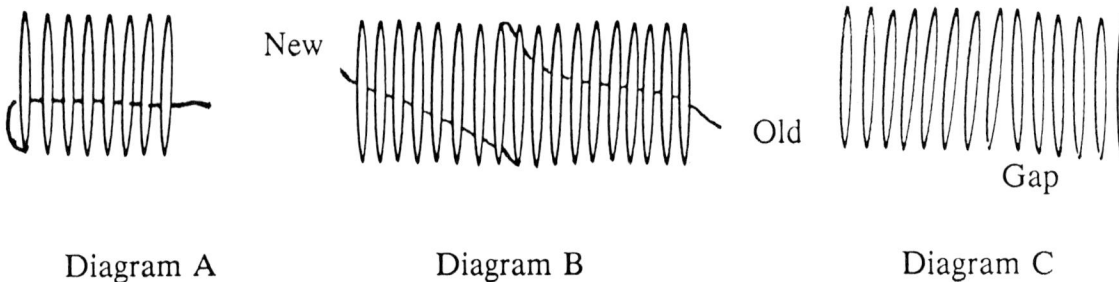

Diagram A   Diagram B   Diagram C

The reason for this is that the straight stitches slant ever so slightly when worked with directional pull. When these stitches are spaced by one, two or more threads, the slant becomes even more apparent. Were you to run the end of the thread back under the stitches, the directional pull would be applied in the opposite direction, thus creating an unsightly gap between the stitches. Diagram C.

In one sentence: You must tie in from the direction you came and out in the direction you are going.

HOW TO BEGIN

The Importance of the Doodle Cloth

Pulled Thread Embroidery patterns, when drawn on graph paper, do not look at all as when embroidered on the cloth. It is therefore difficult to know what a pattern will look like before it is actually stitched. Since one must determine the value in order to balance the design, it becomes necessary to stitch a small swatch on a doodle cloth, preferably of the same fabric as will subsequently be used for the project. Only then can one determine whether the pattern is of open, lacy character or if it will result in a more dense structure, thus lighter in value.

To start, I suggest that you tightly stretch a piece of even weave linen, approximately 10" x 10" in size, in a 6" wooden embroidery hoop. Keep it in your work basket so that it is ready when you wish to try out a stitch pattern. You will then have a good reference sampler when needed. See page 14.

Transferring the Design to Fabric

This can be successfully accomplished in a number of ways. I am listing my preferred method. You probably have your own favorite way.

Since all outline marks must be completely covered or erased so that no traces are apparent and since most of the time the embroidery is executed in white, ecru or other light tints, I stay away from permanent markings, such as Nepo markers or India ink. I trace the entire design onto tissue paper first and then, measuring carefully, I mark a straight line through the design horizontally and vertically. These lines need not be through the center of the design, but somewhere on the paper. They will aid you in placing the design on the true straight of the fabric, i.e. the grain, horizontally and vertically.

Place the tissue paper over the linen in such a way that the straight lines match the fabric threads. A basting line through the fabric, visible through the tissue, will aid in the placing of the design. Pin the tissue to the fabric in several places. With large running stitches, baste the tissue firmly down, always keeping the lines and fabric threads matched.

With a light, but contrasting sewing thread baste through all lines of the design taking small, accurate stitches. When shapes come to a sharp point, such as the tip of a leaf for example, take one stitch into the tip and another backing into the first, so that the tip of the leaf is defined. Use this method in all sharp turns or curves. When all basting is completed, rip the tissue away and the design will be clearly outlined on the ground fabric.

Choosing the Proper Patterns

Not all patterns are suitable for all designs or areas within a design. The size of a pattern, that is the number of threads needed to show its effect must carefully be considered. A small area is best filled with a small scale pattern, while a larger unit may benefit from a larger one. In many instances, the scale of one pattern can be altered by (a) working over a larger/smaller number of threads as shown in Diagram A, (b) by spacing the pattern by one or more threads, as in Diagram B, (c) by adding a complimentary pattern, thus creating a composite, Diagram C.

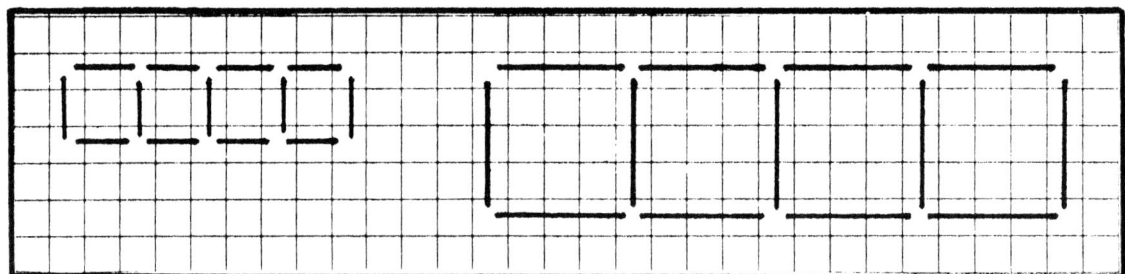

Diagram A

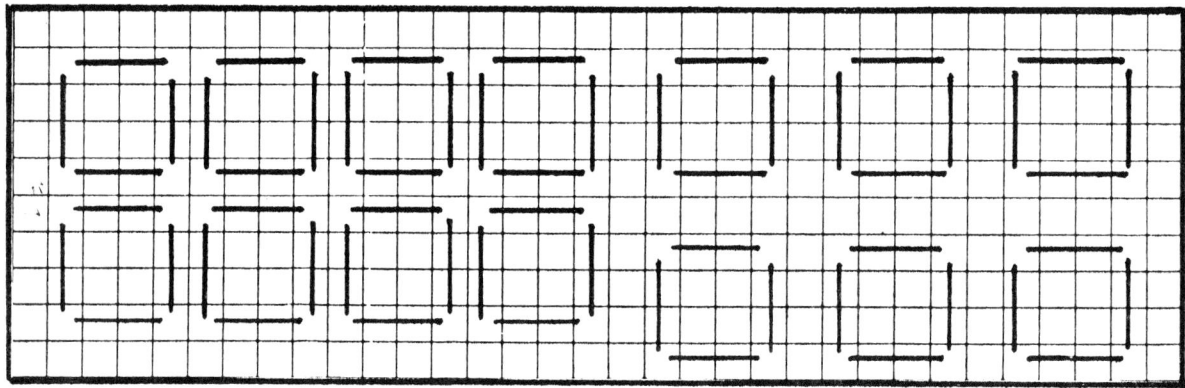

Diagram B

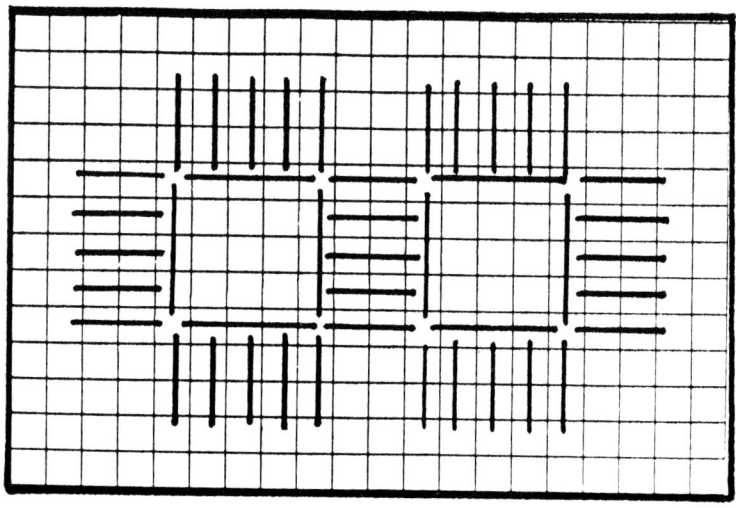

Diagram C

The value or density of the patterns and their proper balance within a design is also important. Please see "COLOR." Shading, contrast in value, page 8.

Another aspect to take into consideration is the look of the pattern in relation to the design element. If filling the wing for an angel you might want to try a light, feathery pattern as pattern No. G-8 or a variation of it. The feathers for a bird would also look nice if a similar pattern were used. Depicting a leaf would be nice if a pattern which can change direction, so that veins become apparent, would be chosen. Here again, the doodle cloth is a must.

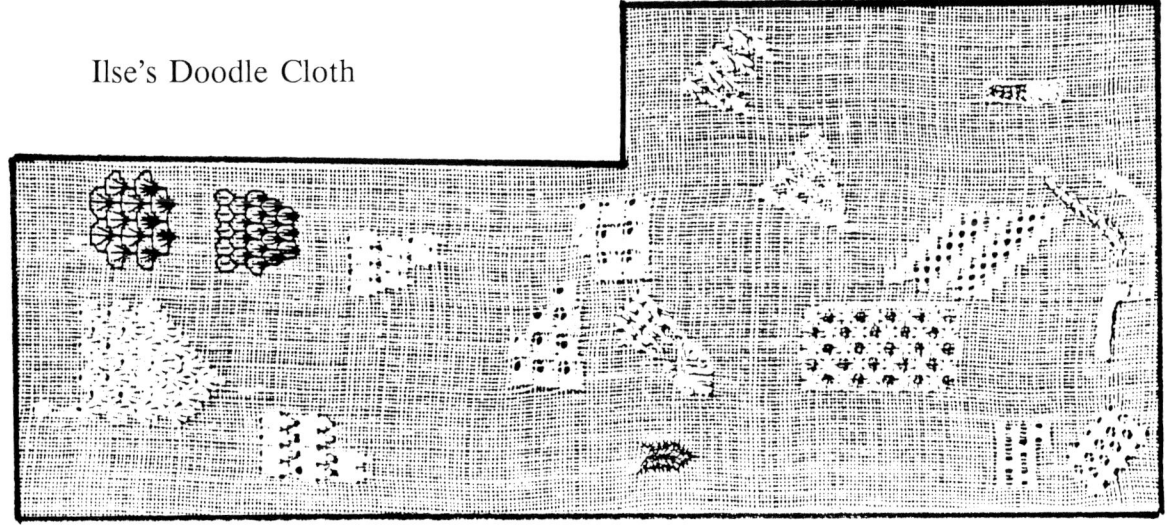

Ilse's Doodle Cloth

IDEAS FOR PROJECTS

Below and on he following pages you will find a few line drawings which you may trace and use for your personal enjoyment. I suggest that you work them as notebook examples to acquaint you with the patterns and their behavior on different ground fabrics and thread count. Then, when you create your own designs you will have a nice collection of reference samplers.

Since it is quite impossible to tell the looks of a pattern when worked on fabric from its graph on squared paper, the following should be taken to heart; for a small area only a small pattern, one which takes up but a few threads per repeat should be used. A larger pattern for which a larger number of threads must be used will only result in too many compensations which will muddle the overall effect. These larger patterns will look stunning when used on very fine fabric (large thread count), large areas, or in borders.

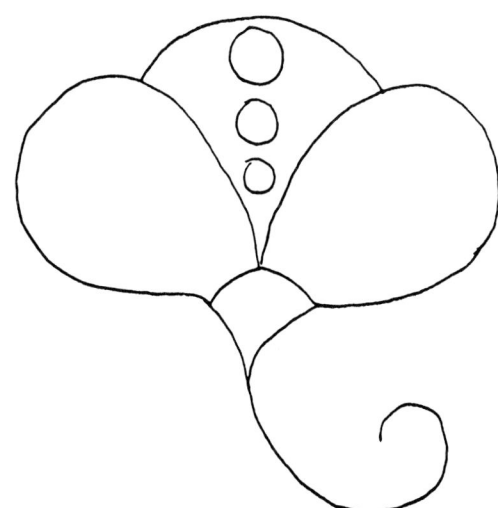

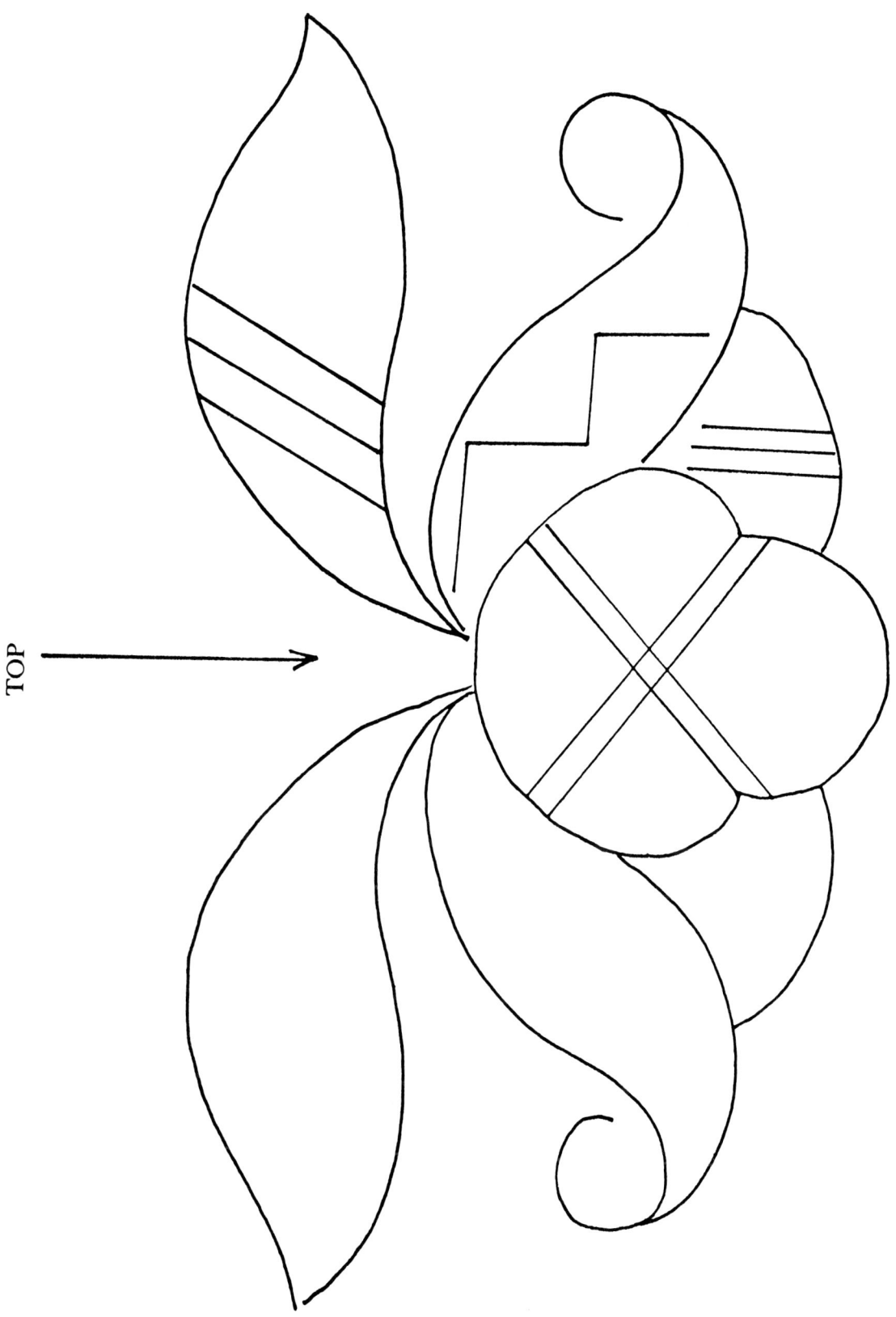

The arrow shows the grain of the fabric. The lines within the shapes are suggesting the direction for a pattern. The choice of the pattern is yours alone.

THE STITCHES

In the following section you will find samplers and stitch diagrams for close to one hundred stitch patterns. These patterns are grouped in families A through G. Each family of stitches is shown on individually embroidered samplers and identified on a "map." Many of these stitches are variations of one particular stitch. These variations are not limited to those shown as many more can be derived from one stitch alone or by simply combining two stitches into one pattern. These combinations are sometimes called composite patterns and are usually more beautiful and intricate than their simpler version.

It would be an enormous undertaking if a diagram for each of these composite patterns would be represented. Some you will find on the samplers and diagrams; they will give you an idea of how to go about combining many more. You will enjoy a pattern that much more when you have made your own combination. A sheet of graph paper, a pencil and eraser is all it takes for that first creative step.

STRAIGHT OR CORDED STITCH - SATIN STITCH

This is the first stitch one must learn. It is the A of the alphabet and without it there would be no Pulled Thread embroidery. Corded also means straight. It implies however, that a straight stitch is pulled into a tight cord. Sometimes, this is also called rope, or rope stitch.

A straight stitch is simply a stitch which comes out at A and goes down at B. This could be in a horizontal, vertical or diagonal line. The diagonal need not be "true diagonal" but can be slanted ever so slightly or to a degree to suit the stitch pattern.

The count can also vary to a great extent. This means that the stitch can cover, i.e. go over two or more fabric threads or intersections of threads. Care must be taken in that the threads don't bunch up but lay nicely side by side. This is especially important when a relatively large number of threads, six or more, are corded or pulled together.

Composite patterns are often combined with straight stitches. Not always are these stitches pulled but more often than not only a slight tension is applied. This will then contrast effectively with the other tightly pulled stitches.

It is possible to become quite creative with the straight stitch as one can vary its tension and size within one area and thus arrive at the desired effect. An example of this can be seen on the embroidered leaves photographed on the cover of this book. The leaf shown below is another example of how the stitch can be used in an unconventional manner.

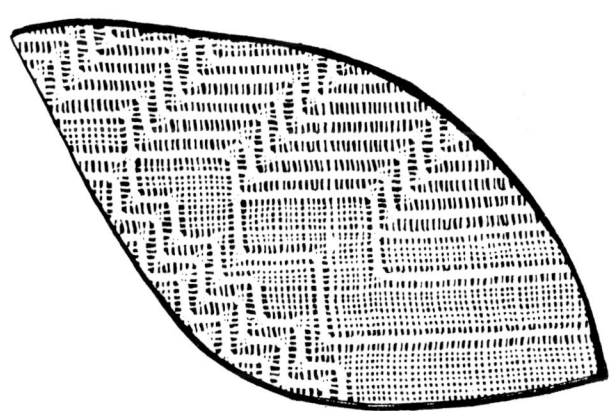

STRAIGHT AND CORDED STITCH SAMPLER

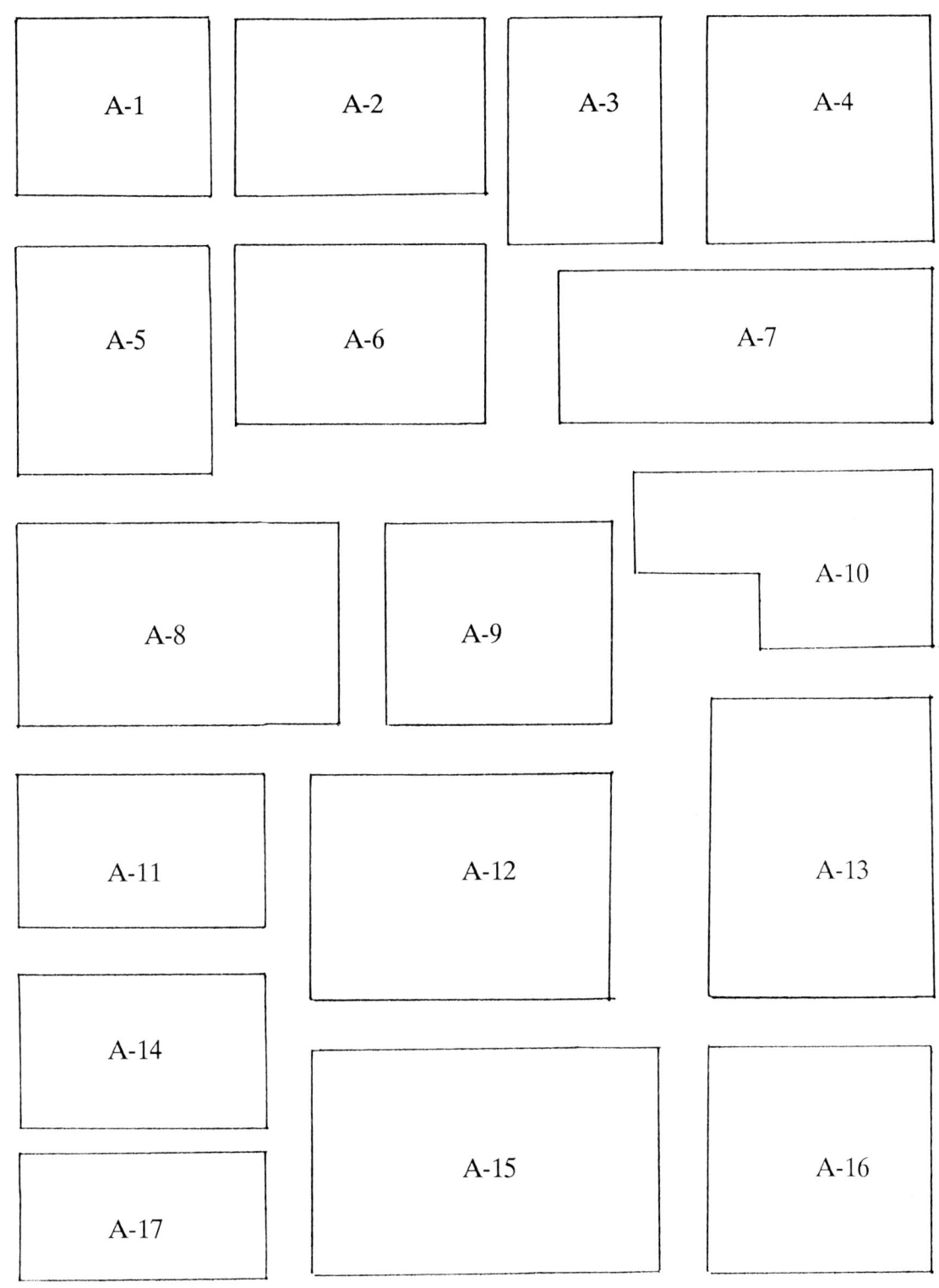

IDENTIFICATION CHART A - STRAIGHT AND CORDED STITCHES

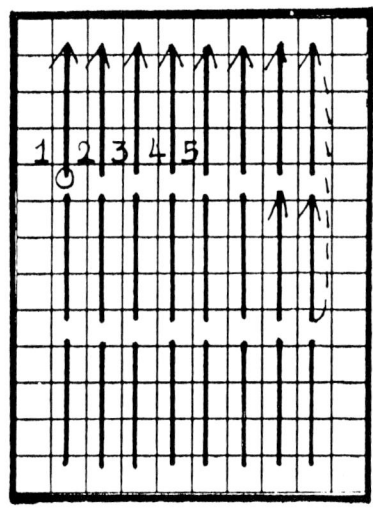

Pattern A-1 - Tight Pull

Work horizontal rows of tightly pulled vertical stitches over four fabric threads.

Pattern A-2 can be found on next page.

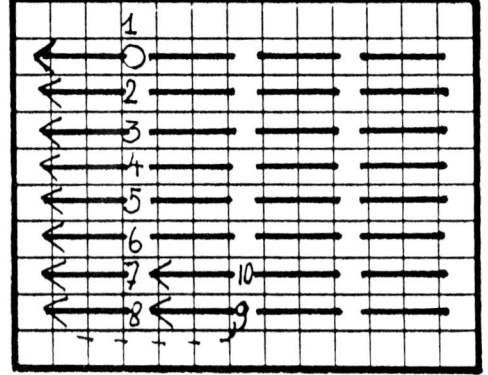

Pattern A-3 - Tight Pull

Work vertical rows of tightly pulled horizontal stitches over three threads.

The direction of stitch/arrow must be maintained to insure the proper pull when proceeding from one row to the next.

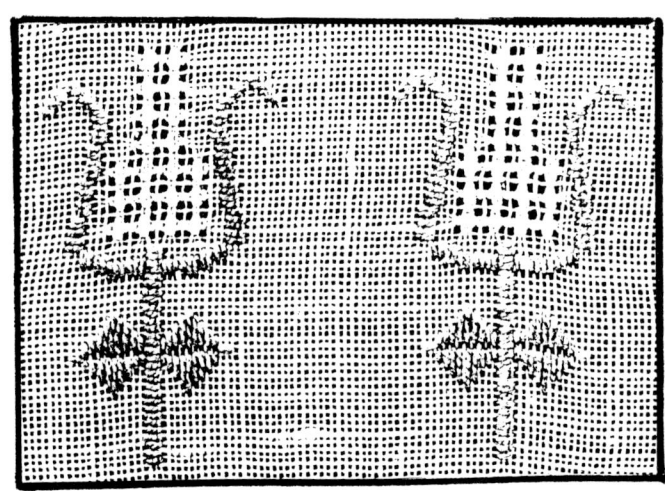

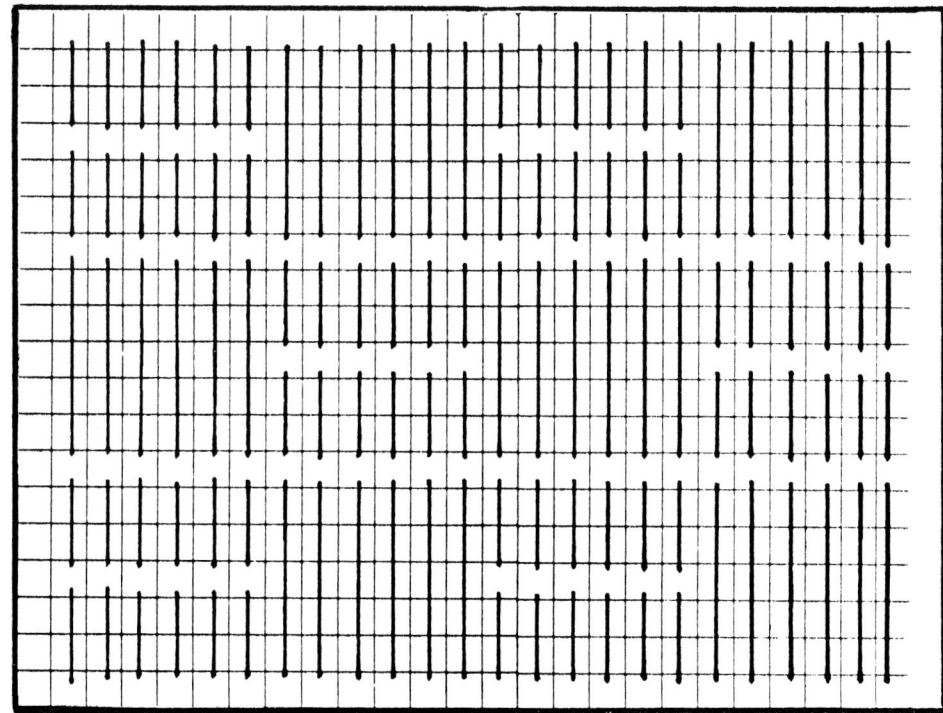

Pattern A-2

Tight Pull

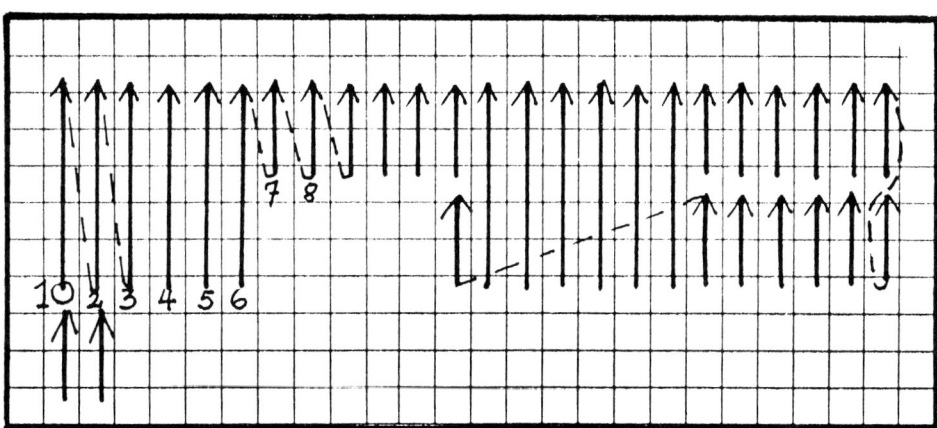

Work six vertical stitches over six fabric threads followed by six vertical stitches over three fabric threads. Repeat this sequence across the row.

Return over the same row by working another set of short stitches placed immediately under the first set. Travel under the long stitches to the next position.

In the next row the position of the long and short stitches is alternated.

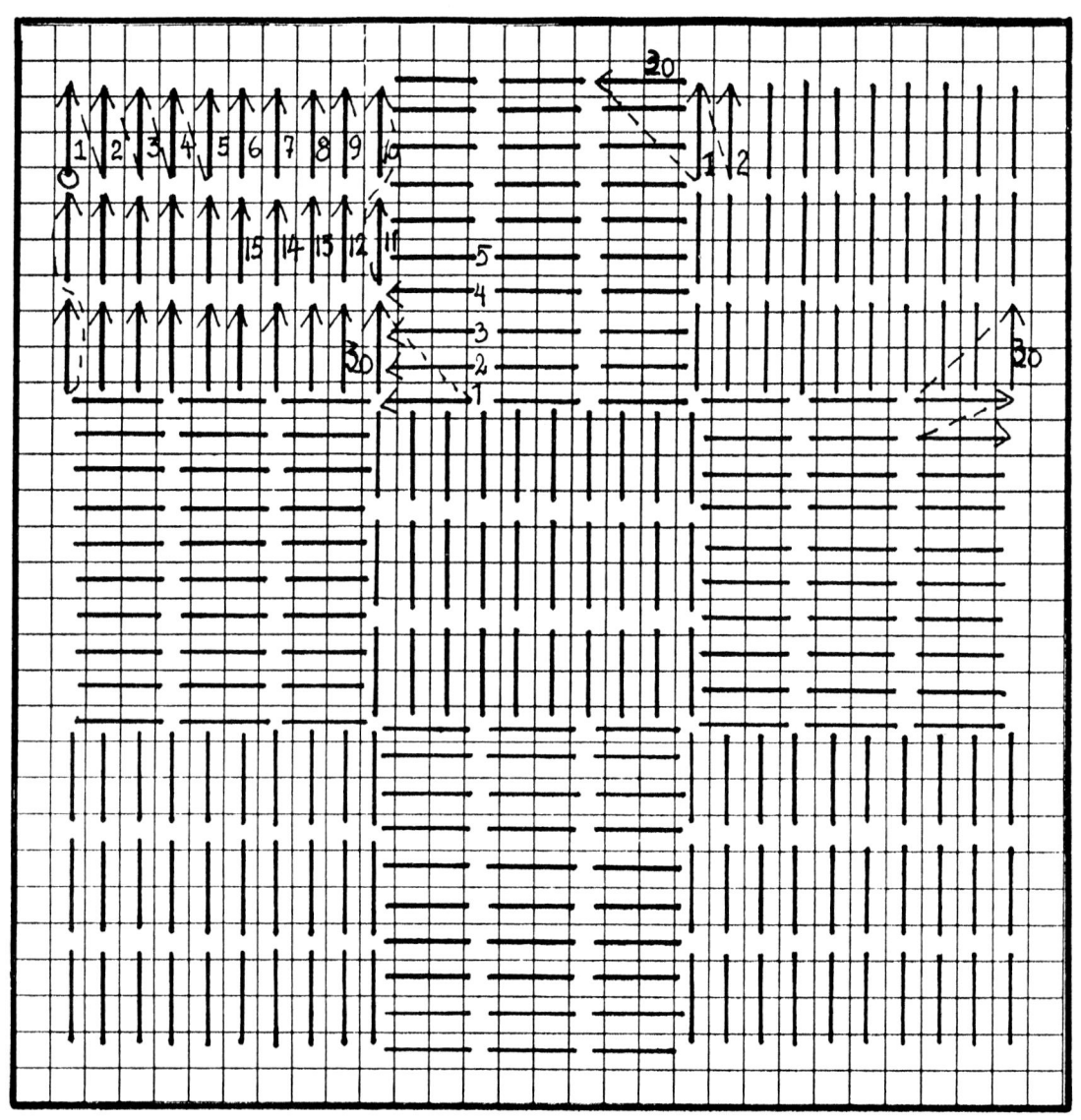

Pattern A-4 - Tight Pull

First Group: Work horizontal rows of ten vertical stitches over three threads back and forth as indicated by numbered arrows.

Second Group: Work vertical rows in the same manner. Travel from last vertical stitch (30) to first horizontal stitch (1) as indicated by broken line.

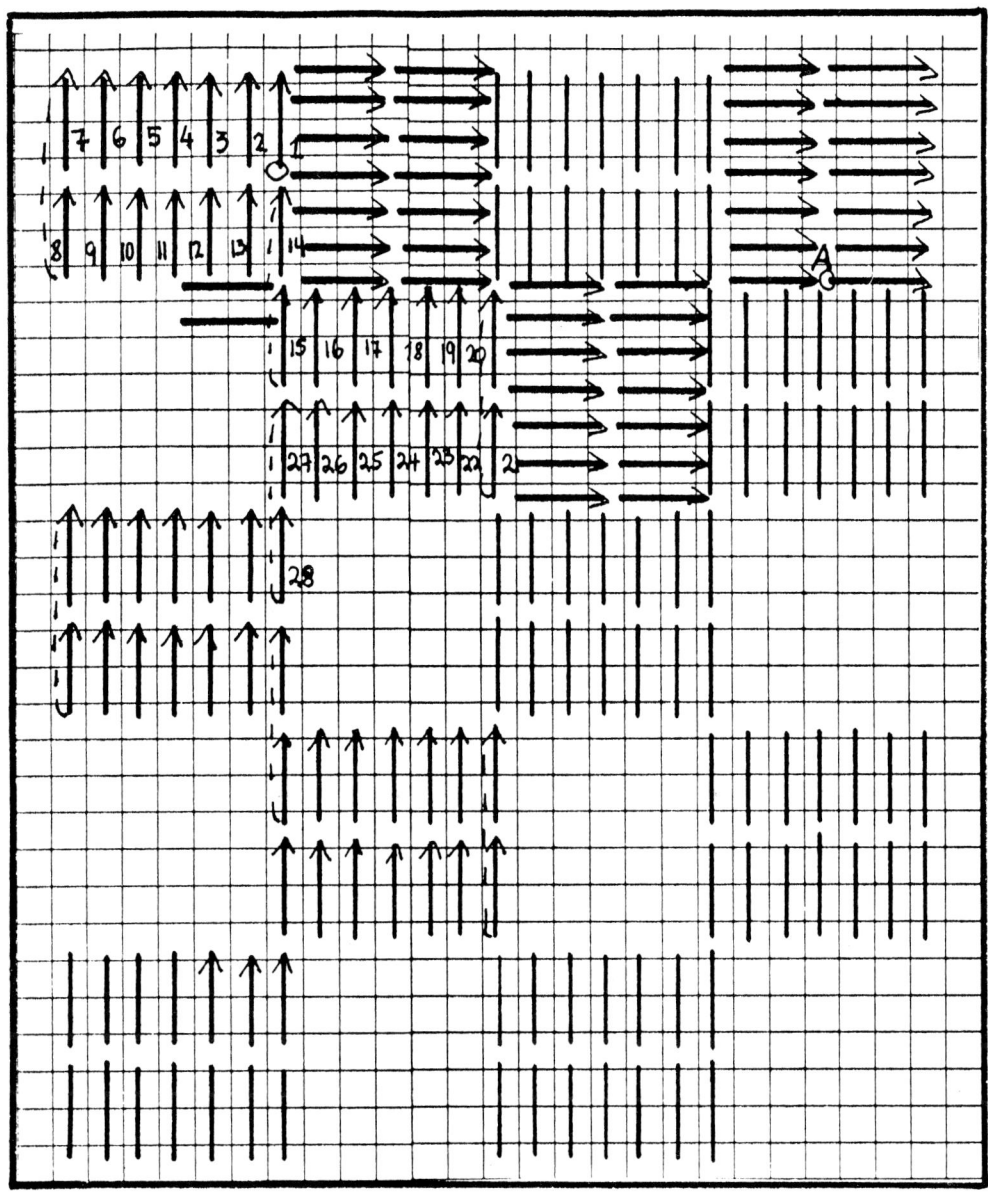

Pattern A-5 - Tight Pull

Work two horizontal rows, back and forth, of seven stitches over three threads. (Stitches 1-14).

Place first stitch of second group (15) immediately under last stitch of first group (14).

Place first stitch of third group (28) immediately under last stitch of second group (27). Continue in this manner placing groups in alternate spaces until shape is filled.

Turn the work 90 degrees and repeat this sequence. See arrow A.

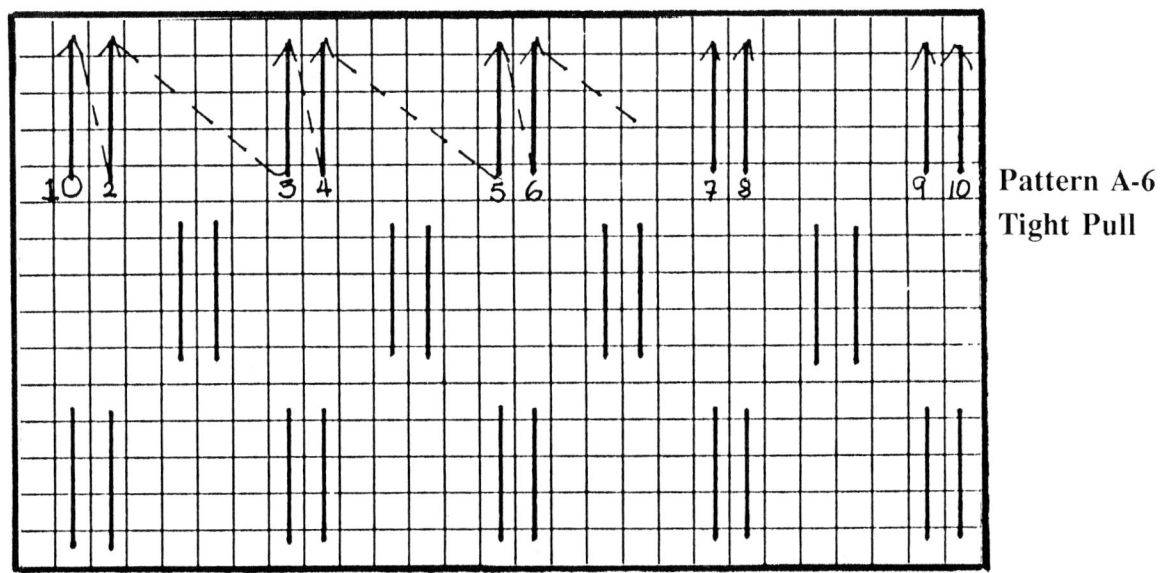

**Pattern A-6
Tight Pull**

Work in horizontal rows. Work two stitches over four threads, spaced by five threads. In the second and all subsequent rows, the position of the stitches alternate.

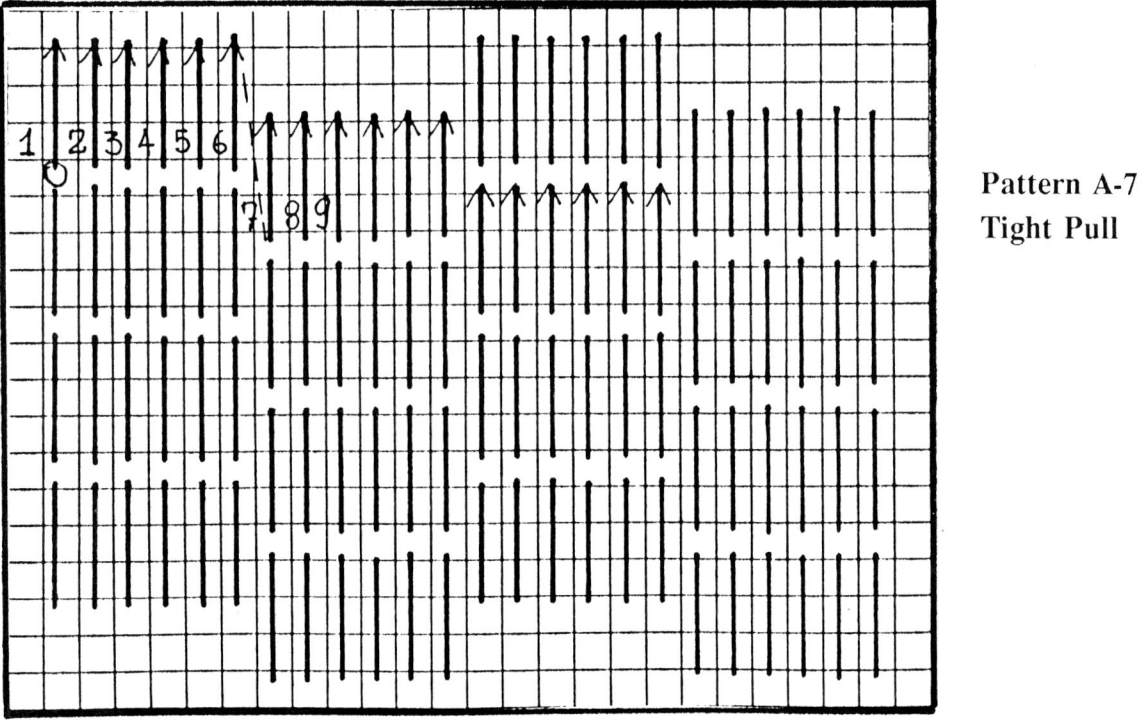

**Pattern A-7
Tight Pull**

Work horizontal groups of vertical stitches over four threads. After the first group of six stitches has been worked, move down by two threads (7) and work another group of six stitches. Repeat across the row.

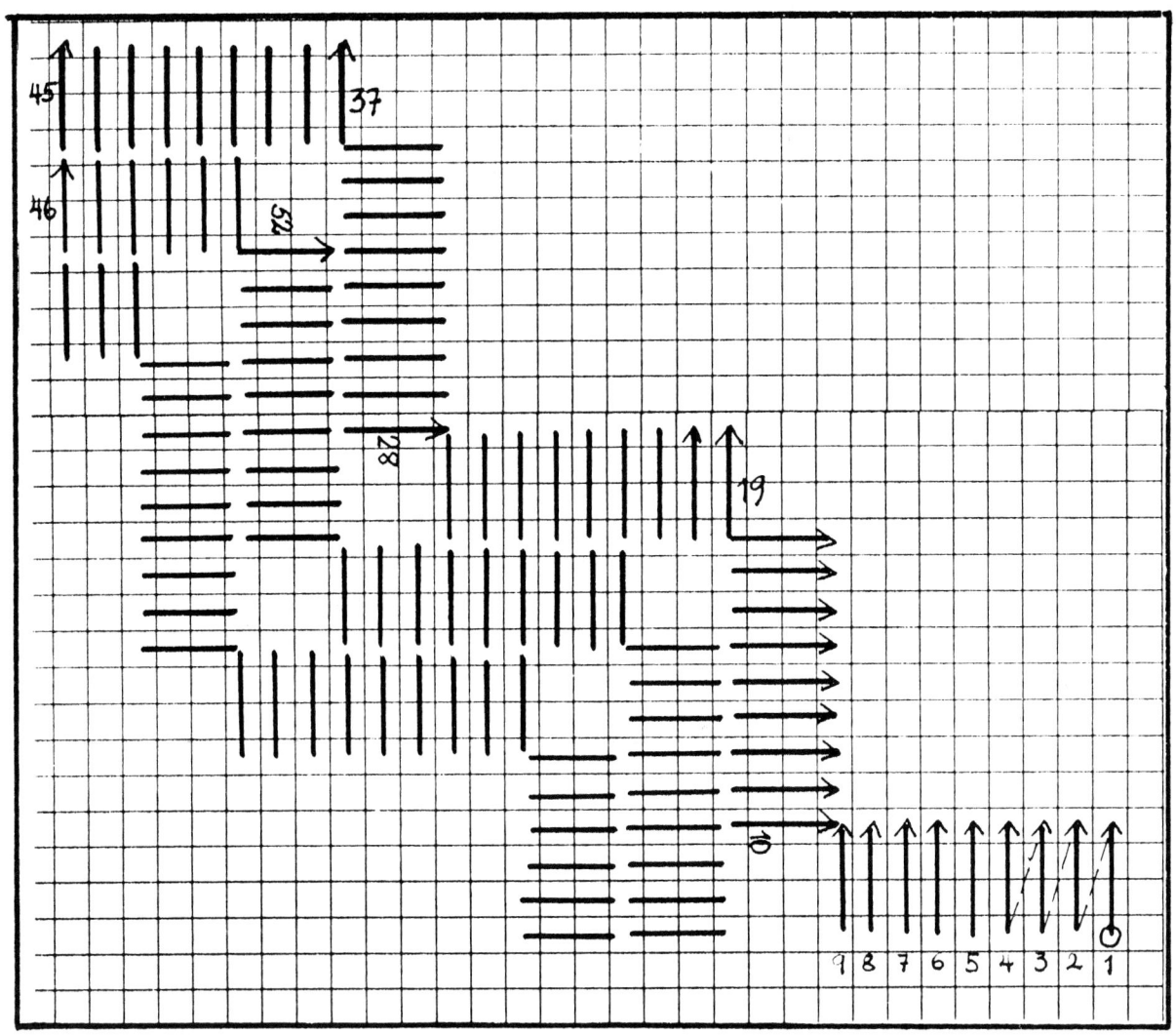

Pattern A-8 - Tight Pull

This pattern is worked in diagonal rows.

Work nine stitches over three threads. (1-9) Change position and work another group of nine stitches. Repeat.

To work second and all subsequent rows, the number of stitches in the first and last group will change, depending on the space being filled. Nine or fewer stitches are worked under the last group, so that three threads remain over which the first stitch of the next group is placed.

Note: If you work a variation of this pattern by working longer rows (more stitches) and wider groups (stitches over more threads), you must work to within as many threads as your stitches are wide. See Pattern A-9.

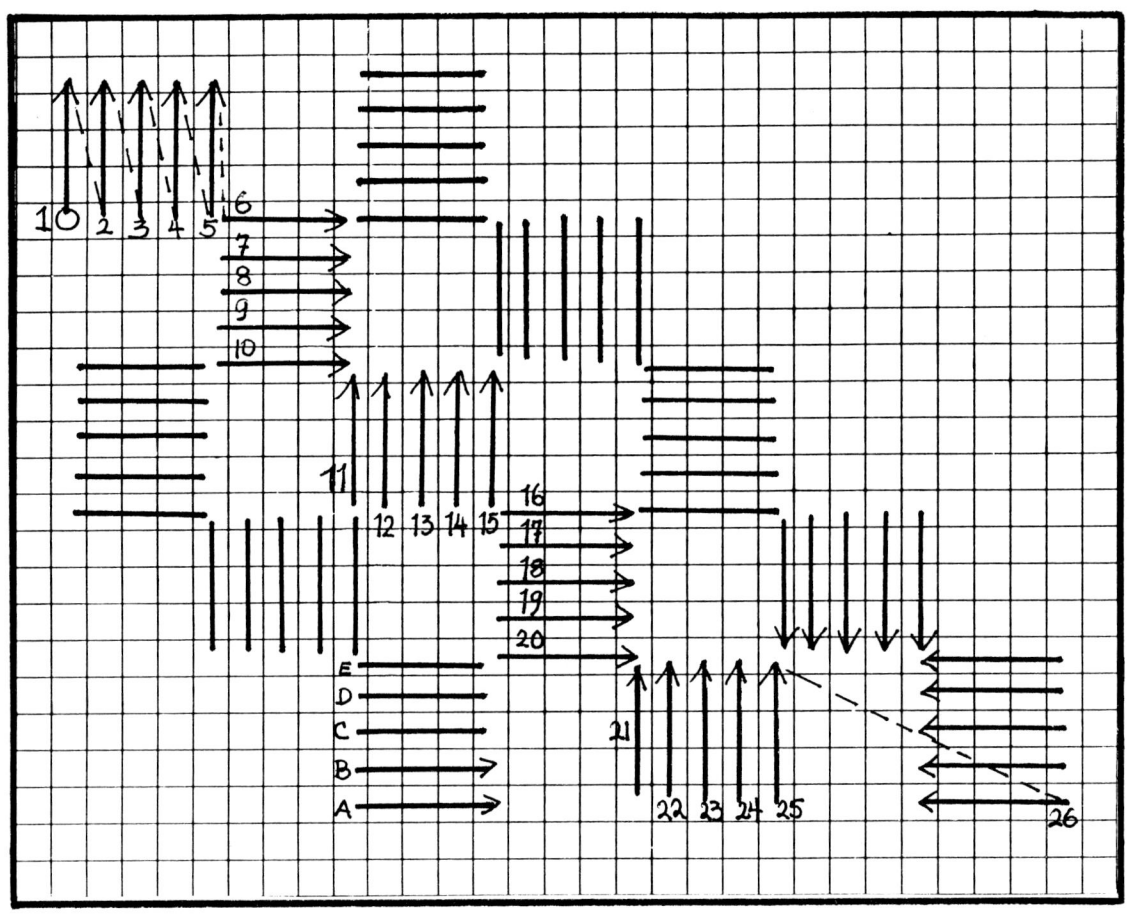

Pattern A-9 - Tight Pull

For working method see Pattern A-8.

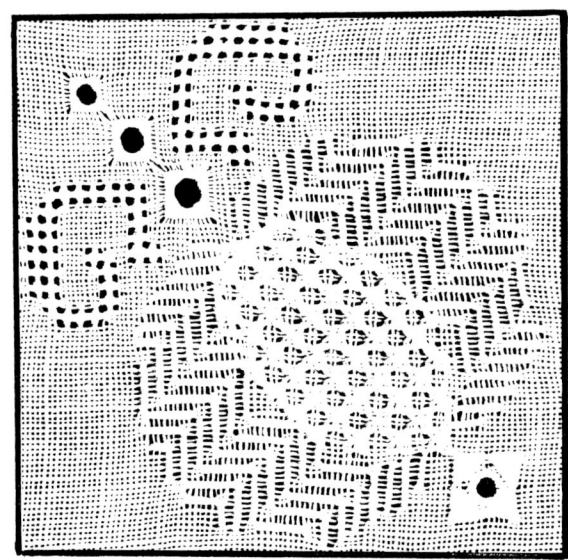

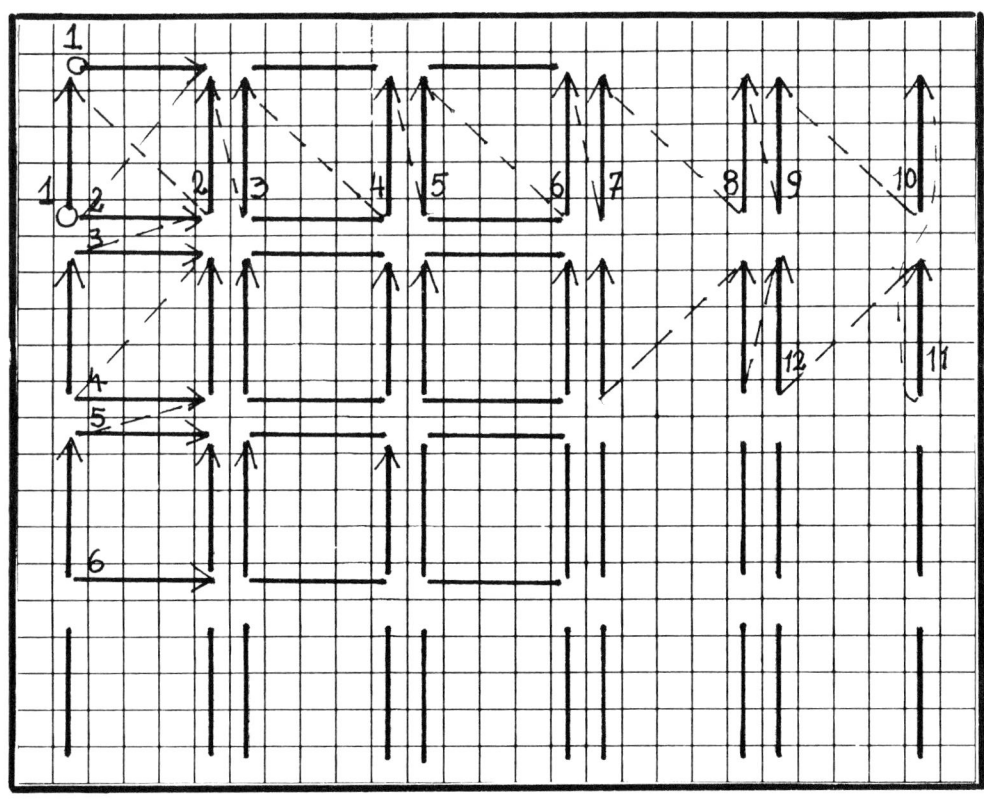

Pattern A-10 - Tight Pull

Work in horizontal rows first and in vertical rows next. Follow numbered arrows.

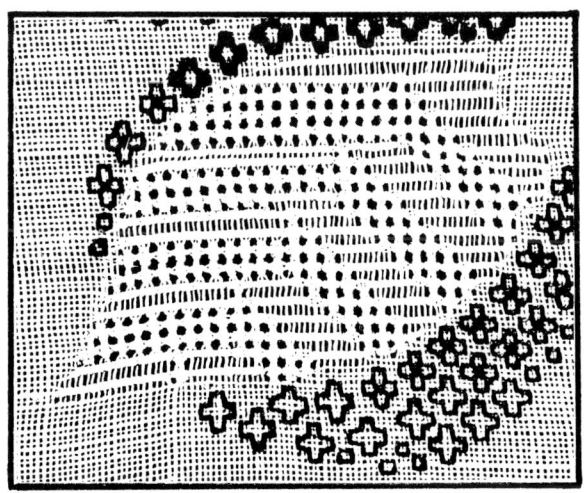

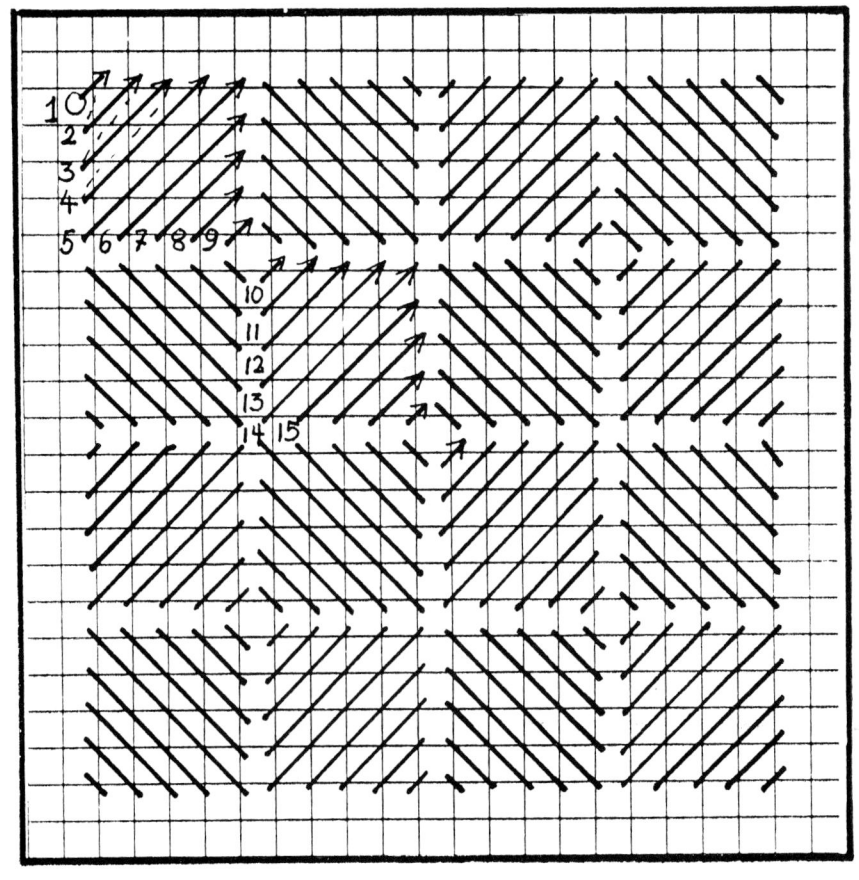

Pattern A-11

Gradual Pull

Pull tightly at first, then gradually relax the tension as stitches get wider.

Work in diagonal rows, in one direction first, in the opposite direction next.

This pattern would look nice if worked in the center of this design.

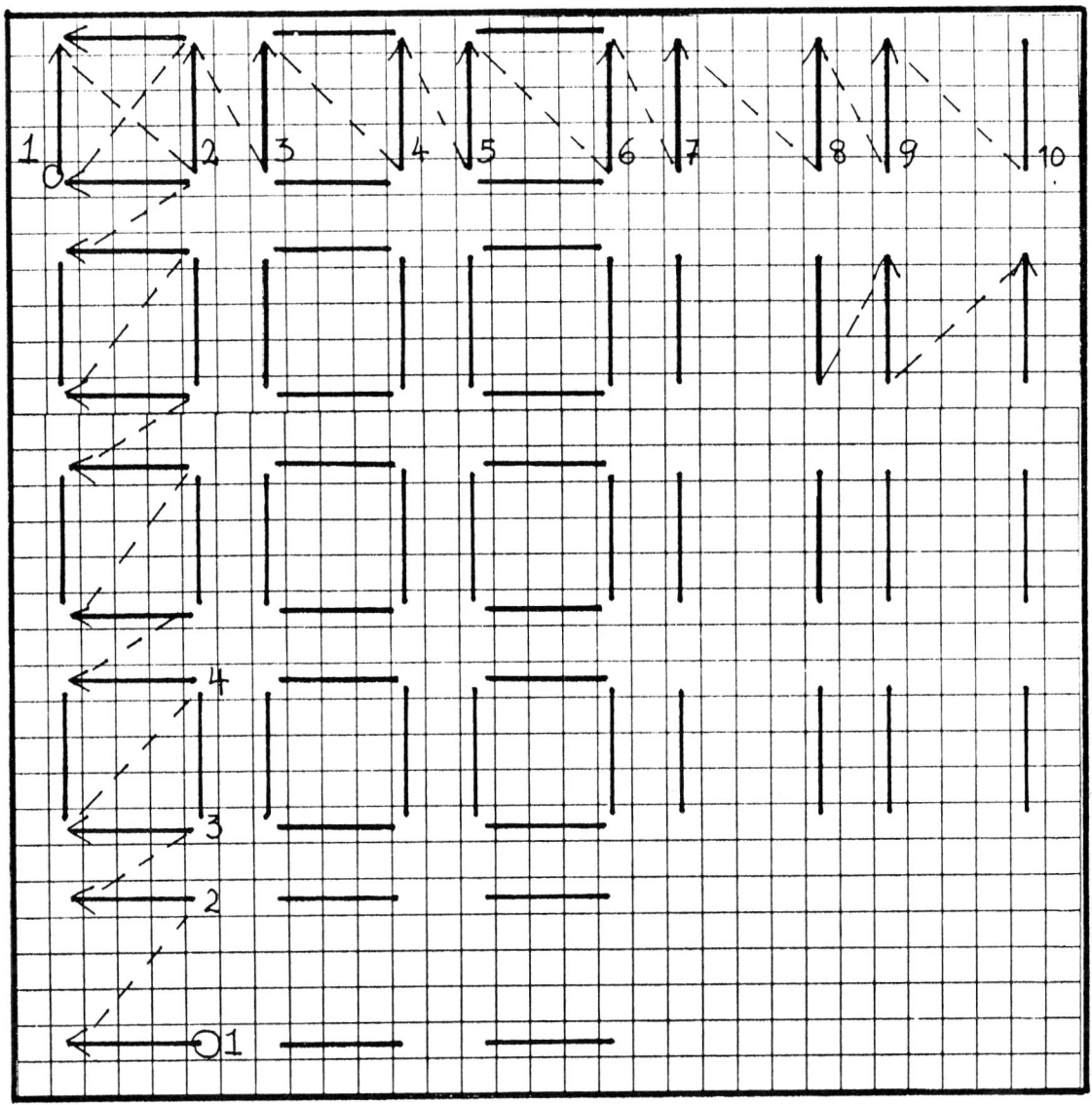

Pattern A-12 - Tight Pull

The pattern is related to Pattern A-10. The spacing between the squares changes from a thread, Pattern A-10, to two threads. This gives the pattern an entirely different look. The length of the stitches, over four threads, should not be shortened when spacing as shown in this diagram. Stitch length may be increased to five threads, or even six, depending on the fabric. Patterns A-10 and A-12 can also be worked as a four sided stitch, spacing is optional.

Pattern A-13 - Tight Pull

Worked as a four sided stitch. Sequence of stitching can be found on page 109.

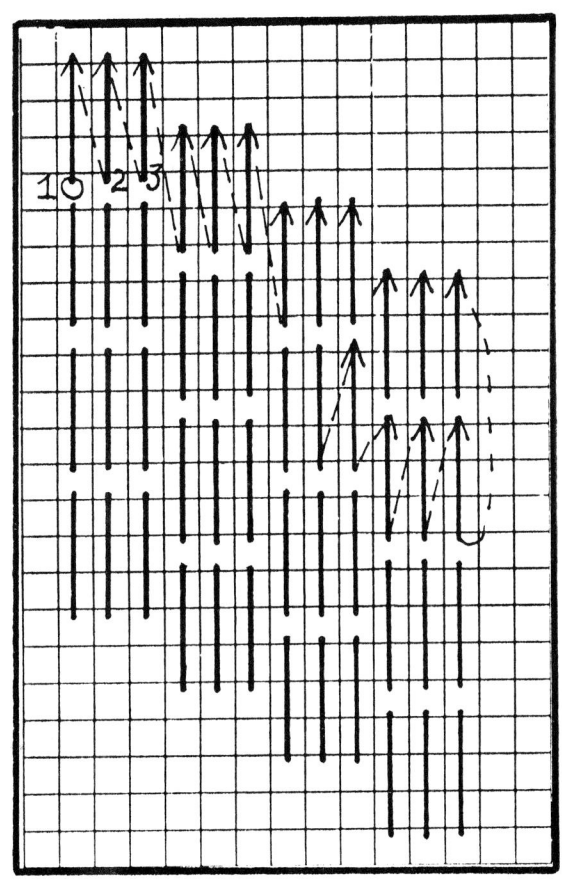

Pattern A-14

Slight Tension

This pattern is most effective when a slightly heavier thread is used. A Perle cotton #8 will work nicely on most fabrics.

Since the pull is only slight, which means that the stitches sit snugly on the fabric and therefore are seen clearly, the somewhat heavier thread is recommended.

Work in diagonal rows in groups of three stitches over four threads.

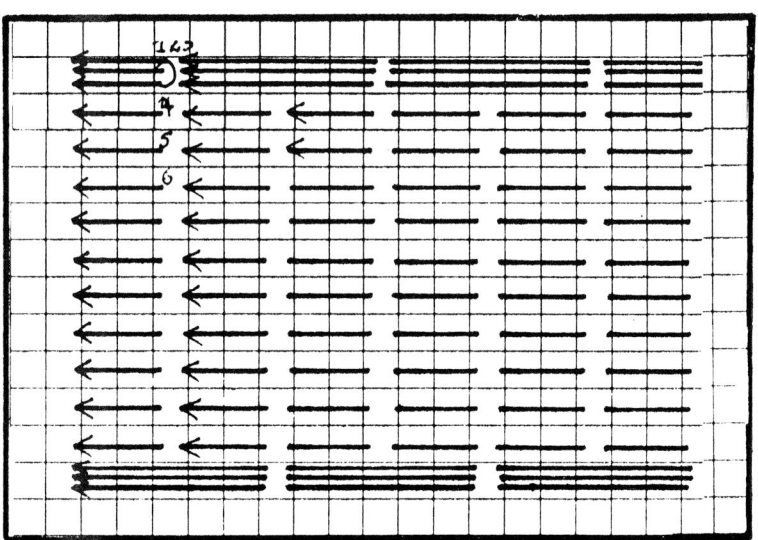

Pattern A-15

Tight Tension

Work three stitches in the same space, one next to the other, going over three threads to start the pattern. Work ten more stitches, one in each space, immediately below the first group.

In the next space, work three stitches over six threads as shown by the longer arrows. Work up again over three threads only and repeat.

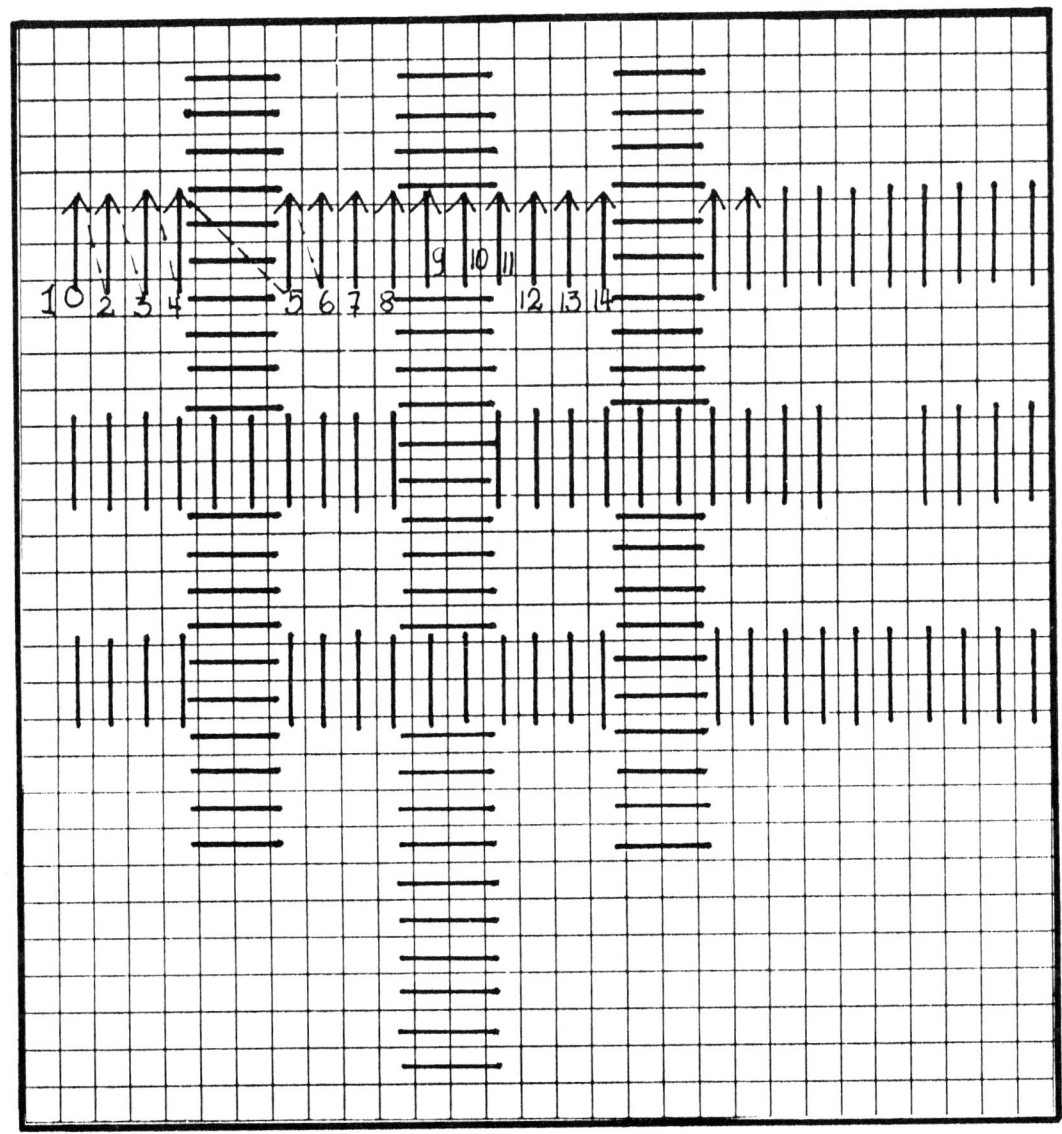

Pattern A-16 - Tight Pull

Work a grid by working horizontal rows first and vertical rows last.

Stitches 1-4 are part of a group of ten stitches over three threads. Work ten stitches, skip three threads. Repeat to end of row.

Space rows three threads apart and stagger or alternate the groups, i.e. spaces. (5-14).

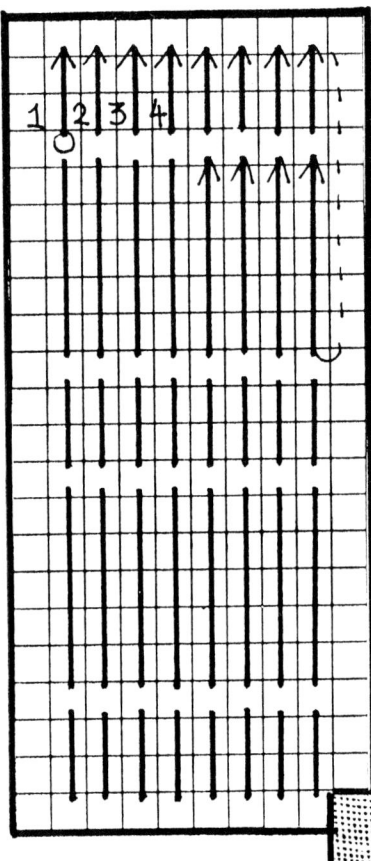

Pattern A-17 - Tight Pull

Work horizontal (or vertical) rows of stitches, alternating over three and over six threads.

Try different ways/counts, for different looks. With this simple stitch one can achieve very striking effects.

As an example, the leaf pictured below shows many changes in stitch width, thus creating an interesting vein formation.

DOUBLE BACK STITCH

The *Double Back Stitch* is one of my favorite Pulled Thread Embroidery stitches. It is suitable for geometric patterns as well as for free form designs.

As with most embroidery stitches, one can find different names for a stitch pattern depending on the technique it is used for; the double back stitch in Pulled Thread work is non other than the stitch used in shadow work, the only difference being that in Pulled Thread a medium tension is applied while in shadow work it is not.

For the Double Back Stitch, two rows of simultaneously stitched back stitches are necessary. These two rows can be stitched vertically, horizontally, diagonally, or if the shape demands it, in any irregular line. The sole requisite is that the stitch be worked over two rows at the same time.

The tension is slight to medium, depending on the distance between the two rows which should never be less than two threads apart nor more than six to eight threads, depending on the threads-per-inch of the fabric. It is best said that the distance should not measure more than 3/8" at most, as the pattern would surely buckle under the tension applied. The tension is needed to produce the holes which gives the pattern its characteristics. It is important that each backstitch shares the hole with the previously taken stitch. A tapestry needle, i.e. a blunt needle, is imperative for this purpose. The thread should not be too fine as the weight of it is needed on the underside for the raised or padded effect. This stitch looks lovely if worked with a slightly tinted thread or one that is a bit darker than the fabric. A good effect can be achieved with DMC color 644 on ecru linen or the palest pastel on white ground.

On the following pages of graphed patterns, the procedure is no longer explained. The numbered arrows (top stitches) and the broken lines (underside stitches) show the sequence in which the back stitches are worked. Diagrams A and B below explain the method further.

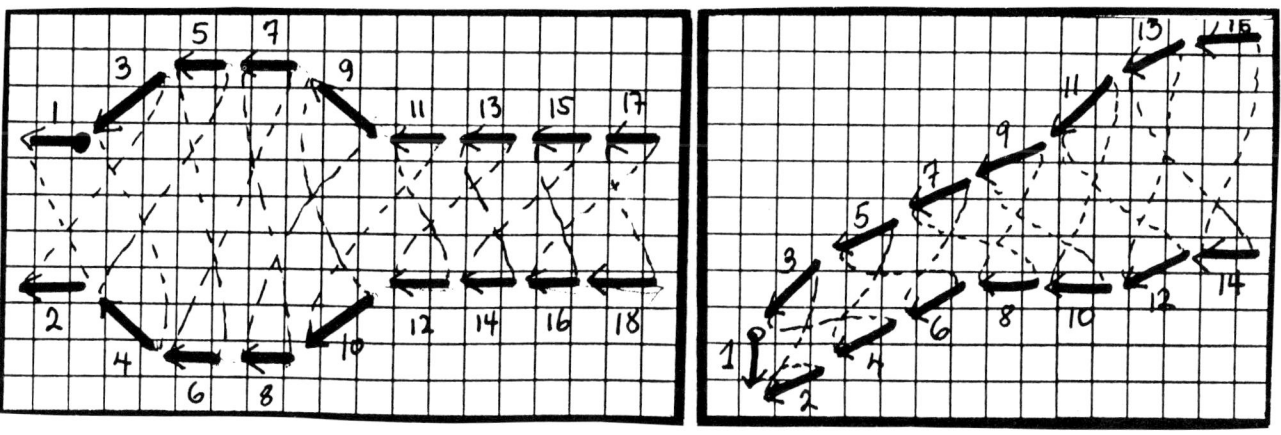

Diagram A - Geometric Pattern   Diagram B - Free Form Pattern

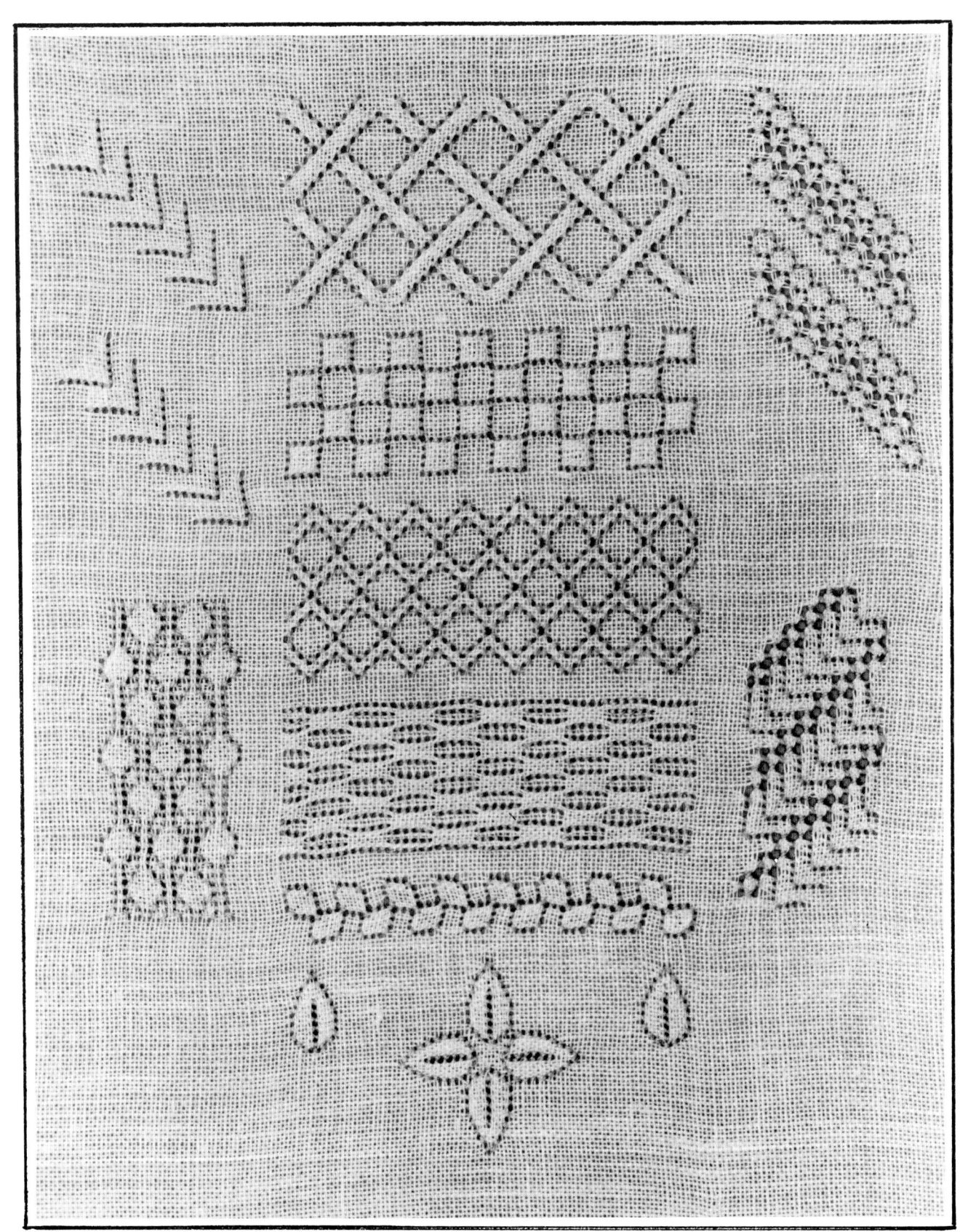

DOUBLE BACK STITCH SAMPLER

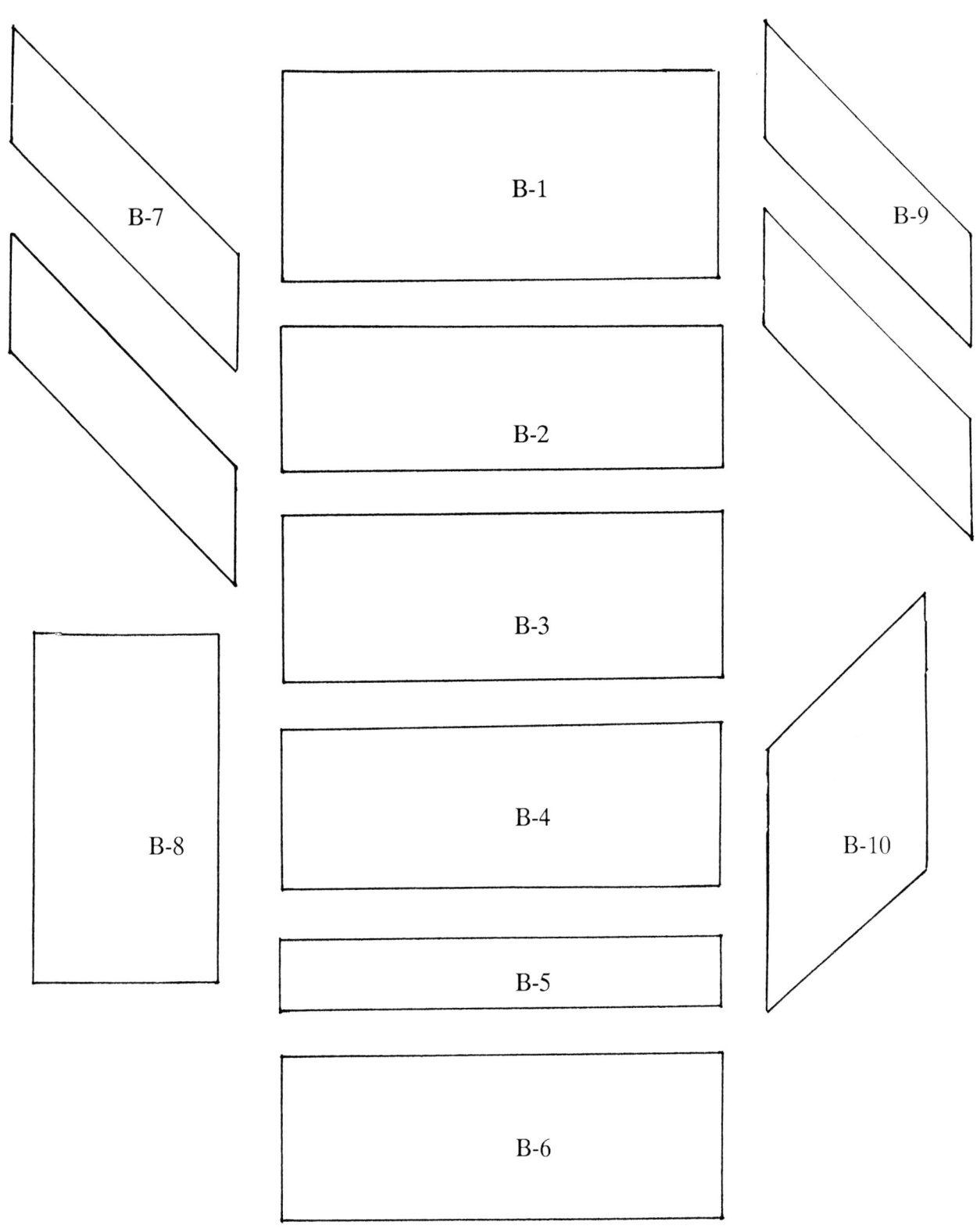

IDENTIFICATION CHART B - DOUBLE BACK STITCH

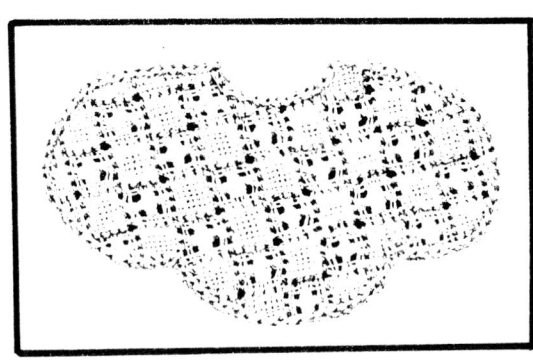

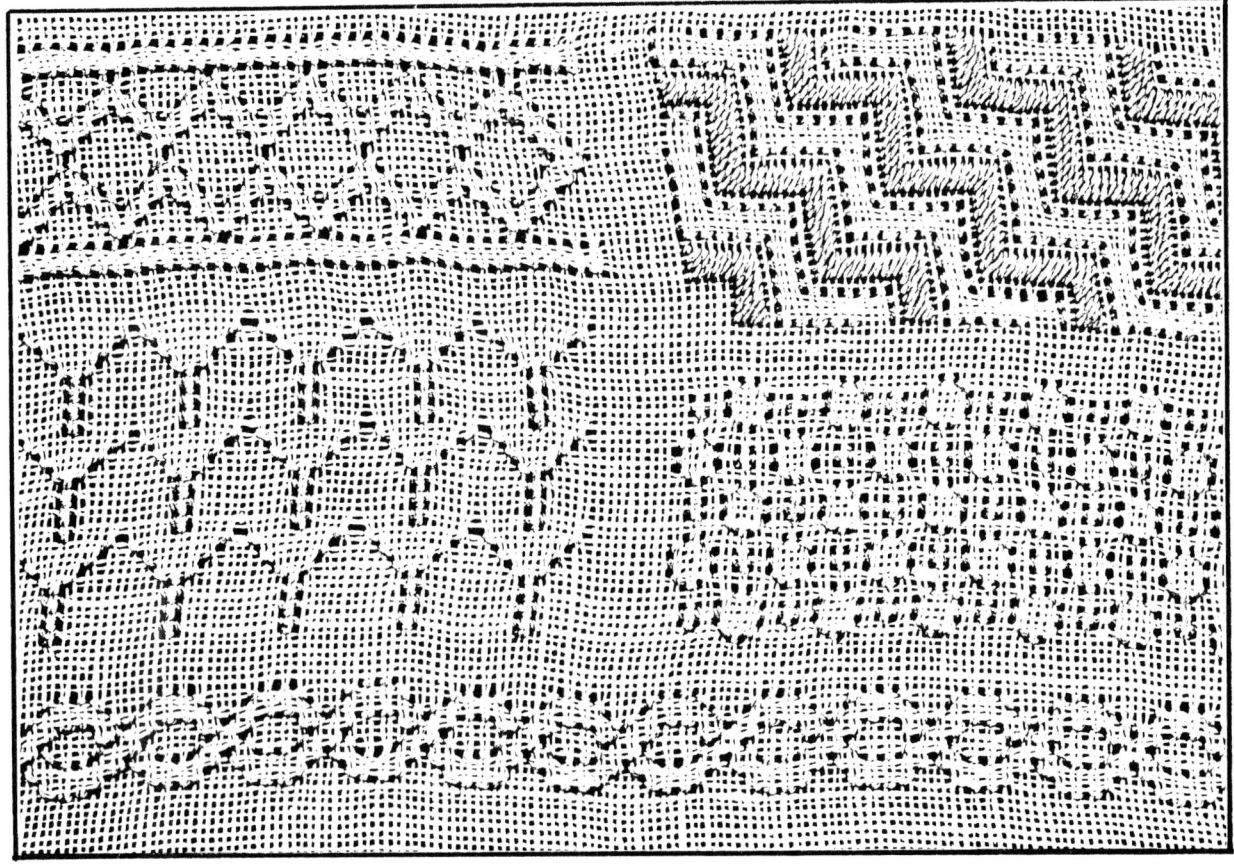

| DOUBLE BACK STITCH | B-11 | SAMPLER II |

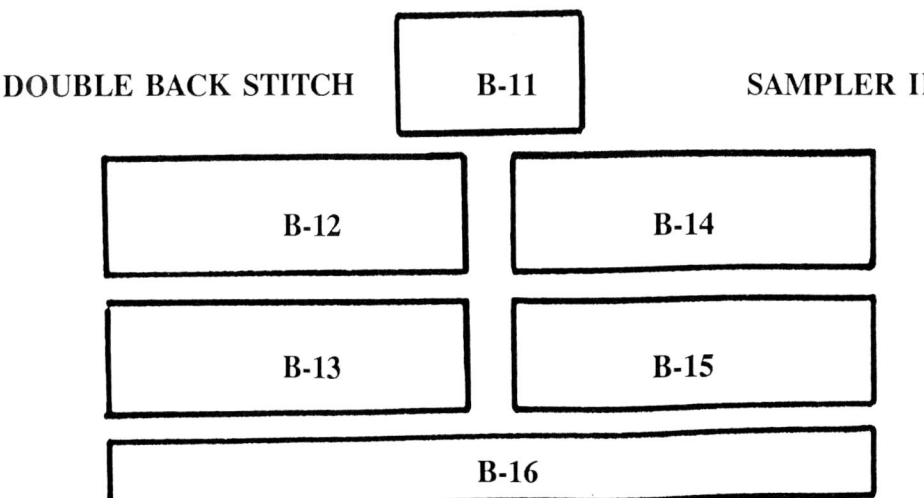

IDENTIFICATION CHART

Pattern B-1 - Slight to Medium Pull

Work in diagonal rows. There are 10 double back stitches in each unit spaced by 4 intersections. Skip 4 intersections between each unit, see arrows #20 and #1.

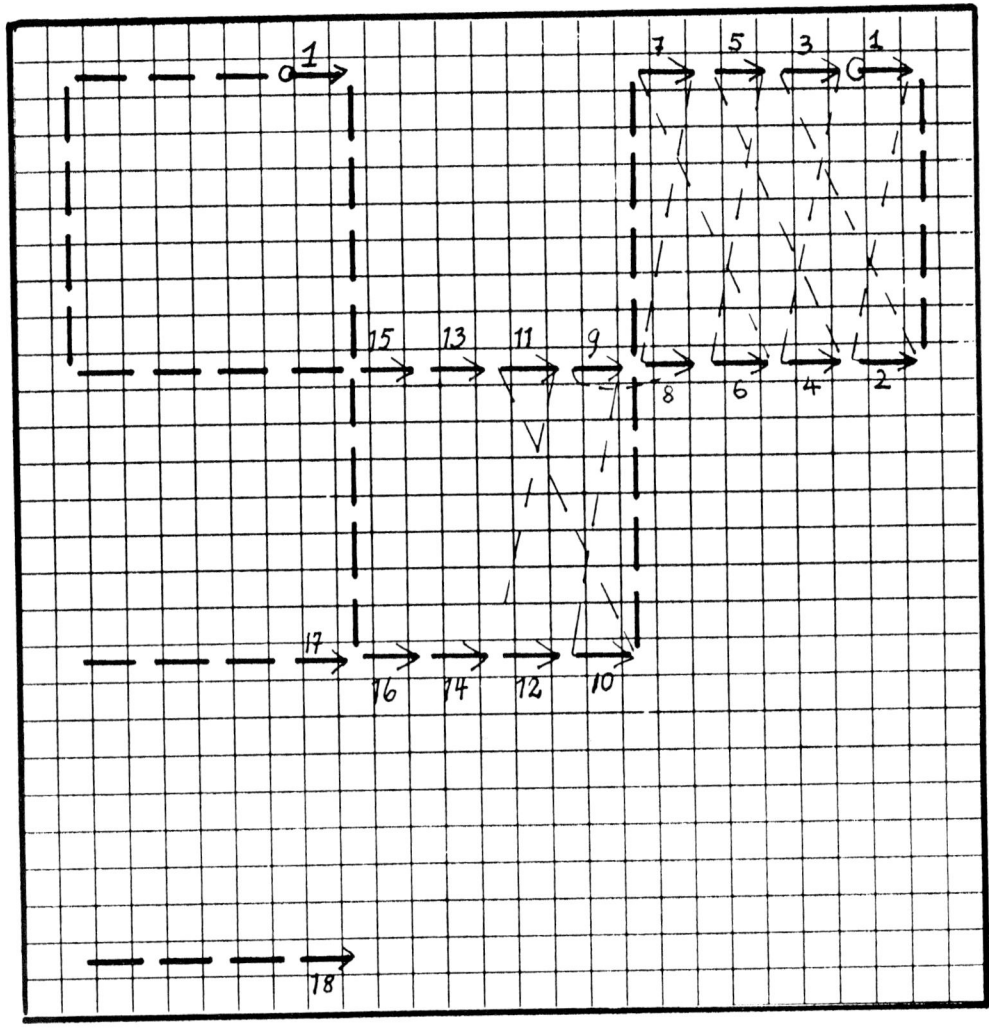

Pattern B-2 - Slight to Medium Pull

This pattern is worked in groups of four by four stitches. It can be varied in that the resulting squares can be smaller or larger, or their shape can be rectangular.

Work four double back stitches over two threads, eight threads apart. Arrows 1-8. Repeat this sequence travelling in a diagonal row. Diagram A.

Return over the same row, working the missing stitches as shown in Diagram B.

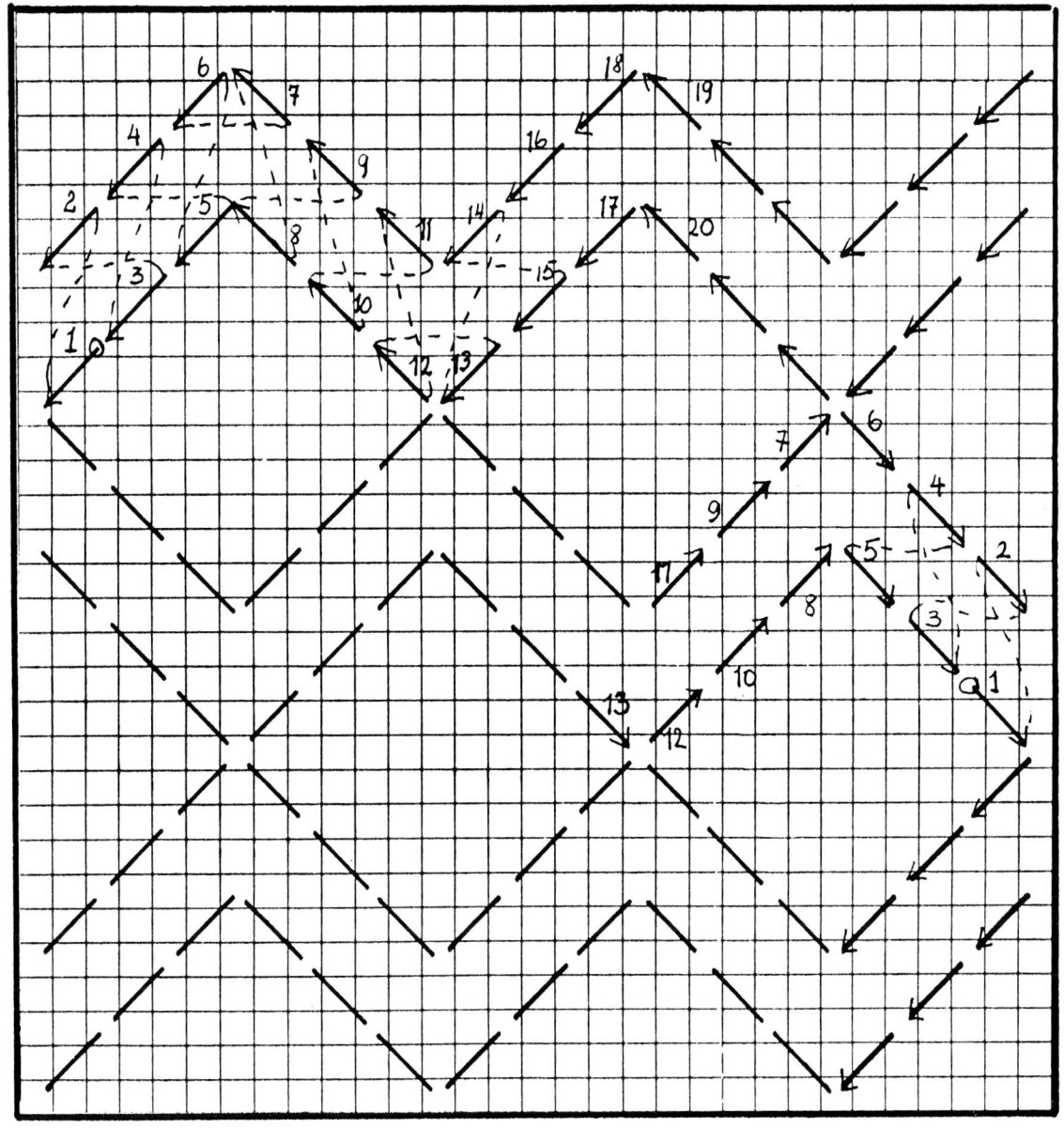

Pattern B-3 - Slight to Medium Pull

This pattern works in a zig-zag motion. Three stitches are worked in each section. This number may be increased for a larger, more open pattern.

The spacing of the double back stitch is by four threads. Notice the change in sequence at the peaks: stitches 6-7 and 12-13. When a peak is reached, the sequence of stitching is reversed.

This pattern looks lovely when further decorated. The empty diamonds can be nicely filled with eyelets, four-sided stitch or Greek crosses, just to mention a few. Let your imagination be your guide.

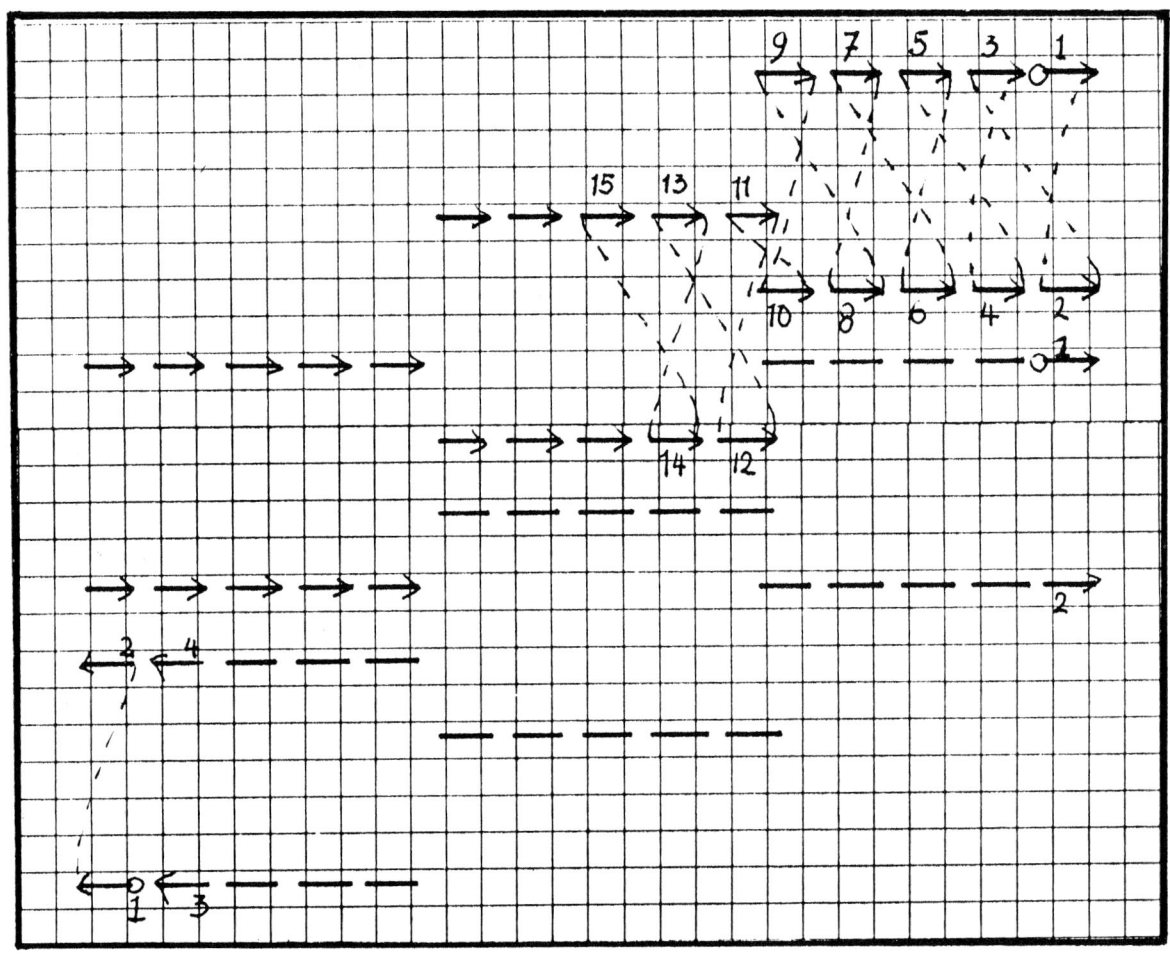

Pattern B-4 - Slight to Medium Pull

This pattern works in diagonal rows. It can be worked from left to right or from right to left as shown. One must reverse the arrows/stitches when working in the opposite direction.

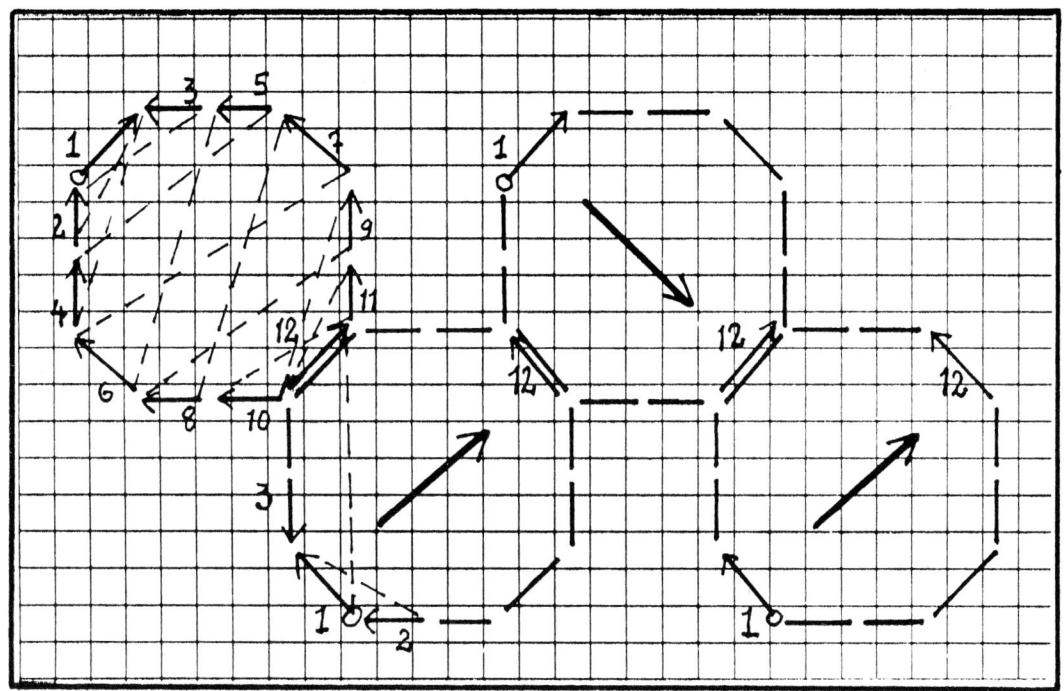

Pattern B-5 - Slight to Medium Pull

This pattern is especially suited for a narrow border. Although in the graph one can see octagons, because of the directional pull, these are distorted into oblong octagon shapes. One shape (leaf) pulls down while the next one pulls up, thus alternating the directional pull every other octagon.

Notice that stitch #12 becomes stitch #7 in the second leaf. This stitch is worked twice.

The large arrows in the center of the octagons show the direction in which the stitch is pulled.

Suggestion: One could enlarge the octagon by one stitch or work two or more octagons in one direction before switching the pull. Try this on your doodle cloth, it may very well give you the effect you are looking for.

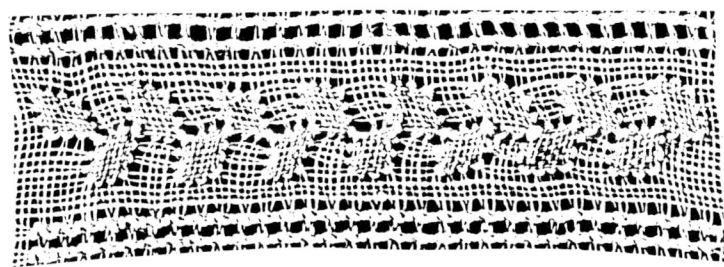

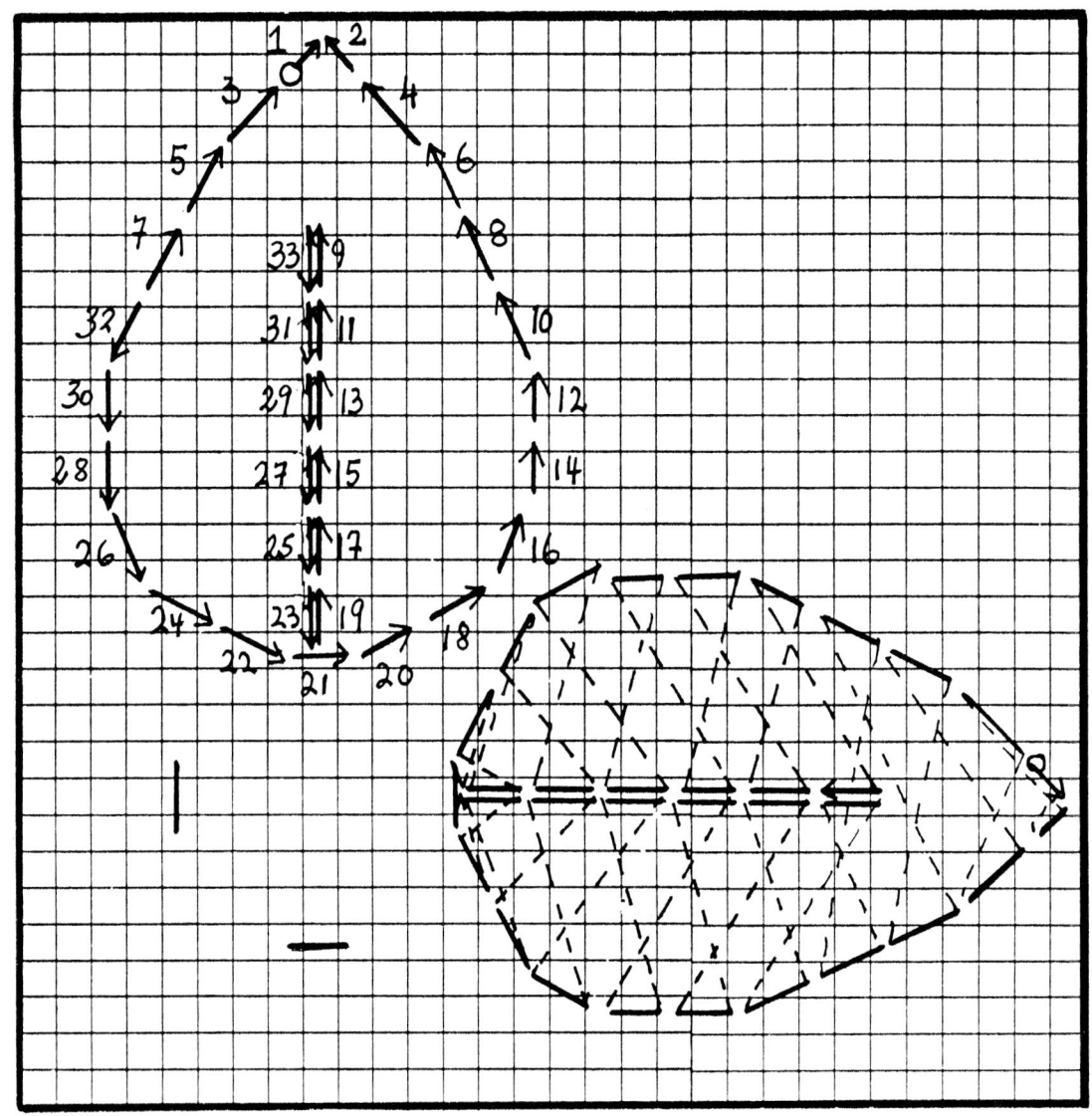

Pattern B-6 - Slight to Medium Pull

Fancy little leaves or flowers can be worked using this pattern. Notice that after stitch #8 the leaf is split, thus forming a vein in its center. The reason for this is that the stitches would get too long or far apart which would in turn create buckling of the shape, distorting it too much.

Work down one side of the shape first and subsequently work up the other side. Notice the inverted arrows/stitches on the left side. The center or vein stitches are worked twice, i.e. the holes are shared. These holes will become well pronounced as they are first pulled to the right and then to the left.

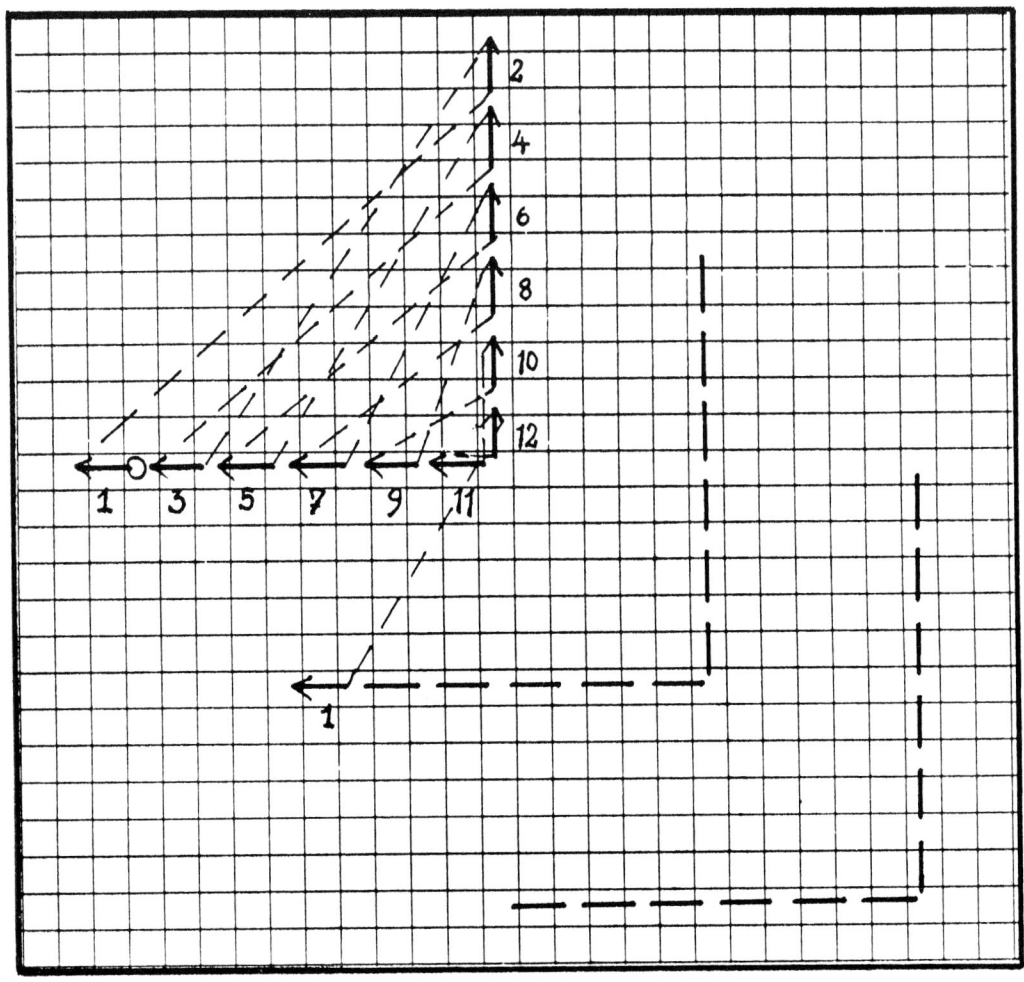

Pattern B-7 - Slight to Medium Pull

This pattern works in neat little triangles which look like arrow heads.

The pull is on the diagonal and the number of stitches can be successfully varied to change the size of the shape.

This pattern combines very well with other patterns, especially when combined in diagonal rows.

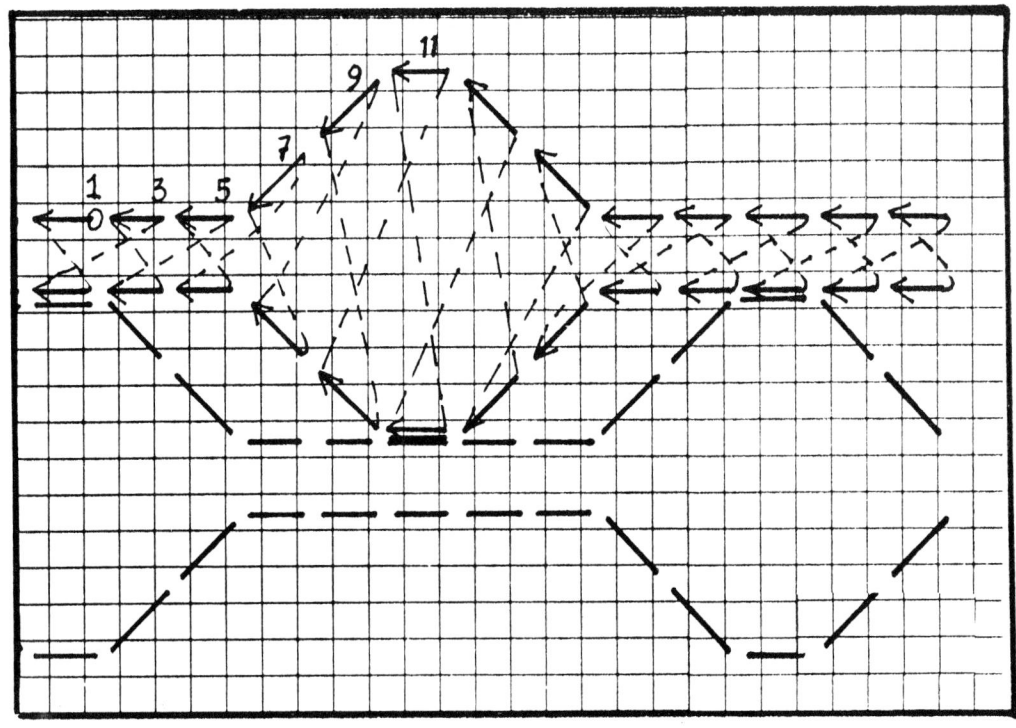

Pattern B-8 - Slight to Medium Pull

This pattern can be worked either horizontally or vertically. Rows can be closely placed as in the above graph in which the top and bottom stitch of the octagon shares holes with the stitches of the next row. The rows can also be spaced by several threads. Another neat pattern.

Another nice pattern will result when placing the rows so that the octagons are on top of each other rather than alternated as in the graph. The resulting rectangular hexagons can then be filled with additional decorations (stitches) or they can be left empty. Try using a group of four-sided stitches, faggotting or reverse faggoting as fillers.

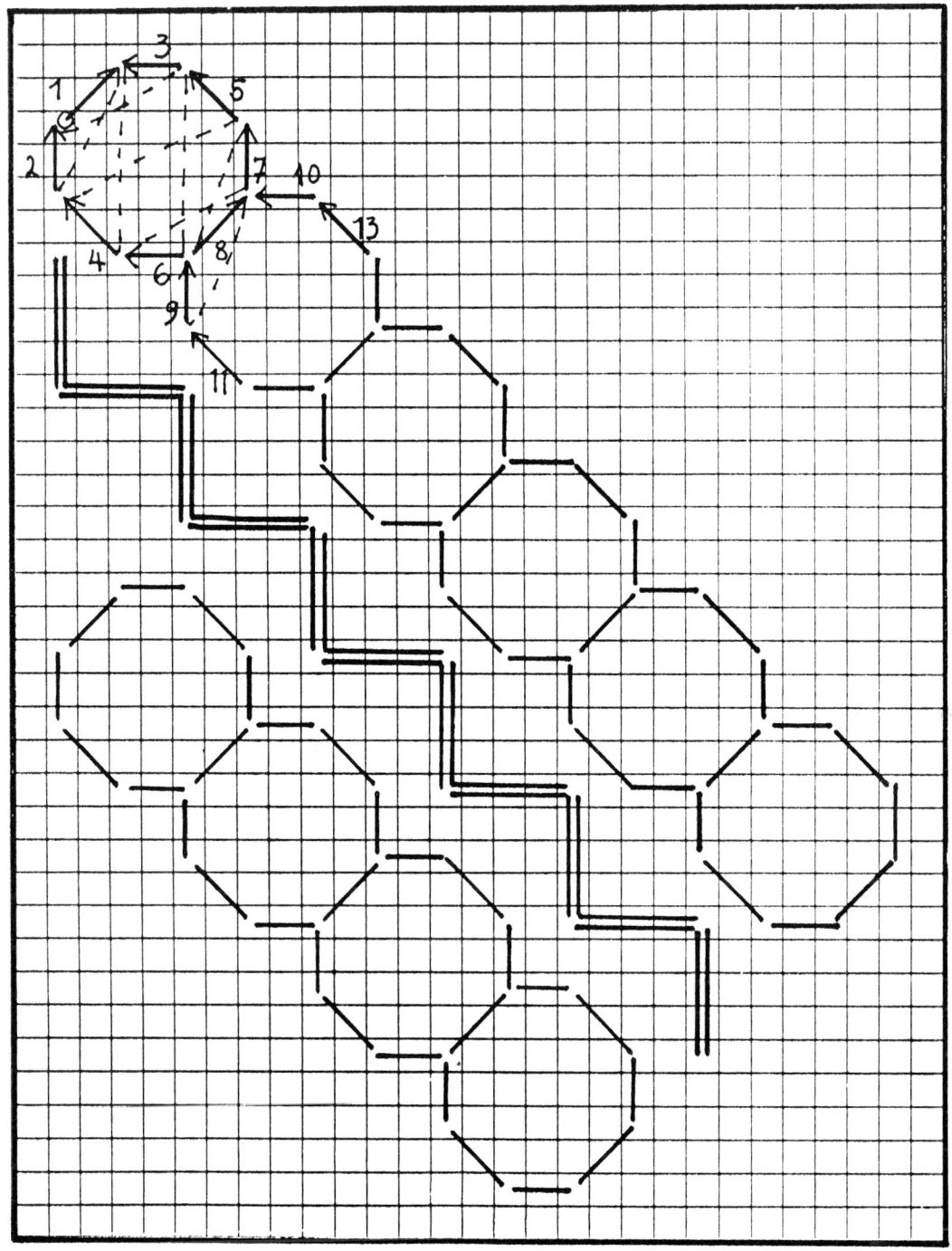

Pattern B-9 - Slight to Medium Pull

The small octagons are worked in a continuous diagonal row. Spacing the rows by several threads and placing an additional pattern in the space created adds much interest to this pattern.

In the above graph, the resulting spaces are filled with the faggot stitch, each stitch taken twice for a more defined hole. See D-1

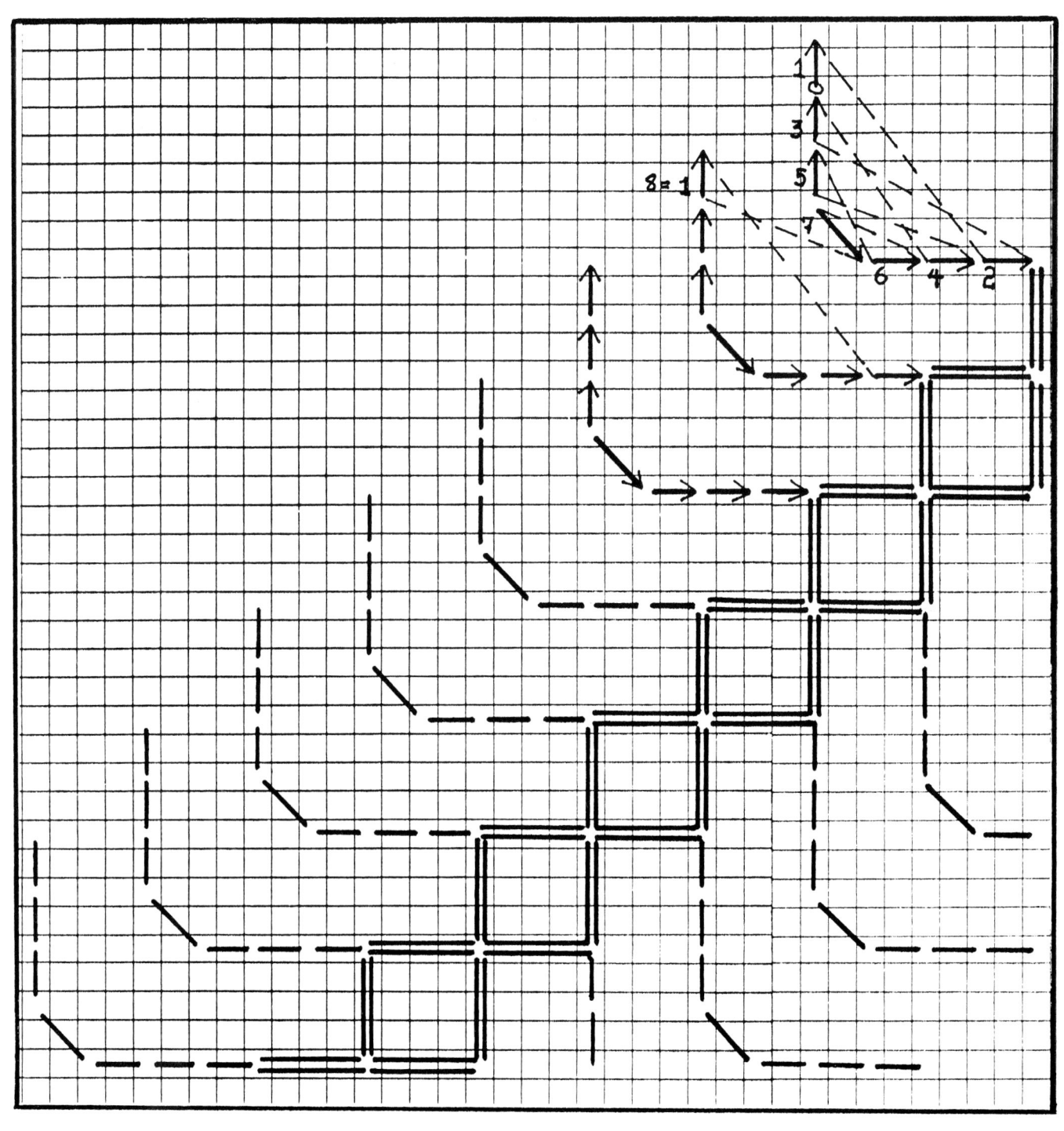

Pattern B-10 - Slight to Medium Pull

Rows of diagonal triangles are worked. This time the triangles do not come to a point as in Pattern B-7, but show a diagonal stitch instead, stitch 7. The rows are then alternated with two rows of faggotting in which each stitch is taken twice for a more defined pattern. Method of working the faggot stitch can be found on page 72.

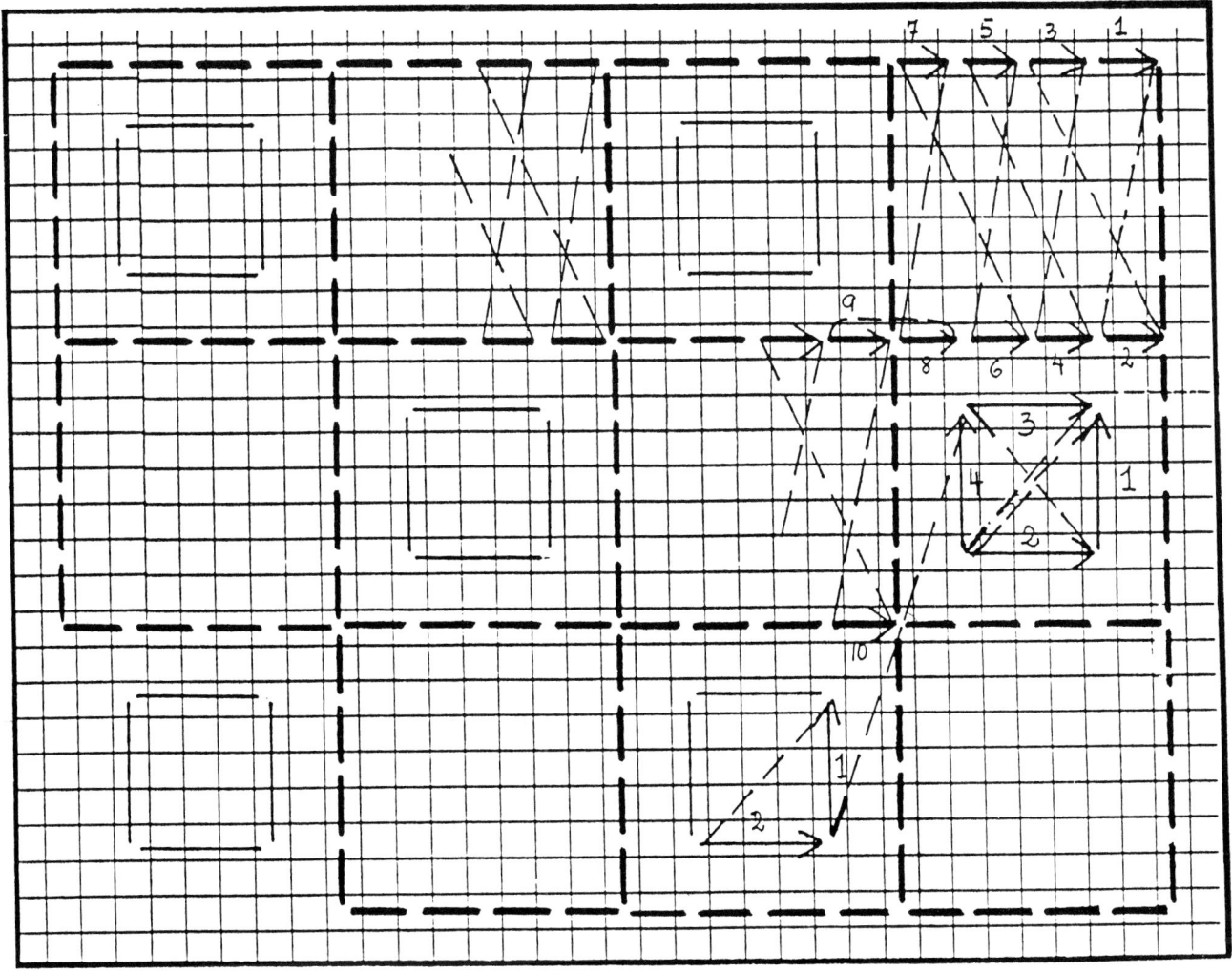

Pattern B-11 - Slight to Medium Pull

Work padded squares as in Pattern B-2. Fill empty, non-padded squares with the four-sided stitch, travelling in diagonal rows.

For a variation try filling the empty squares with a Greek cross (C-5) or an eyelet (G-1). One could also fit four of either the Greek cross, eyelet or four-sided stitch.

Pattern B-12 - Slight to Medium Pull

This pattern makes a nice border. It is a combination of Pattern B-3 and a horizontal row of double-back stitch two threads wide and four threads high.

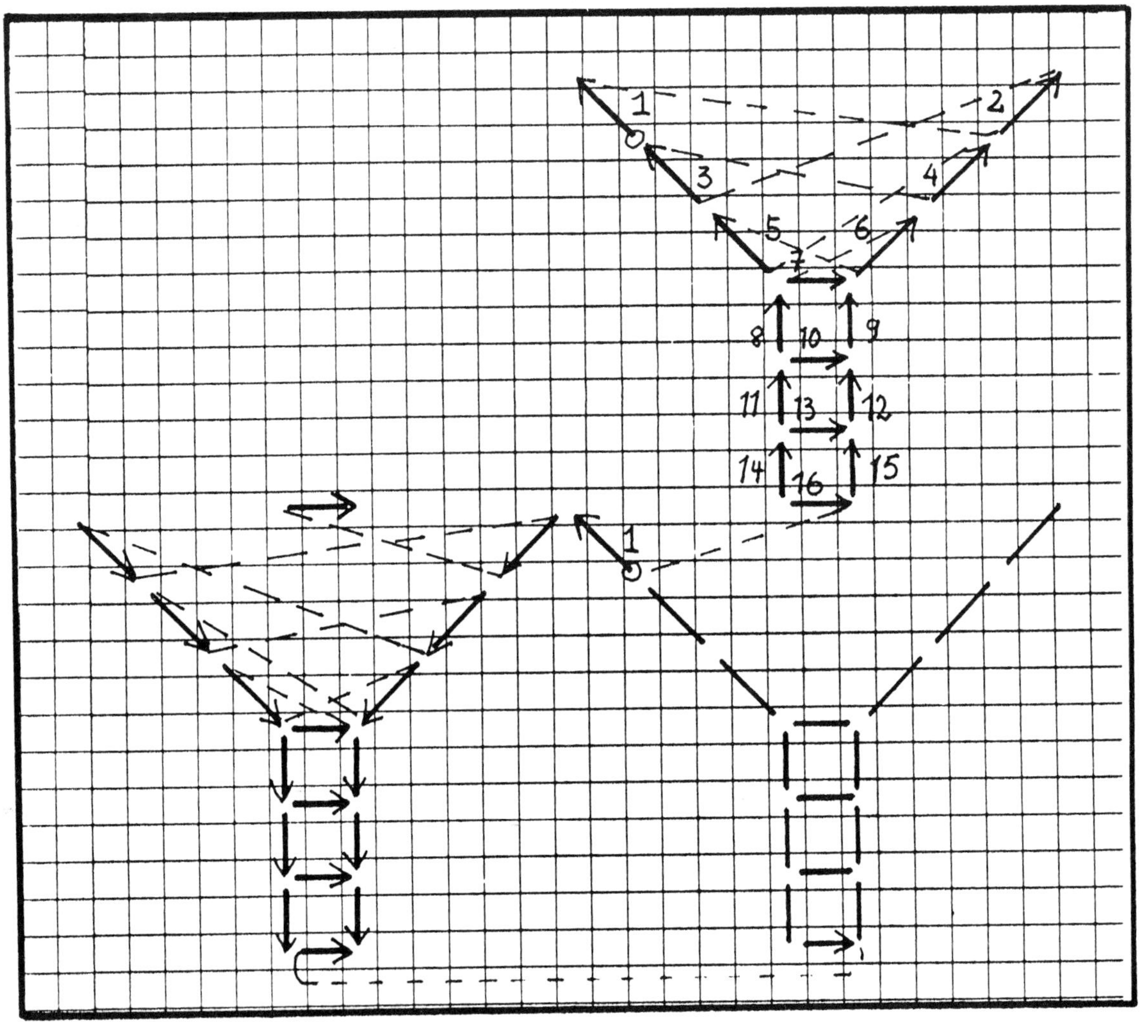

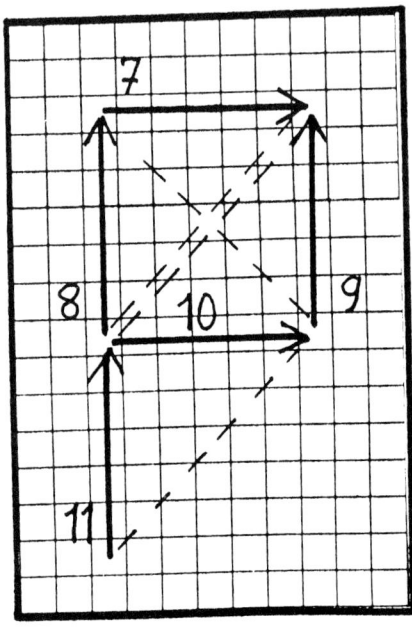

Pattern B-13 - Slight to Medium Pull

This pattern is worked in vertical rows. Start by working the upper right side unit. Three double back stitches are worked first followed by three four-sided stitches. Repeat this sequence. An enlarged diagram of the four-sides stitch was graphed to clarify the stitching sequence.

After the vertical row of patterns is completed, work up forming a second row. Notice that arrows/stitches point down

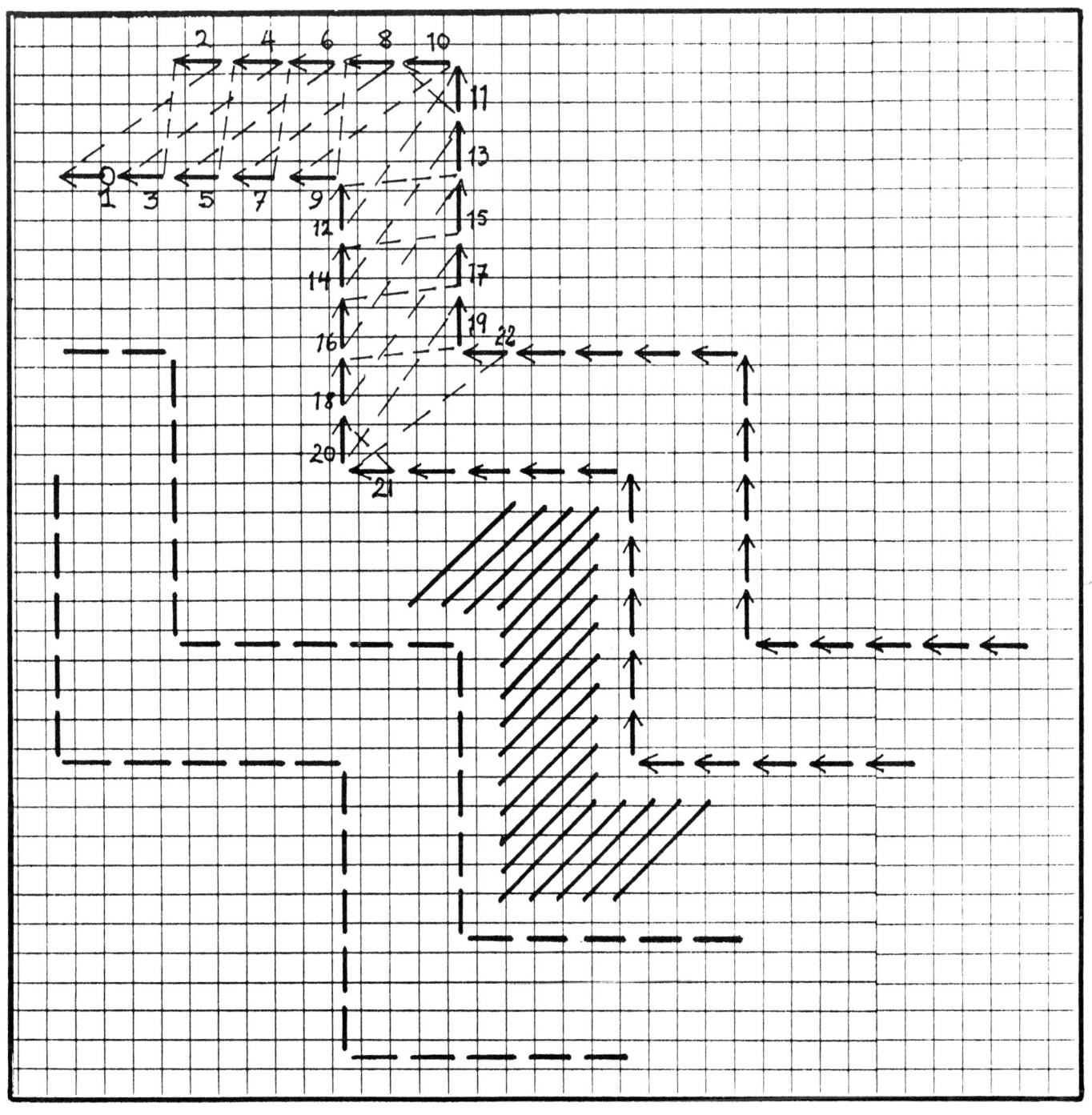

Pattern B-14 - Slight to Medium Pull

The double back stitch is worked in large zig-zag patterns, spaced here by six threads which are subsequently filled with diagonal stitches. These can be pulled into cording or can be left flat. If left flat, they could be worked in a slightly darker shade or in a soft pastel color.

Work the double-back stitch as arrows indicate. Notice in the outer corners, arrows #10/11 and #20/21, the sequence of stitching is reversed

CROSSED STITCHES SAMPLER

The **Crossed Stitches** are very effective when used alone or in combination with other pulled thread stitches. They can be varied and combined in many different ways, put only a few can be included in this book. It gives the stitcher much pleasure to "invent" new and different combinations.

The tension will vary with each pattern and number of threads over which a pattern is worked.

The basic stitches can be found in the sampler shown on the next page. Variations and adaptations are subsequently diagrammed.

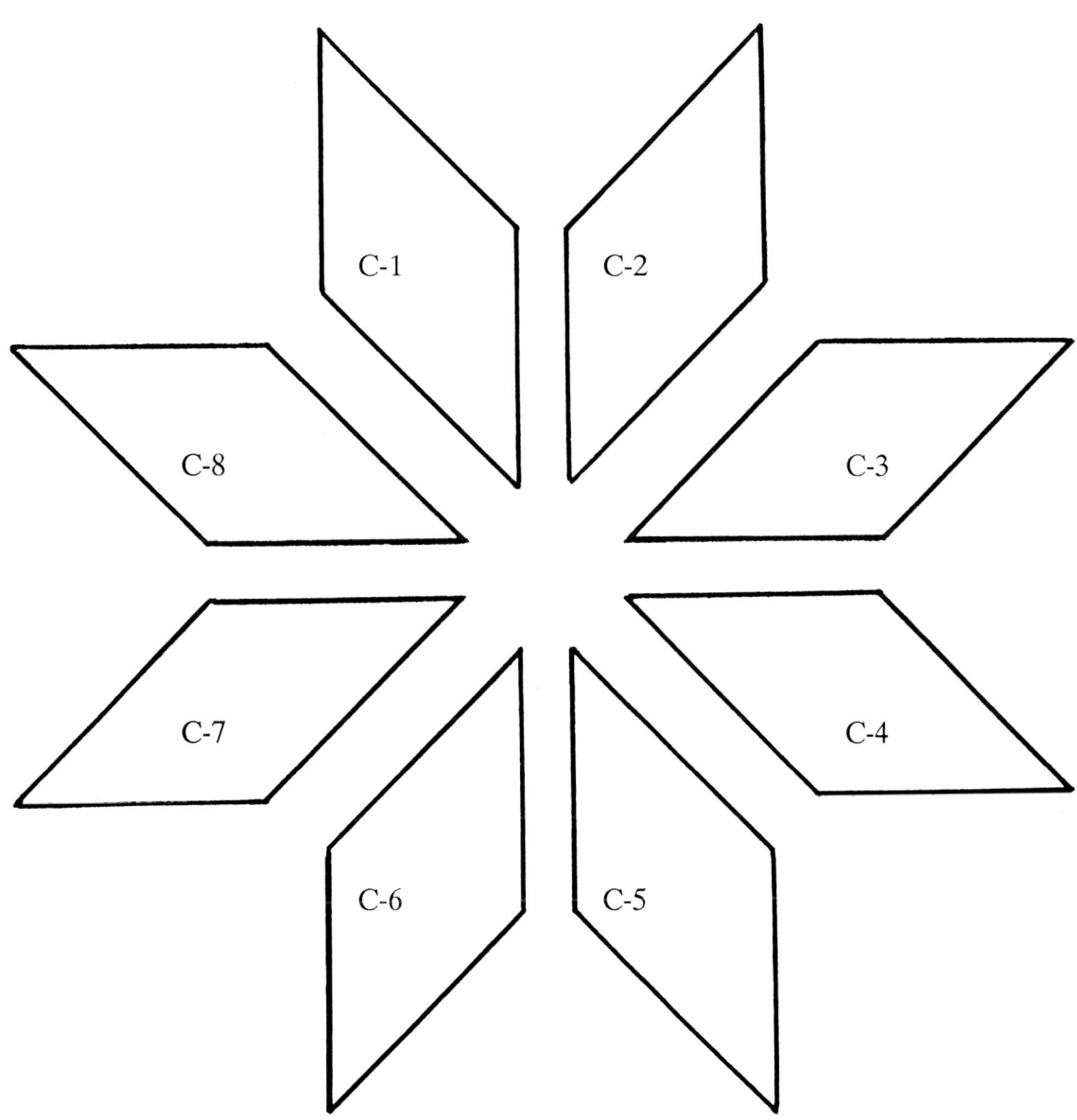

IDENTIFICATION CHART C - CROSSED STITCHES

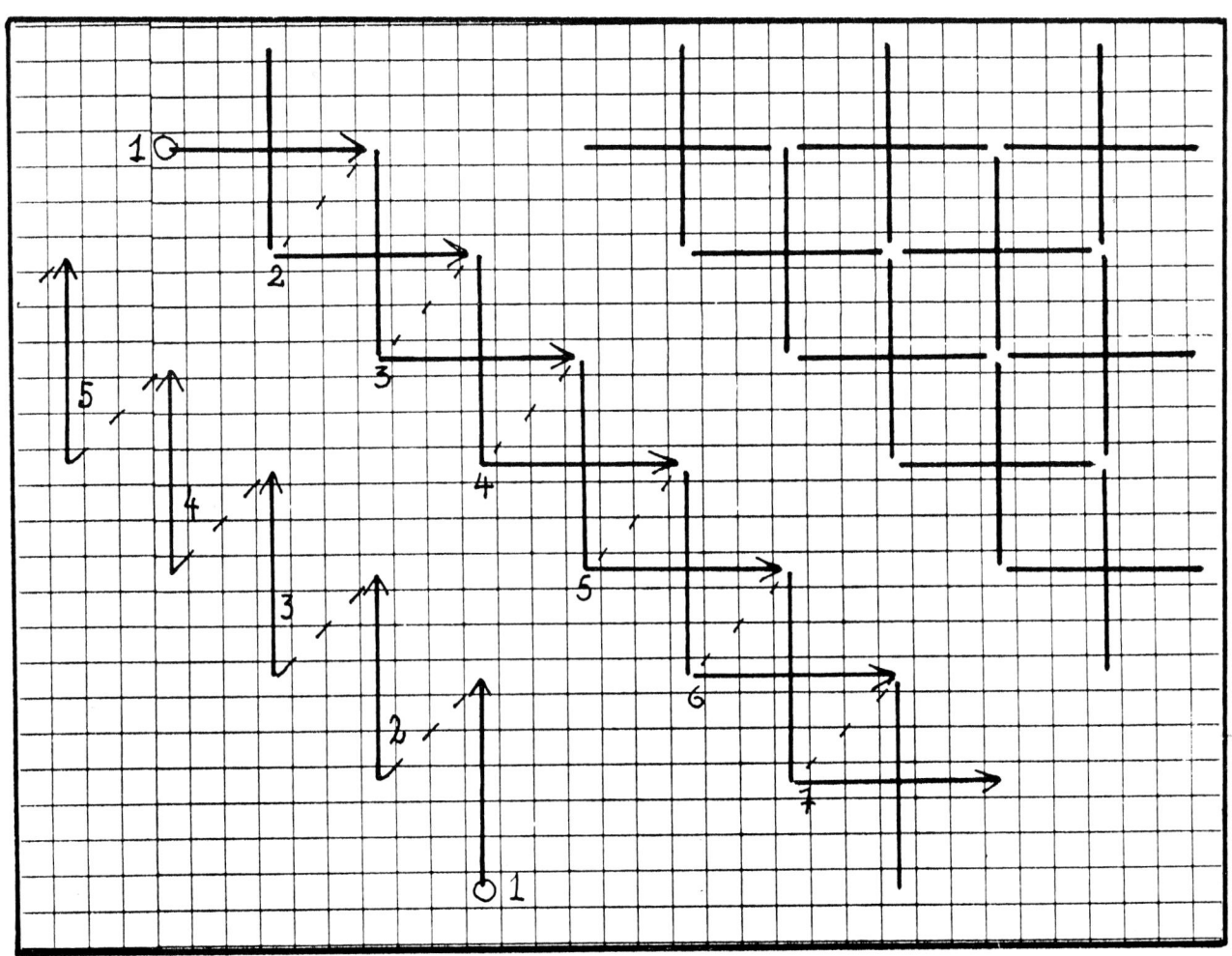

Pattern C-1 - Medium to Tight Pull

This pattern is composed of diagonal rows of straight crosses which are worked in two journeys.

Work up starting at arrow/stitch #1, here shown over six threads. Bring needle up three threads down and three threads to the left, arrow/stitch #2. Continue in this manner until row is completed. Work down crossing the previously made stitches as shown.

For an overall pattern, the rows are attached, i.e. they share the same holes with the previously worked row.

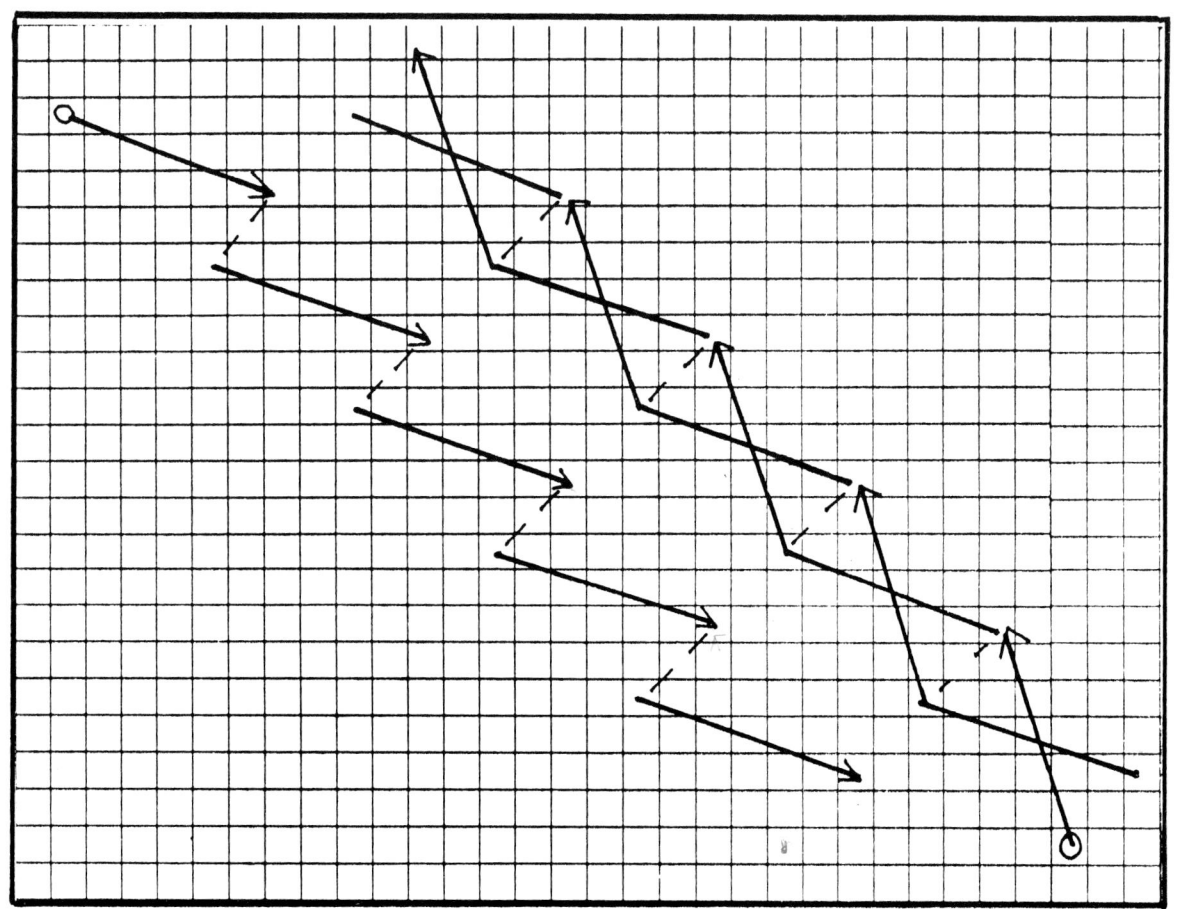

Pattern C-2 - Medium Pull

Slanted crosses are lined up in diagonal rows. Here stitches are shown over six and down two threads.

Work first journey down as numbered arrows/stitches indicate. Cross these stitches on the way up.

Rows are spaced by two intersections where crosses join.

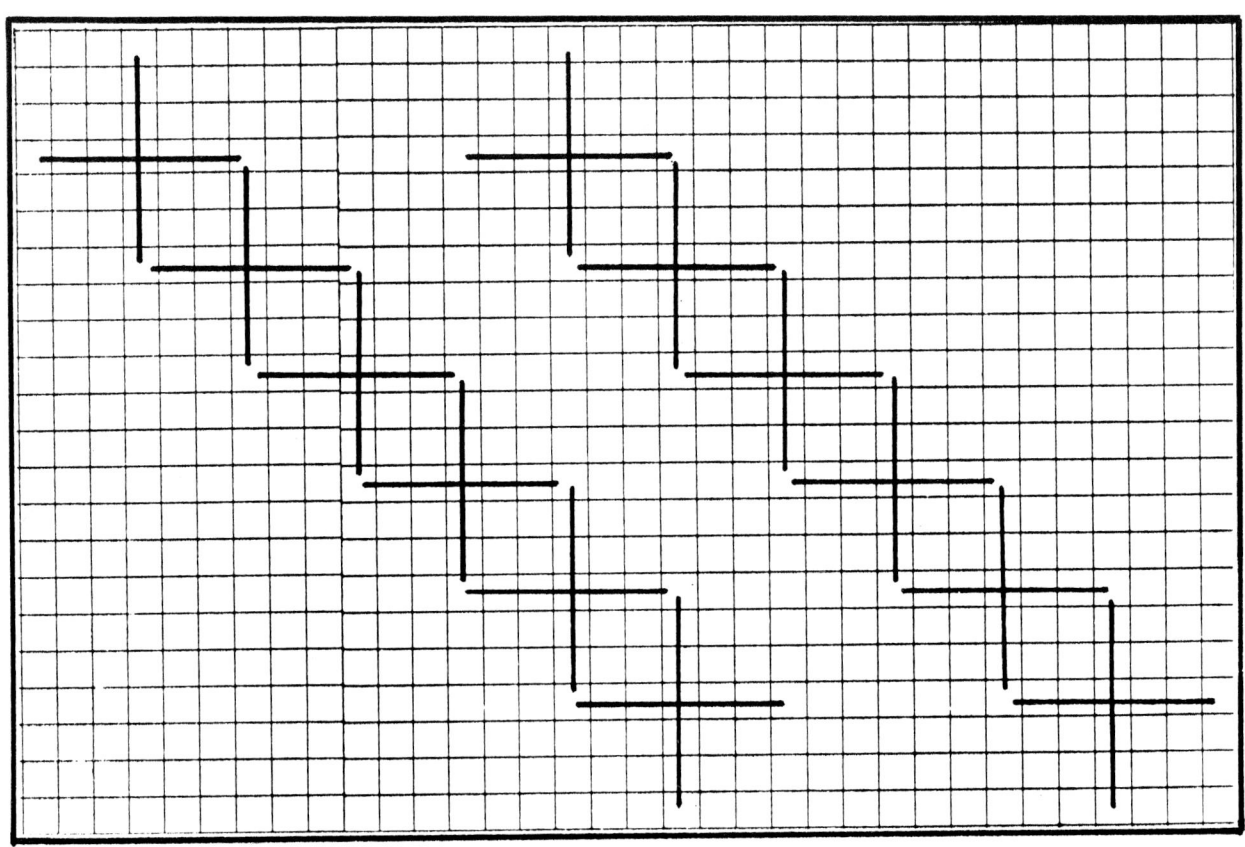

Pattern C-3 - Medium to Tight Pull

Work pattern C-1. Space rows by six threads as shown on above graph. Work all rows in one direction first. When completed, cross rows by turning your work by 90 degrees and work pattern again in the opposite direction. See graph on next page.

Notice that you will have to skip every other cross as these have already been worked. If you find it easier, you can also work all crosses, i.e. going over the one already worked; it will be hardly visible.

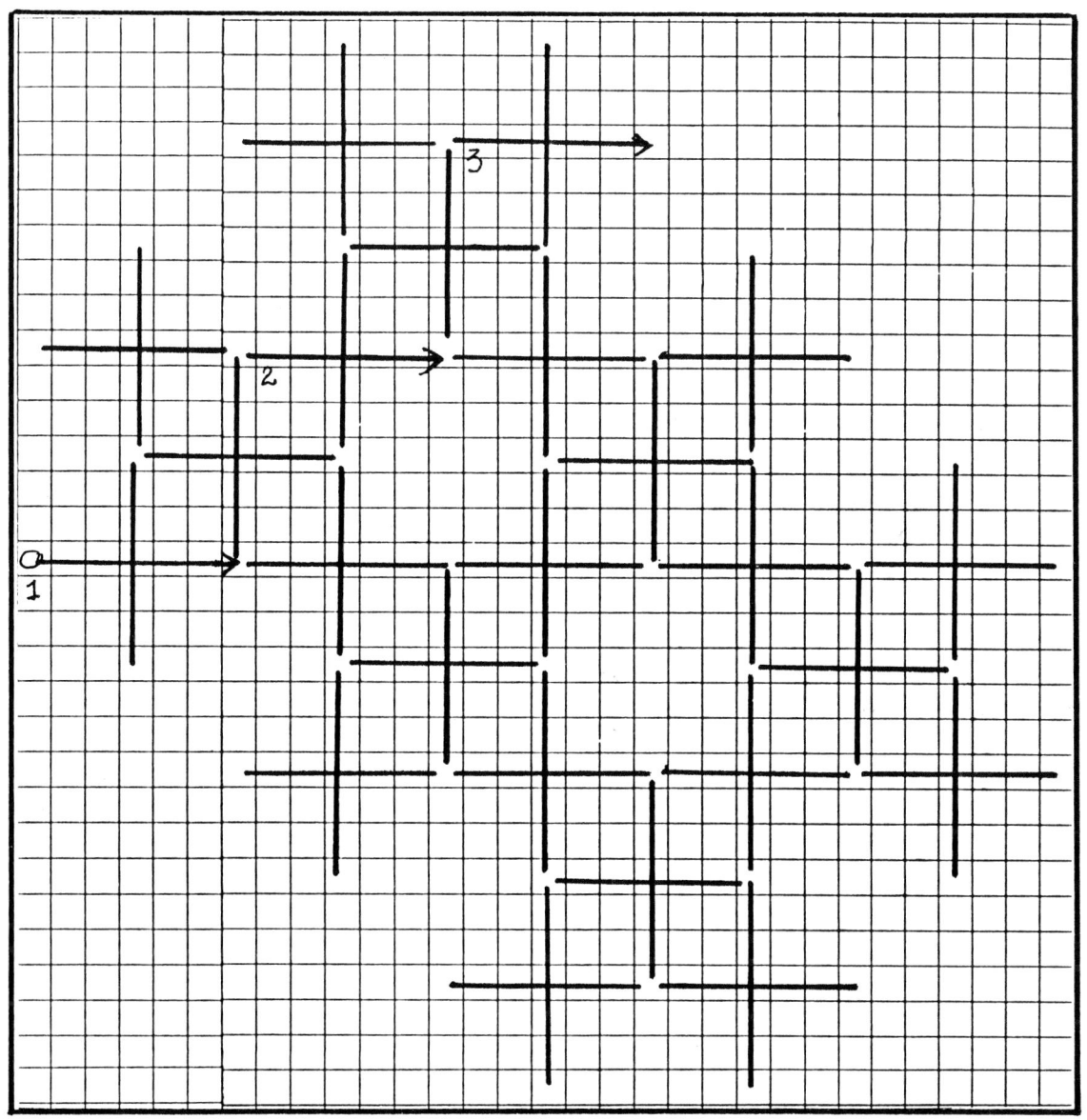

Continuation of Pattern C-3

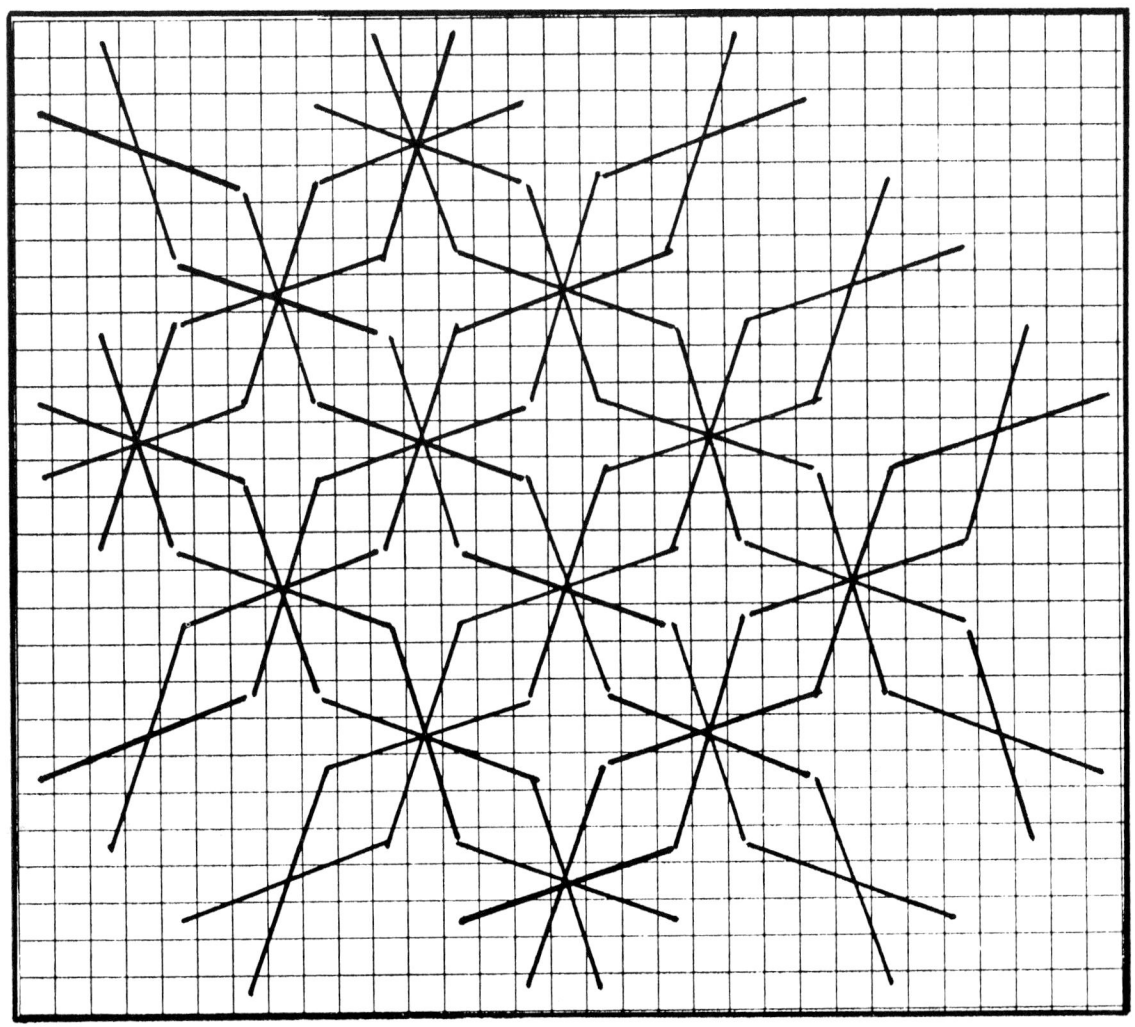

Pattern C-4 - Medium Pull

This pattern looks best when worked in a slightly heavier thread so that the little stars show up, since it is a rather dense pattern with only small holes.

Work Pattern C-2 spacing rows as shown. Work all rows in one direction first. When completed, cross rows by turning your work 90 degrees and work the pattern again in the opposite direction.

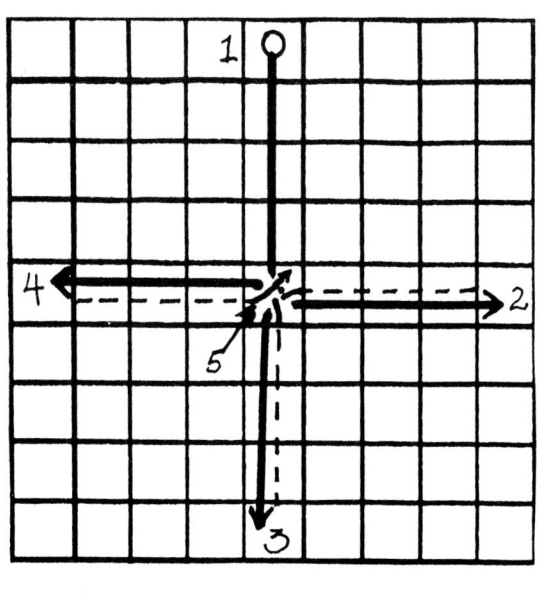
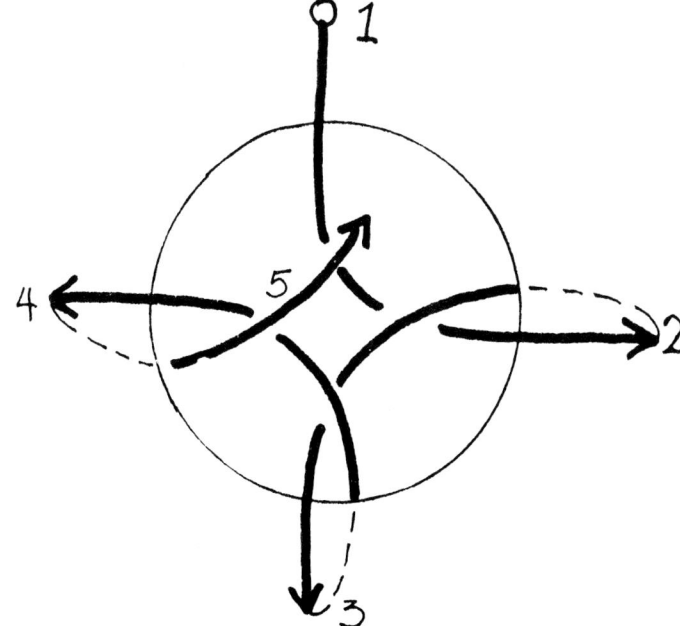

Diagram A   Diagram B

The *GREEK CROSS* stitch deserves to be mentioned on its own since, when correctly worked it is a very versatile stitch. It can be used in various ways for filling pattern and it also adapts very well in a combined filling or composite pattern. Several pages are dedicated to this stitch. I urge you to read all instructions before stitching on the doodle cloth.

First, let's analyze the stitch in itself. If you are familiar with Hardanger embroidery, one could assimilate the Greek Cross with the Dove's Eye or Lace filler; the difference being that one is worked through the fabric while the other is worked in the air. My favorite way to explain this for both techniques is that either stitch is composed of four blanket or, as more often called, buttonhole stitches which converge in the center.

On Diagram A the needle comes up at 1 and in one motion goes down at 2, leaving a loop or slack thread. The needle comes up in the center, that is four threads down of #1 and four threads to the left of #2; needle goes down at 3 and comes up in the center; needle goes down at 4 and comes up in the center. Each of these motions is pulled TIGHTLY. A small stitch is still needed to pull these four stitches together. It is shown as 5. Stitch 5 remains in the center hole, catching only the two "working" threads.

Diagram B will give you a clearer picture as to what is actually happening in the small center hole, here shown enlarged and inside the circle.

In conjunction with these two diagrams, you would want to check Diagrams A-D on the following page as these will give you the direction in which you must proceed to the next unit. It is necessary to follow this direction in order to achieve the correct pull.

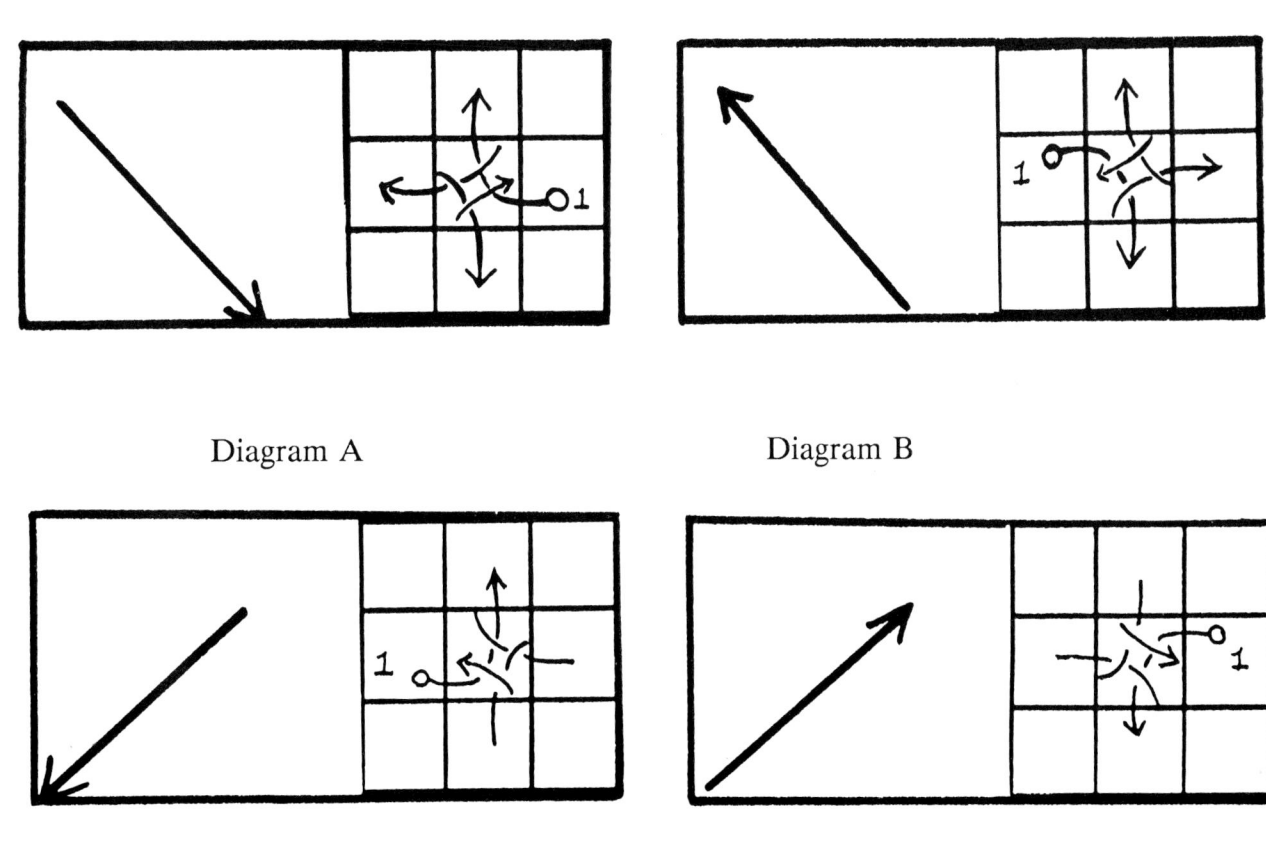

Diagram A   Diagram B

Diagram C   Diagram D

Directional Pull Chart

Let's assume that you are filling a square. Perhaps you would like to place your first unit in the upper left hand corner. Since the only way to proceed would be to the bottom right side, you would choose Diagram A, arrow point pointing in the direction you want to travel, thus you must start your first and each subsequent stitch of that row by coming up in position 1. Your second row would then travel from bottom right to upper left side. You would now start in position 1 of Diagram B. Notice large arrow!

Stitchers who prefer to work with their left hand may prefer to use Diagram C and D or, of course, if you are filling an irregular shape you might need to use these diagrams as well.

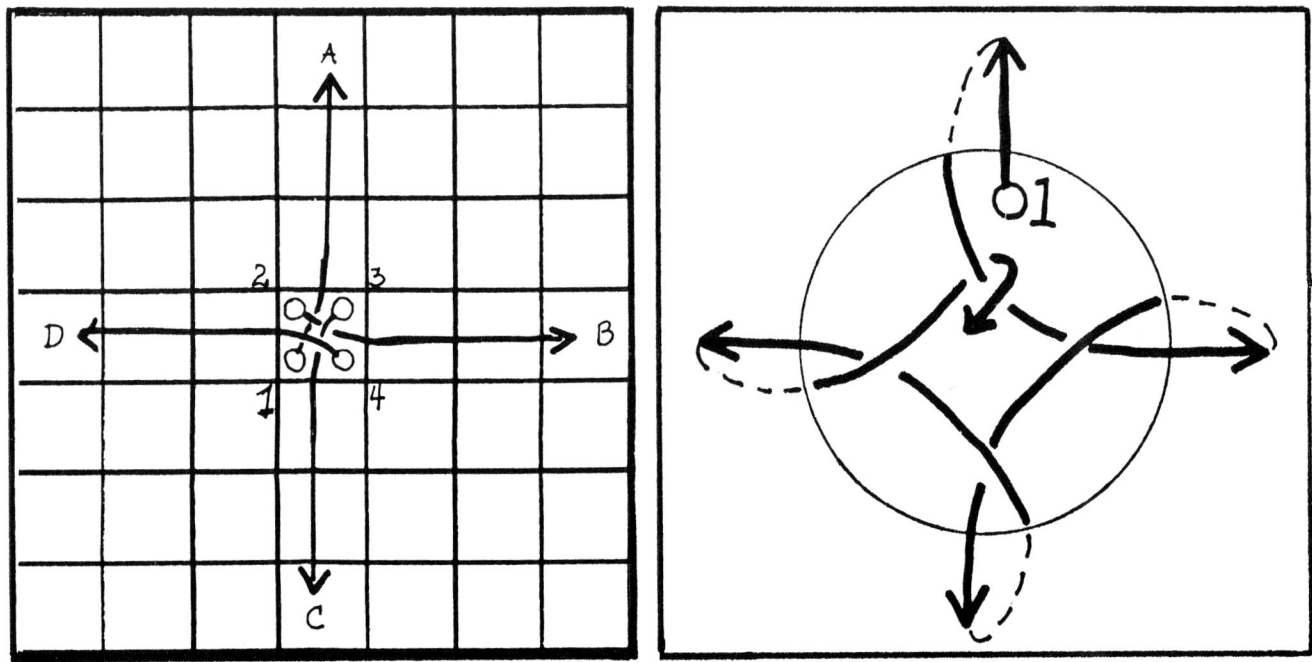

Diagram A   Diagram B

AND THEN THERE IS ILSE'S WAY!!

I like to come up in the center of the unit and make four blanket/buttonhole stitches into the center rather than working the first two "arms" in one sweep. Furthermore, I like to challenge myself by placing a perfect tiny little, correctly worked Dove's Eye in that tiny little center hole! It will be minute, but it is there and oh joy! when seen through a magnifier.

Diagram A shows my working method, enlarged for better understanding and Diagram B shows how to achieve that perfect, tiny little Dove's Eye in the center of the Greek Cross!

METHOD OF WORKING

Diagram A: Come up in center, position 1. Work over a chosen number of threads, 4-5-6, depending on fabric, here shown over three threads. Insert needle at A, come up in center again, in position 2 and insert at B. Come up in center position 3 and insert at C, come up in center position 4 and insert at D.

Diagram B: Come up once more in center position 1, work over stitch 4/D and under stitch 1/A, insert for the last time in very center of all.

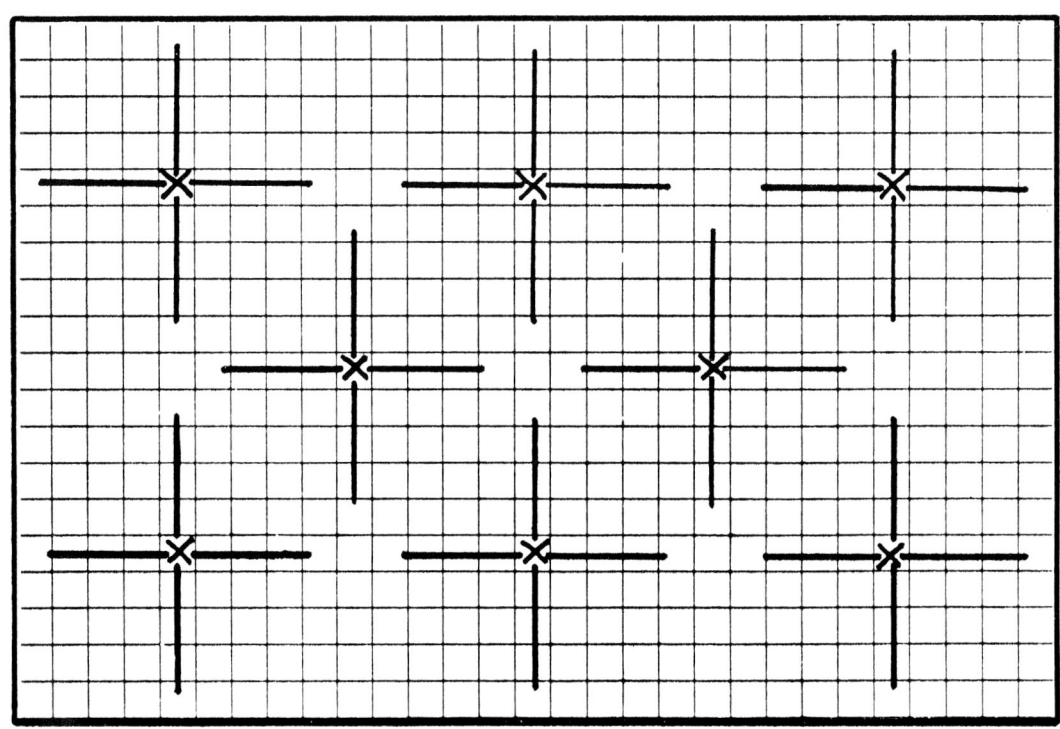

Pattern C-5 - Tight Pull

Greek Cross spaced by two intersections. These two intersections form the design shown with the 2 by 2 threads inside the hole. Method of working is diagrammed and explained on previous pages

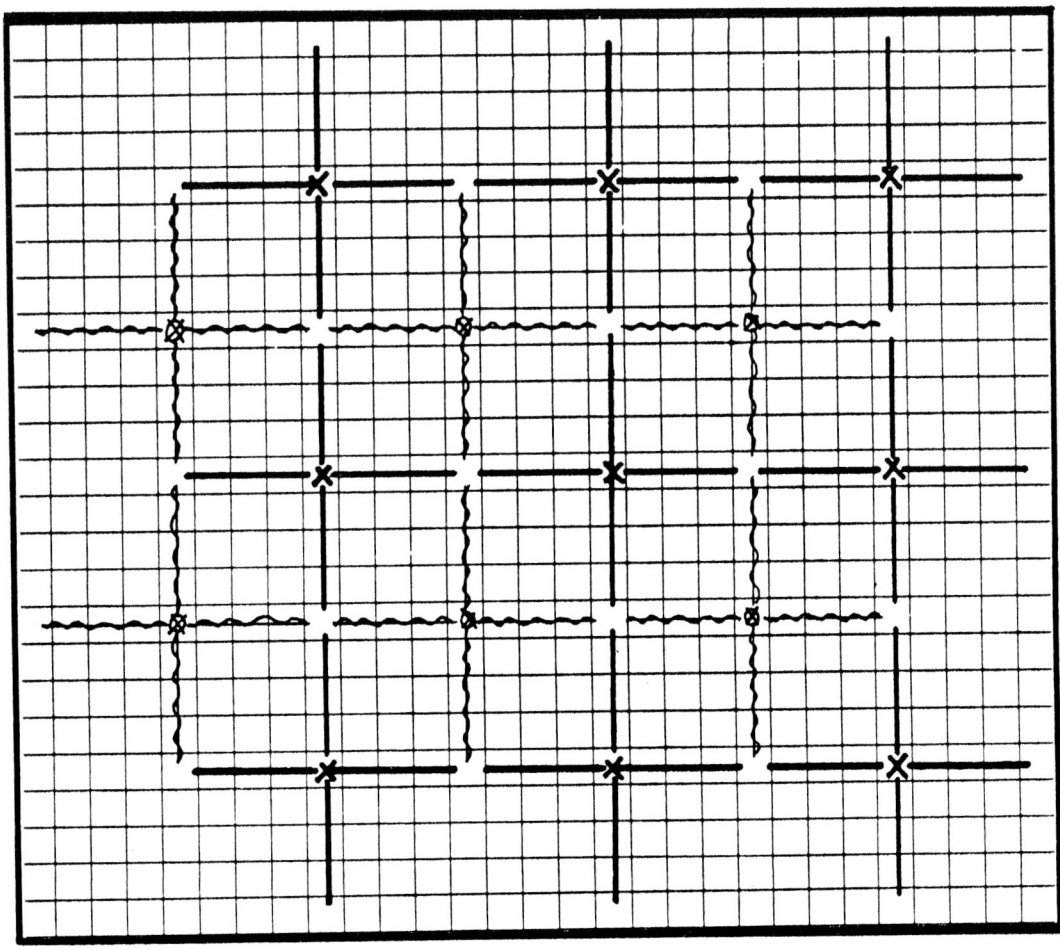

Pattern C-6 - Tight Pull

Here the Greek crosses are worked close together. Each cross shares the hole with the next. To show this more clearly, every other cross was drawn with a wavy line. Method of working is diagrammed and explained on previous pages.

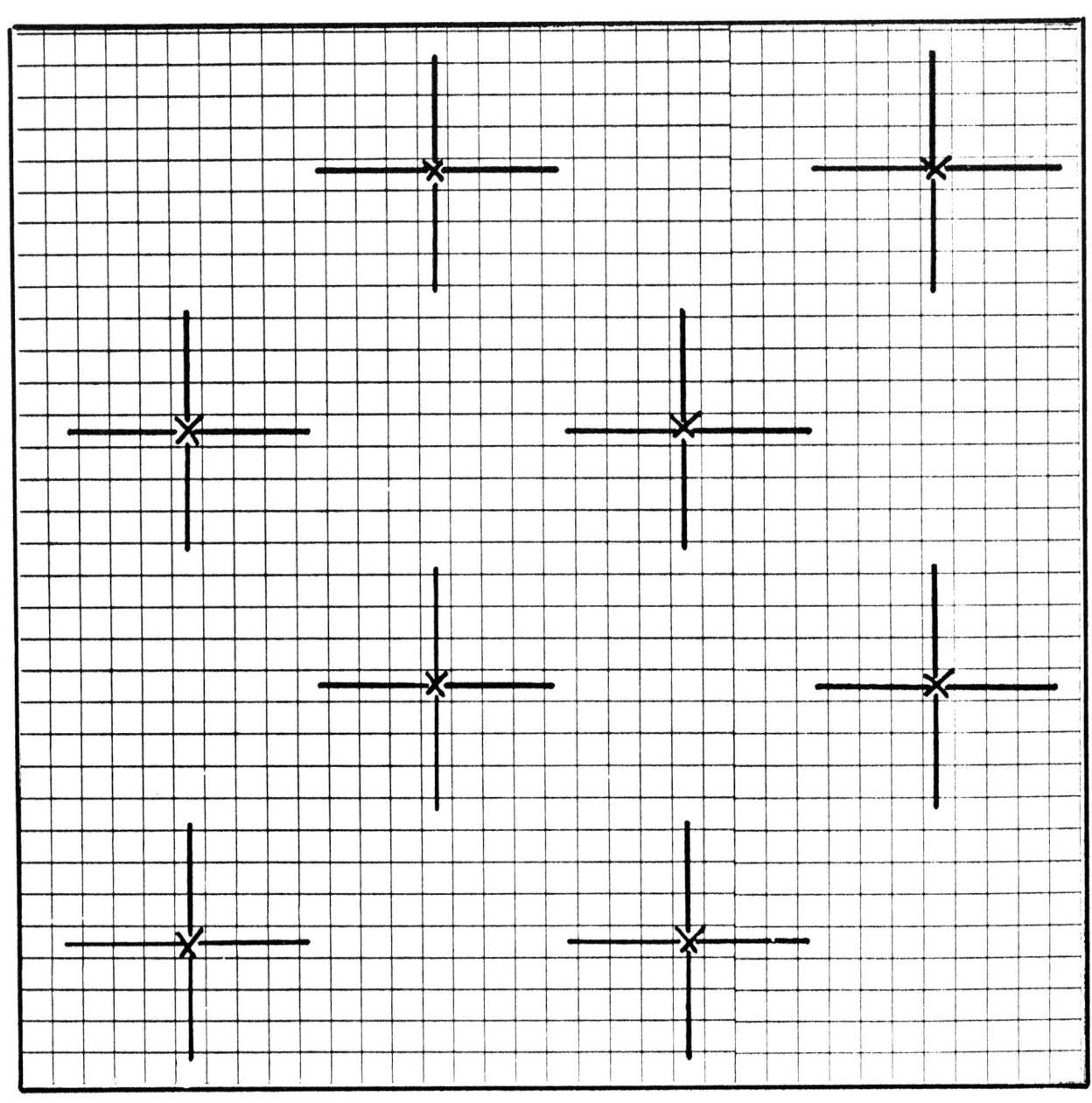

Pattern C-7 - Tight Pull

The Greek crosses are spaced far apart, giving this pattern a light, airy appearance. Method of working is diagrammed and explained on previous pages.

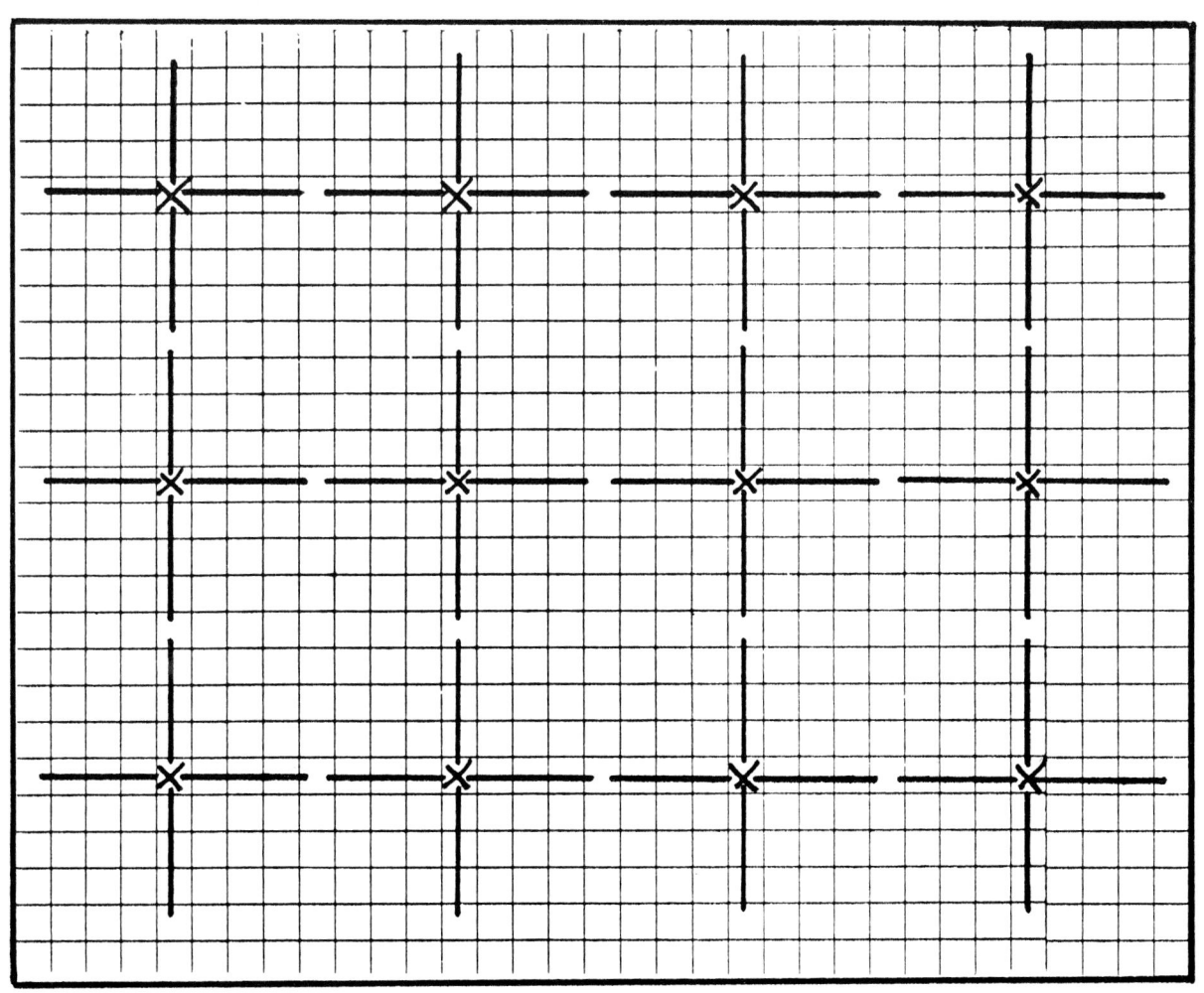

Pattern C-8 - Tight Pull

By spacing the Greek crosses as shown, an illusion of circles is created. Method of working is diagrammed and explained on previous pages.

THE FAGGOT STITCH

This very versatile stitch should not be missed in anybody's repertoire. It is as important as the straight stitch or the four-sided stitch and is used not only in Pulled Thread embroidery, but in other techniques as well; Hardanger being one of them.

The faggot stitch is used as much on the front as it is used for the effect it produces on the back, when it's name becomes reverse faggot. On the front the stitches are worked over the straight of the goods or grain of the fabric, while on the reverse they are worked on the bias or diagonal. It is always worked in diagonal rows. The stitches may pull together 2, 3, 4, 5 and even 6 threads. The larger the number of threads being pulled, the larger the holes will be but, as in all stitches, one must avoid the bunching up of the fabric. Here again, the type of ground fabric will determine the number of threads to be worked over.

You will find in some of the forthcoming graphs that the longer stitches are drawn twice in the same position. This means that the stitch must be repeated once more or gone over again before the pattern continues. Long stitches definitely benefit from this double stitching as the holes will be more rounded and, since these stitches are more often used in larger patterns or areas to be filled, they will be better suited in "weight" and appearance.

The faggot as well as the reverse faggot stitches combine beautifully with other patterns. One or two rows of either, alternated by several rows of some formation of straight stitches for instance, will make up the most beautiful and intriguing composite patterns. It would be a never-ending job to graph out all the possibilities. Many composite patterns will be found throughout this book. Many others, I am sure, will be discovered by you.

In the execution of the stitch, it is of utmost importance that the sequence of working the stitches be strictly adhered to. Just making the stitches "look" like they are drawn on the graph is not enough. When in doubt, check the underside of the work and see if you are getting the look of the faggot, i.e. reverse faggot stitch. If inadvertently you have changed the sequence of stitching, you must take the stitches out, even if no error can be readily seen on the right side of the work. The error will be highlighted with subsequent rows!

As a helpful hint in working procedure, you can think of the faggot stitch as a back stitch worked in a zig-zag fashion. The reverse faggot stitch however can be thought of as a "forward stitch" (the opposite of a back stitch!) worked over two rows. See Diagrams A and B.

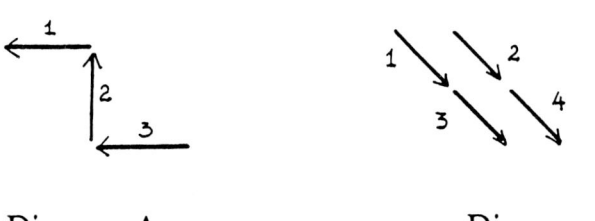

Diagram A   Diagram B

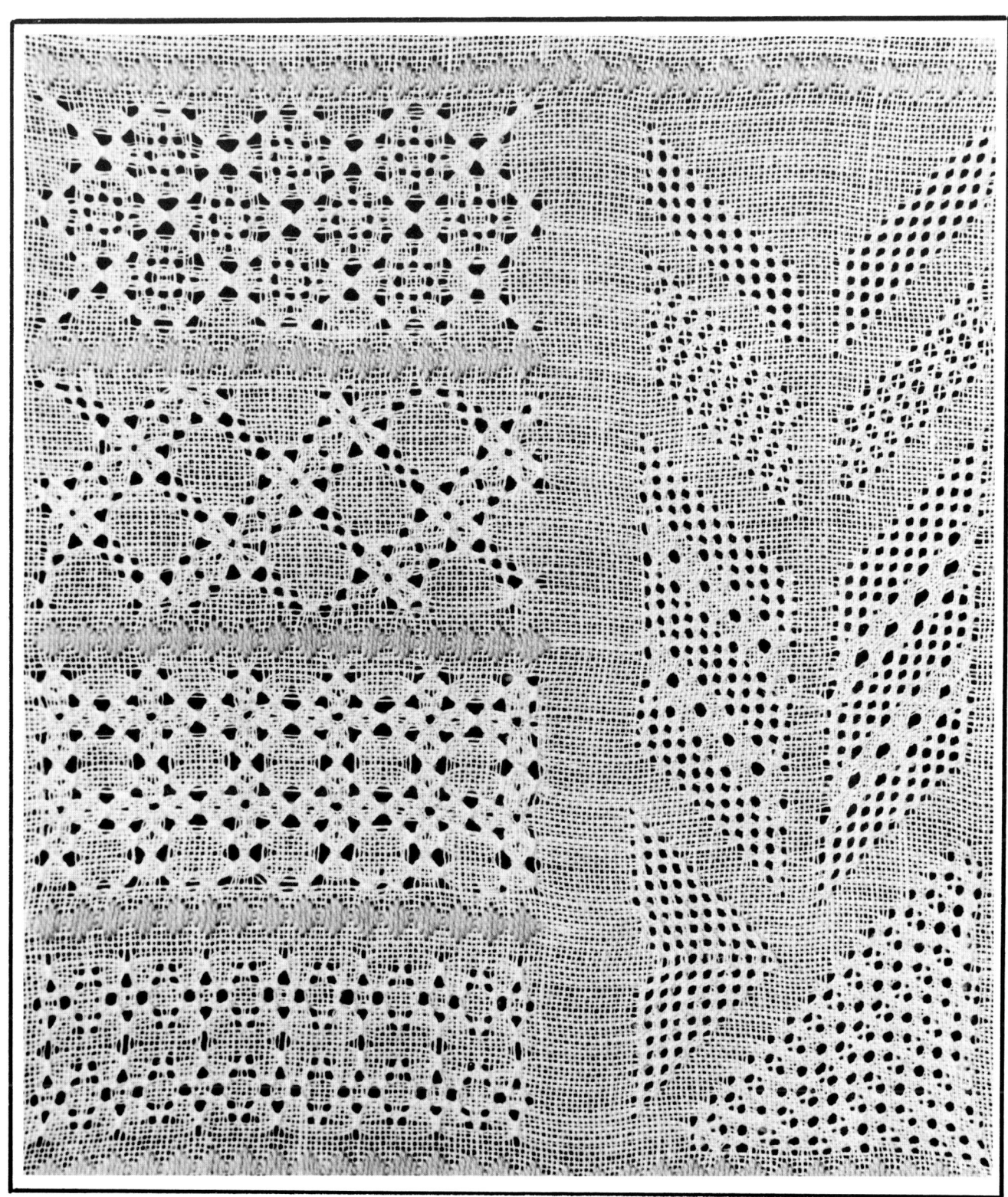

FAGGOT STITCH SAMPLER

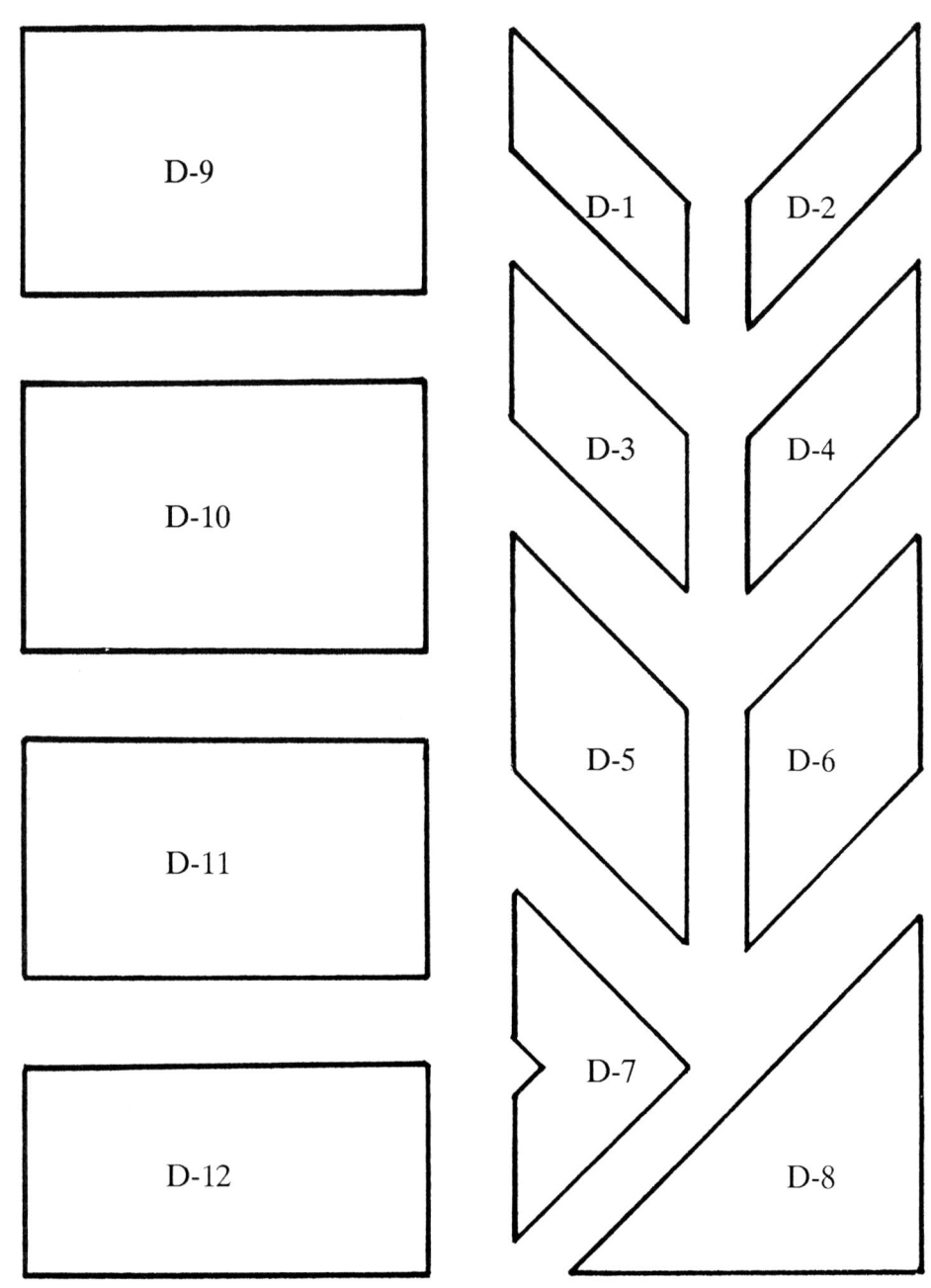

STITCH IDENTIFICATION CHART D - FAGGOT STITCHES

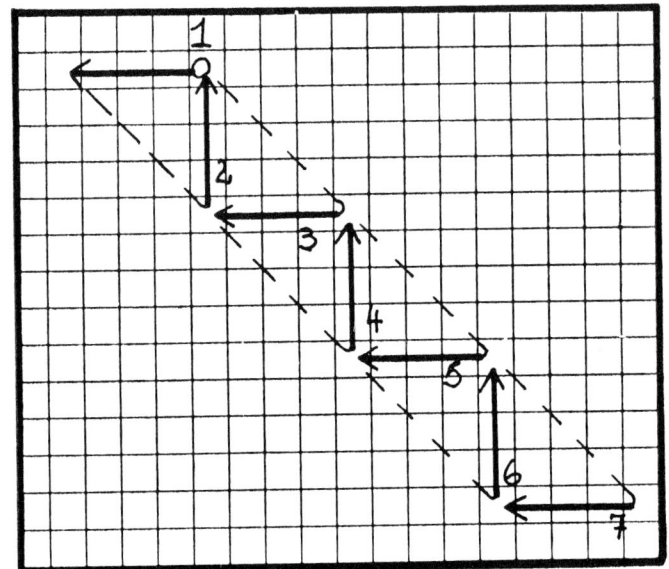

Diagram A

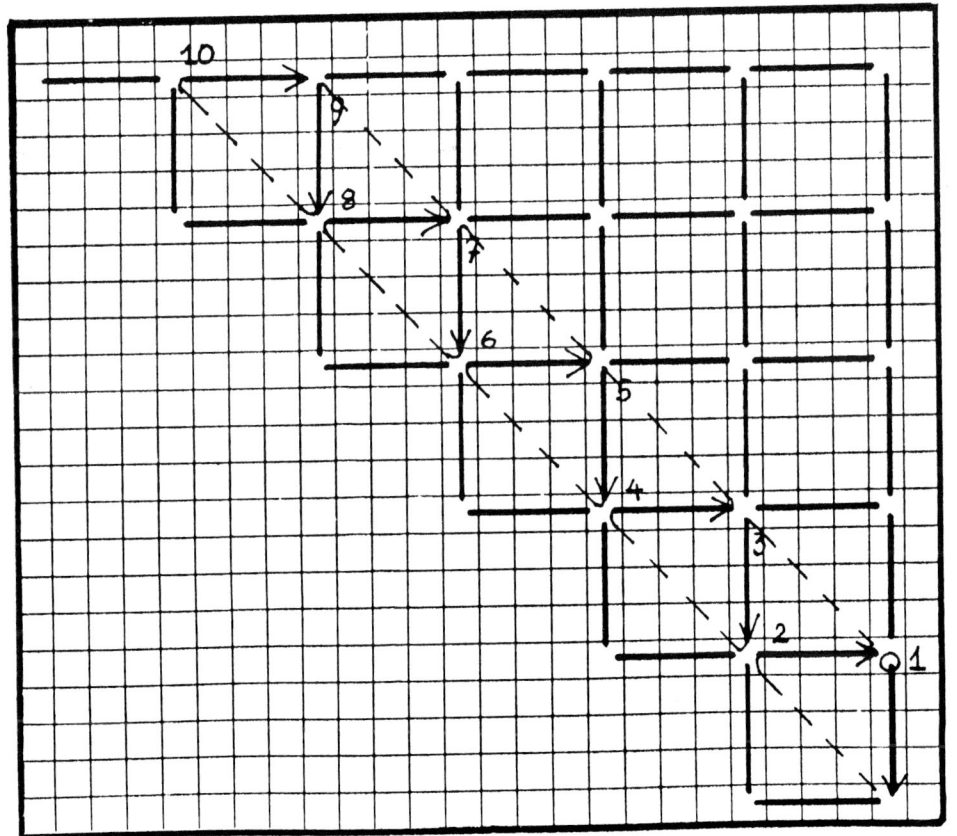

Diagram B

Pattern D-1 - Faggot Stitch - Tight Pull

Work horizontal and vertical stitches in a diagonal row as numbered arrows indicate. Diagram A.

Diagram B shows placement of subsequent rows when stitch is used to fill a shape.

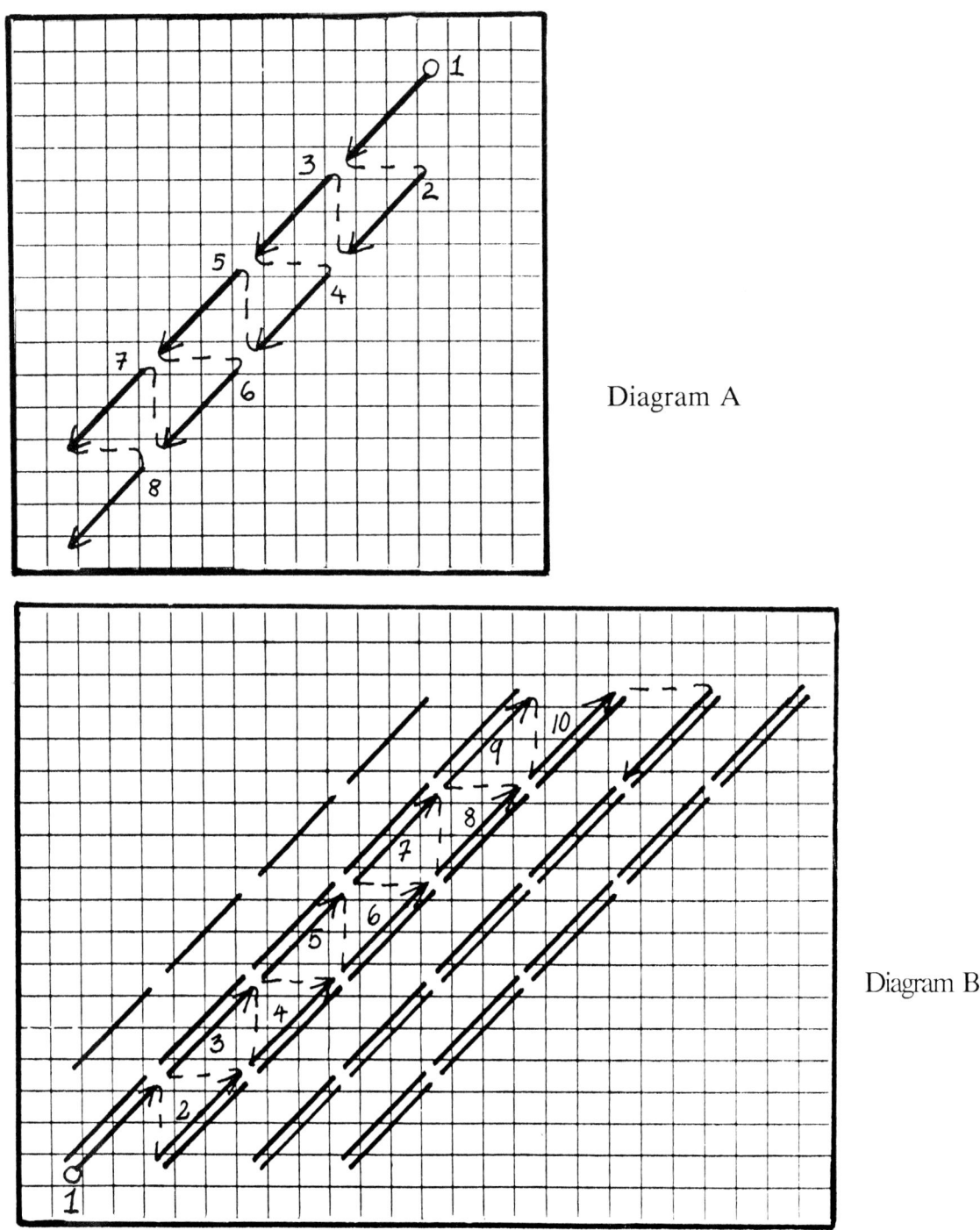

Diagram A

Diagram B

Pattern D-2 - Reverse Faggot Stitch - Tight Pull

Work diagonal stitches in a diagonal row as numbered arrows indicate. Diagram A. Diagram B shows placement of subsequent rows when stitch is used to fill a shape.

This pattern is most effective when used in double rows, i.e. two rows. These can be crossed in various ways so that squared areas appear. The filling of these areas adds interest to the pattern.

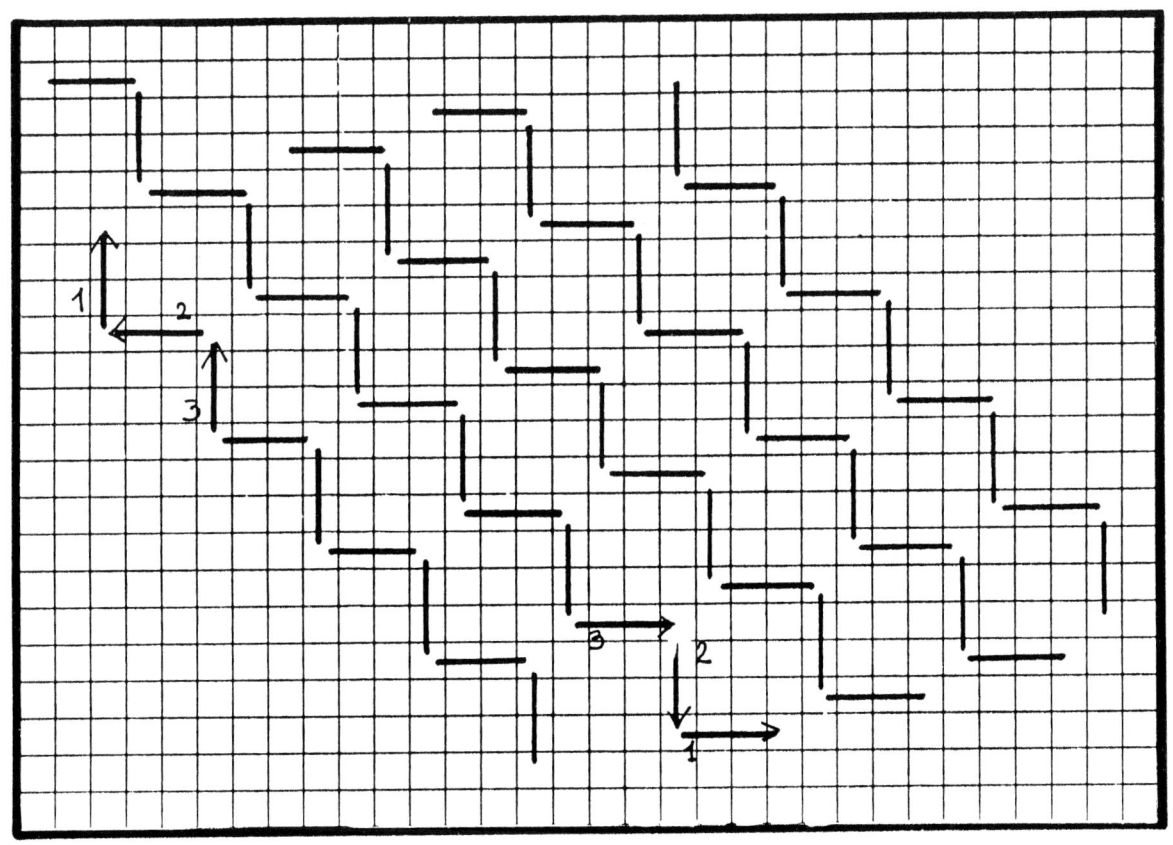

Pattern D-3 - Tight Pull

Work rows of faggot stitches spaced by one intersection where peaks meet.

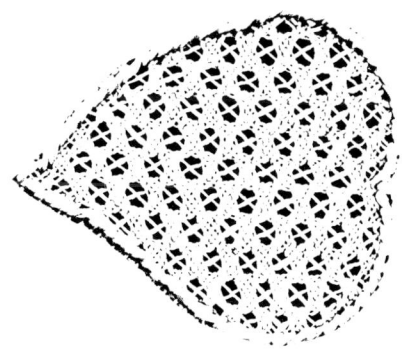

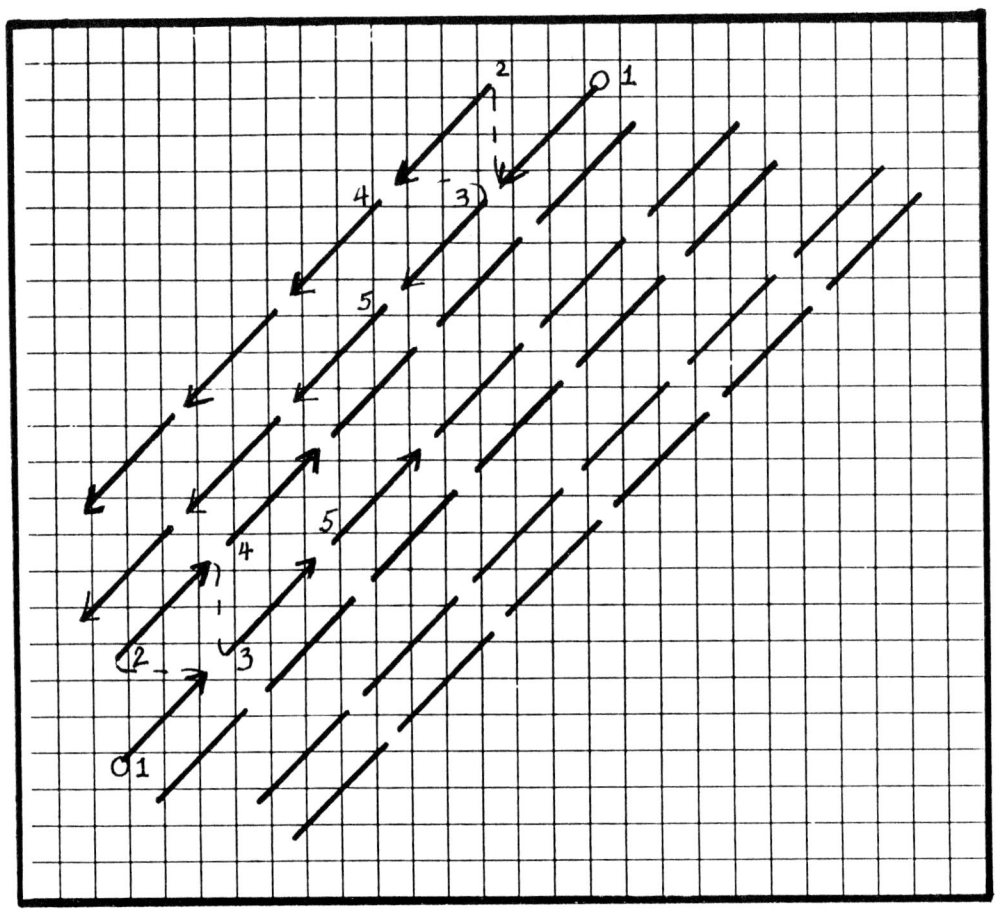

Pattern D-4 - Tight Pull

Work rows of reverse faggot stitches spaced by one intersection.

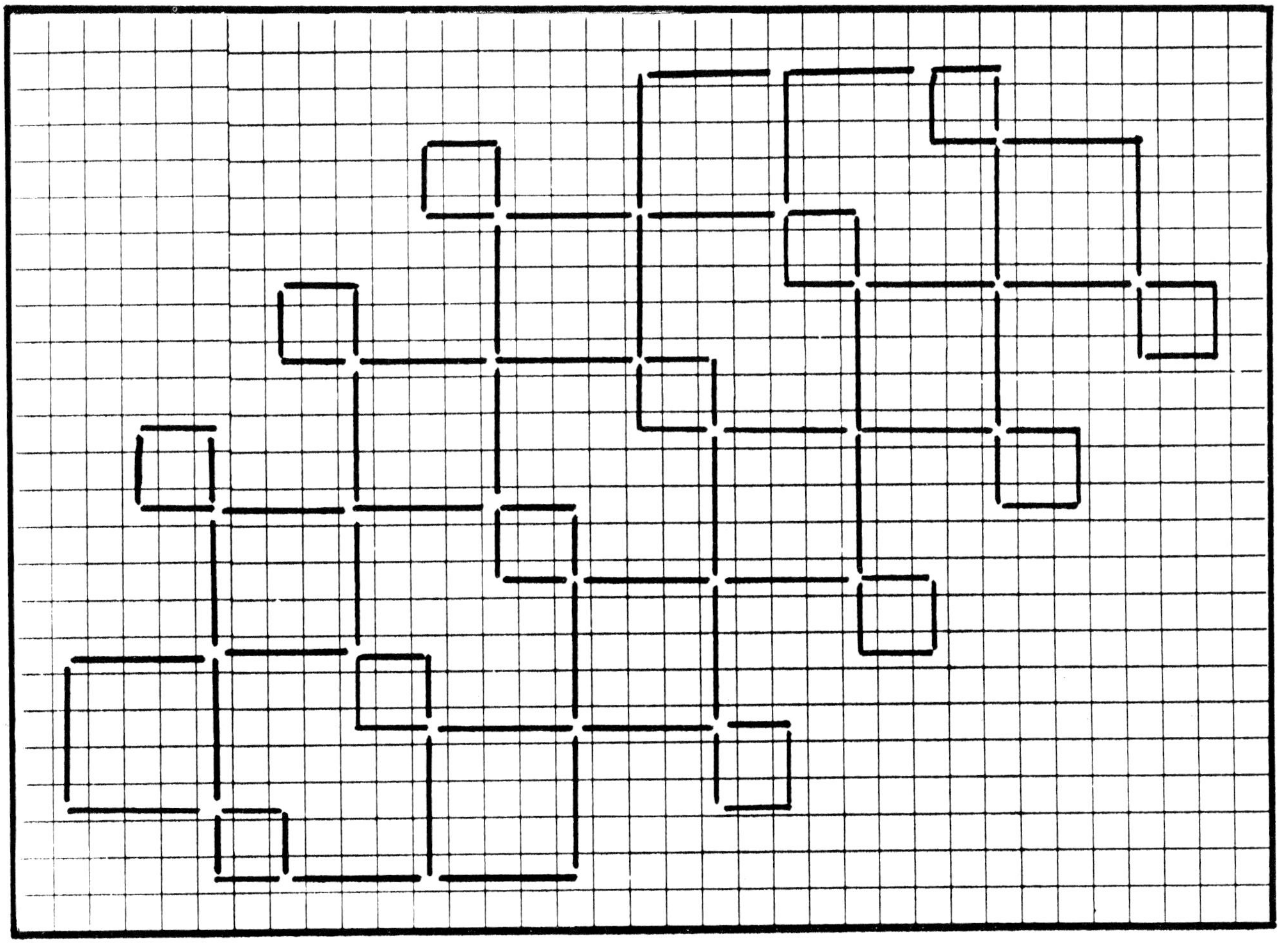

Pattern D-5 - Tight Pull/Medium Pull

Work four diagonal rows of faggot stitch over three threads, pulled tightly. Alternate with two rows of faggot stitch over six threads; use a medium pull on these only, as stitches are too long for a firmer pull.

You might want to try to stitch the longer stitches twice, pulling tightly. The effect is more pronounced when stitched in this manner.

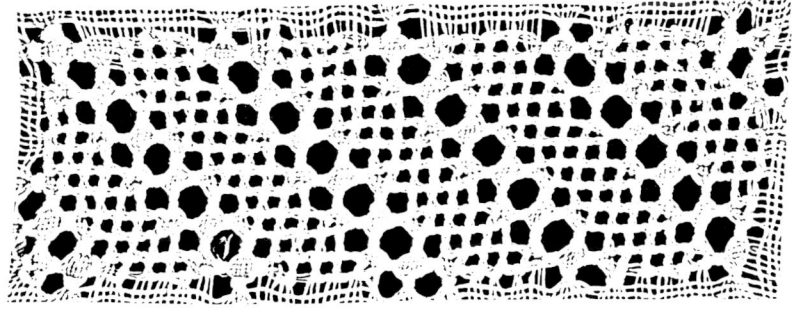

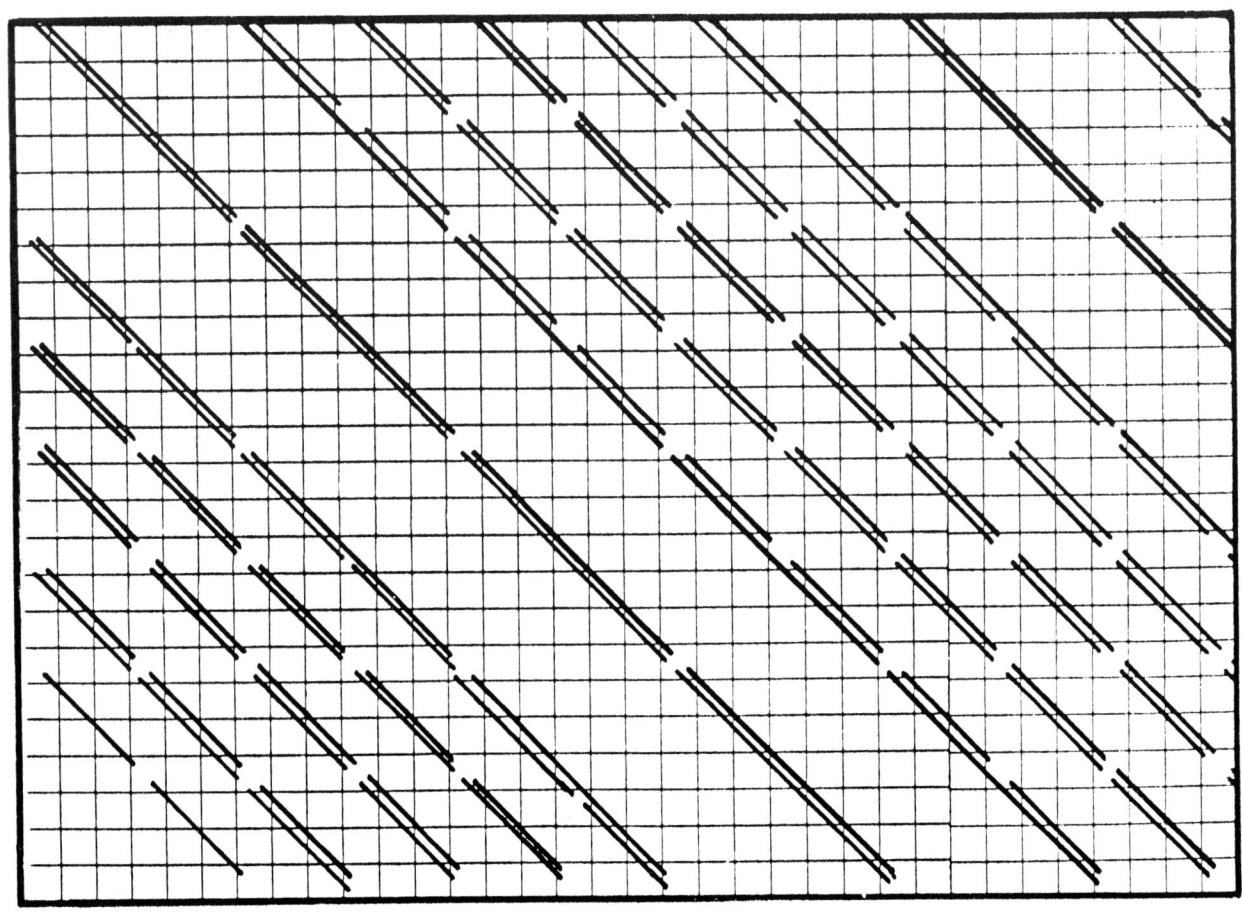

Pattern D-6 - Tight Pull/Medium Pull

Work four diagonal rows of reverse faggot stitch over three intersections, pulling tightly. Alternate with two rows of reverse faggot stitches over six threads, medium pull.

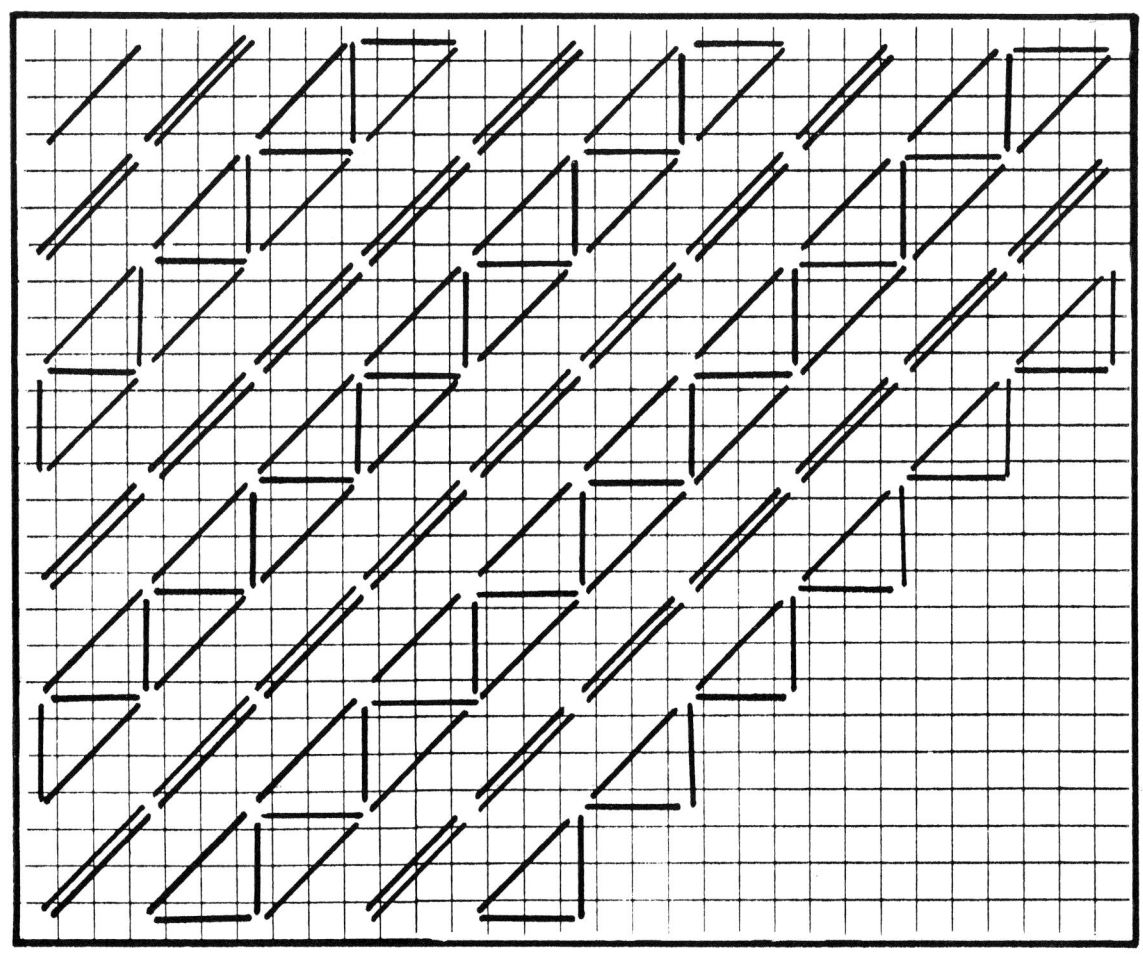

Pattern D-7 - Tight Pull

Work one row of faggot stitch alternated with one row of reverse faggot stitch. Here both are shown over three threads. The number of threads for each stitch must be the same or one may be double in length.

Try the suggested variations out on your doodle cloth and see the resulting difference in pattern.

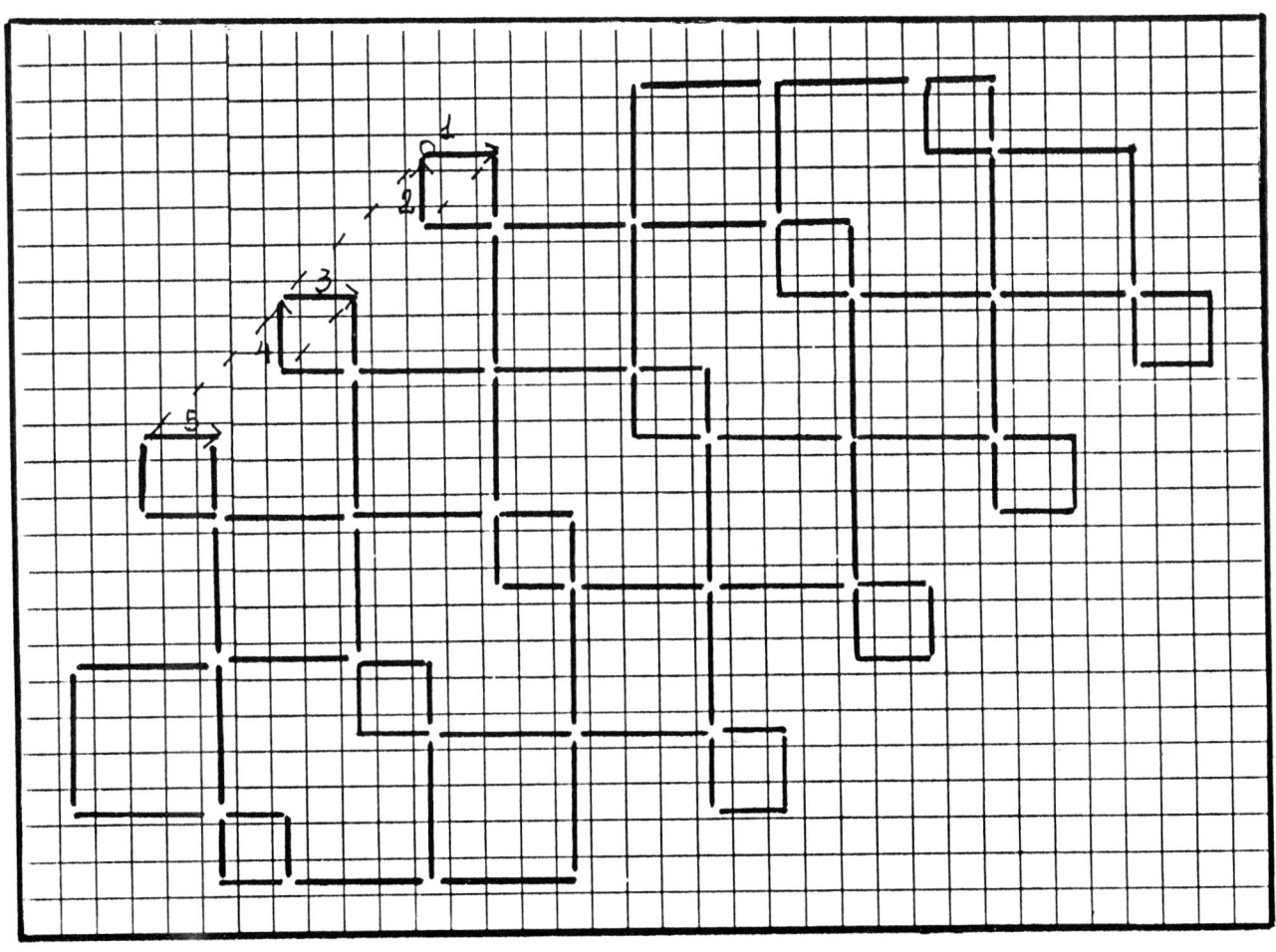

Pattern D-8 - Tight Pull

Work two rows of spaced faggot stitch over two threads, alternating with two rows of faggot stitch over four threads.

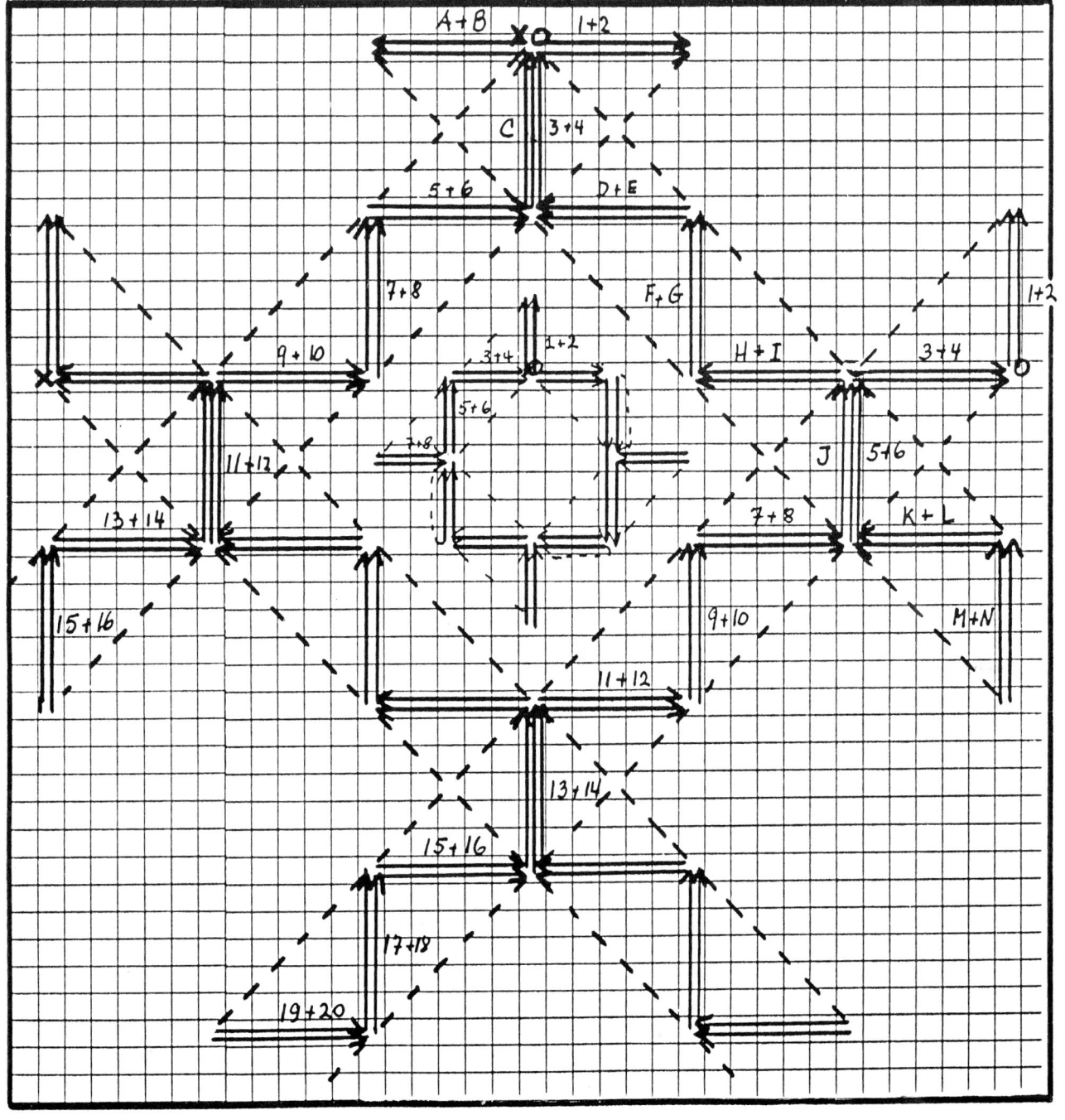

Pattern D-9 - Tight Pull

Description for this pattern is given on the following page.

Pattern D-9 - Tight Pull

This is a fairly large pattern which requires enough space to show various repeats. Only then can the pattern be appreciated. A repeat requires 24 fabric threads in width by 18 threads in height.

Work diagonal rows of twice stitched faggot stitches over six threads. For spacing see graph. Cross the rows by working in the opposite direction. *Notice* that only one stitch is made where the rows cross. (Total of three stitches in this space.)

Fill the resulting centers with a small unit consisting of stitches over three threads only.

Pattern D-10 - Tight Pull

The graph for this pattern can be found on the following page.

This pattern requires enough space to show various repeats. Only then can it be fully appreciated. This pattern consists of reverse faggot stitches combined with faggot stitches of varying lengths. Back stitches are added where required.

Notice that all stitches are worked twice.

Start at circled arrow/stitch 1+2 on the upper right corner. Follow the numbered arrows in their correct sequence, always coming up at the arrow's base and inserting the needle at the arrow's point, and you will have no trouble following the pattern.

Work a companion row starting form the bottom and bringing the needle up at arrows/stitches A+B, marked by an X. The striped motifs are subsequently filled with eyelets.

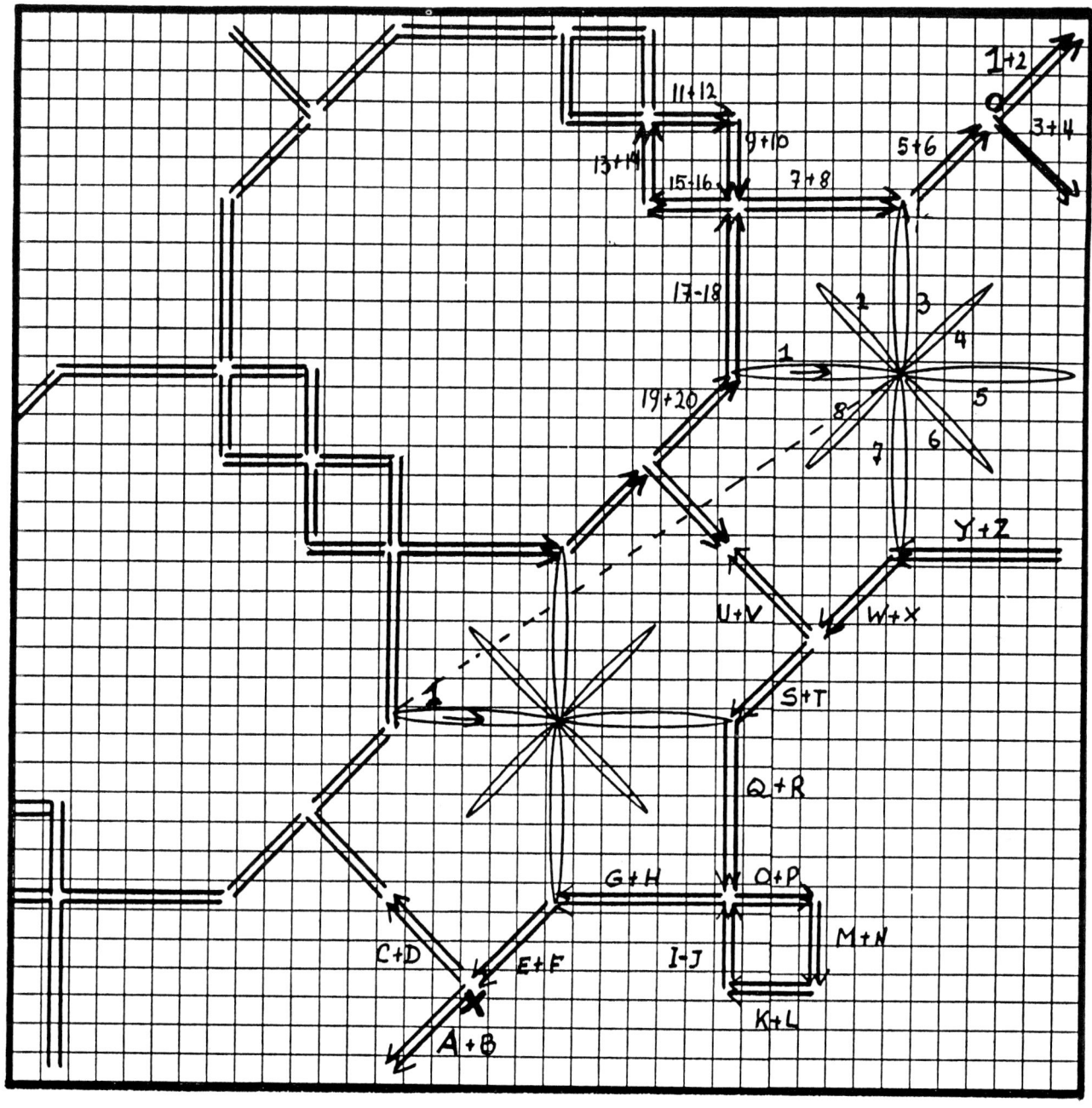

Pattern D-10 - Tight Pull

Description for this pattern is on the preceding page.

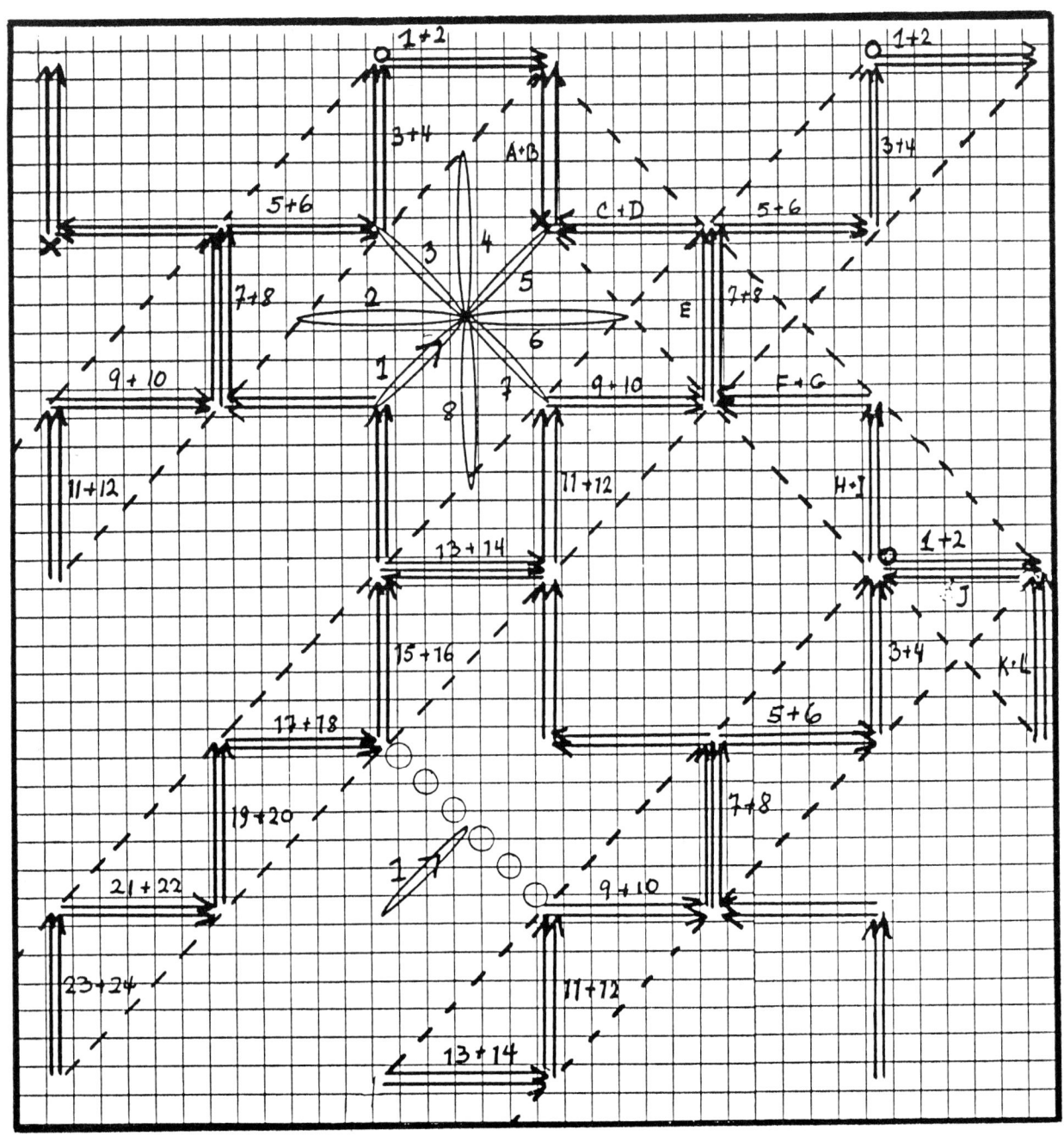

Pattern D-11 - Tight Pull

Work faggot stitch twice over six threads following numbered arrows. Work in diagonal rows spaced by six intersections opposite peaks.

Work diagonal rows in the opposite direction, but working the crossing stitch only once.

Work eyelets in the resulting open spaces.

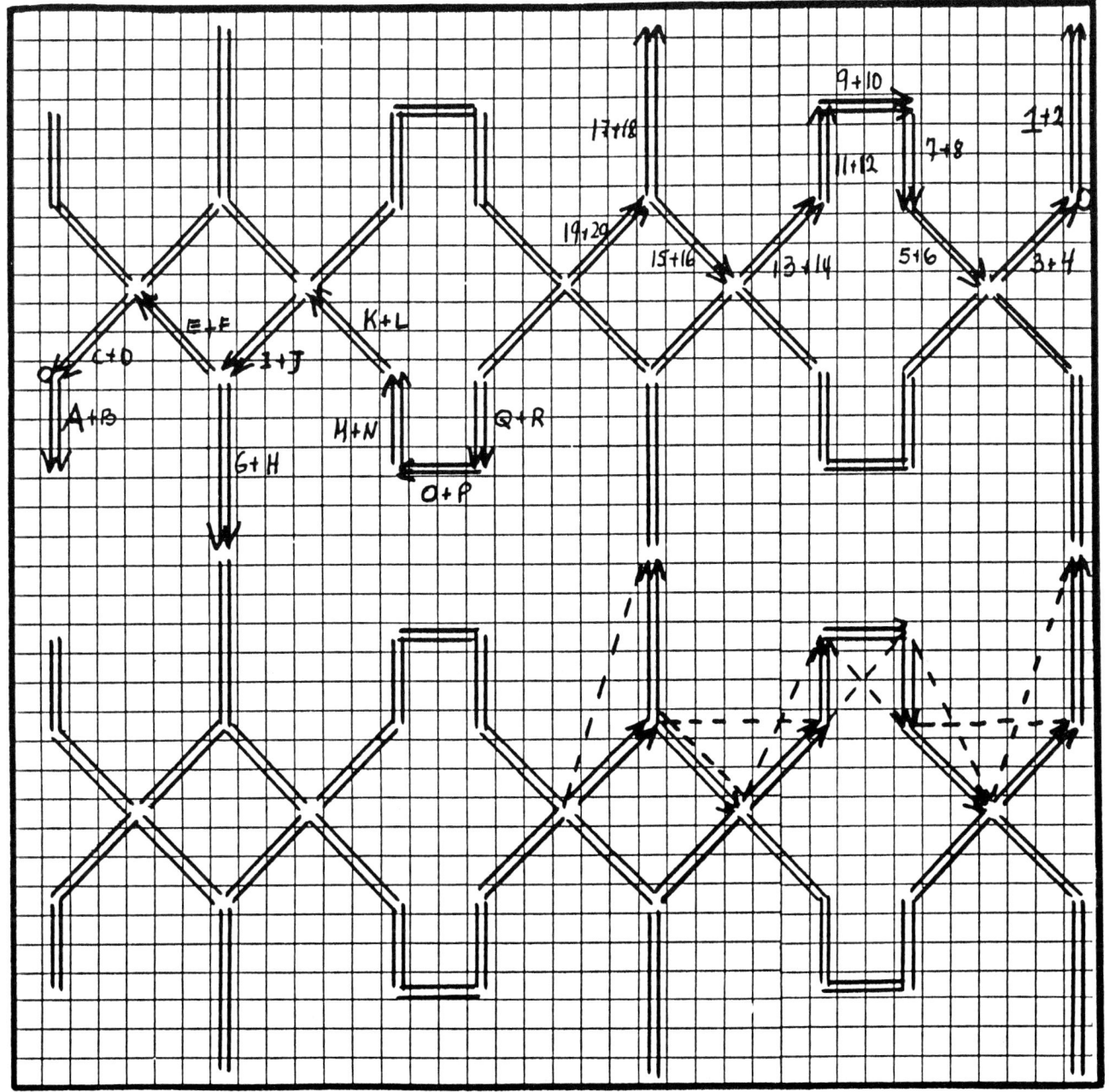

Pattern D-12 - Tight Pull

Work a combination of diagonal, vertical and horizontal stitches. Each is worked twice.

Work in horizontal rows in the fashion of back stitch. Follow numbered arrows.

The return trip completes the pattern; see Arrows A+B. The broken lines on the second row also show the travelling path.

The occurring empty spaces can either be filled or left open.

THE WAVE STITCH

The wave stitch and its many variations are other fine stitches which should not be missed. They work wonderfully in borders as well as in overall patterns.

The reverse side of the wave stitch is as charming as the front and is frequently used for overall patterns as well as for borders when combined with other stitches. See patterns E-6, E-9 and E-10. We call this stitch the Reverse Wave stitch. In Europe the wave stitch is referred to as the "knit" stitch as it indeed resembles its sister stitch in a knitted item worked in stockinette stitch. The stitch is used to add color patterns to the already knitted background. The reverse wave stitch is called the "purl" stitch for the same reason.

The stitch can be varied in length and thread count to suit the shape of the units in a design and the whimsy of the stitcher.

If the stitch is sewn rather than stabbed, a right-handed person must stitch the horizontal rows of wave stitch from right to left which means that the work must be turned around when the row is completed. A left-handed person would do the opposite for comfort in sewing. The reverse wave stitch is sewn in the opposite direction for ease in stitching. If you prefer the stab method, either direction is comfortable. Sewing is my preferred method since in most wave stitch patterns the needle picks up vertical threads only, which means that the needle is in a horizontal position at all times. There is an easy rhythm to the process which makes the wave stitch a fun and fast one to do.

In the diagrams that follow, some stitches are graphed on the straight of the fabric; these are reverse wave stitches, while others are graphed on the bias or slant; wave stitch. Some stitches are repeated, meaning they are stitched twice and others are squeezed together in the narrowest way possible. Most wave stitches will benefit from fine thread with the exception of E-3 and E-4, the honeycomb stitch and its variation. The doodle cloth will aid you further in picking the right thread for the look you are aiming for.

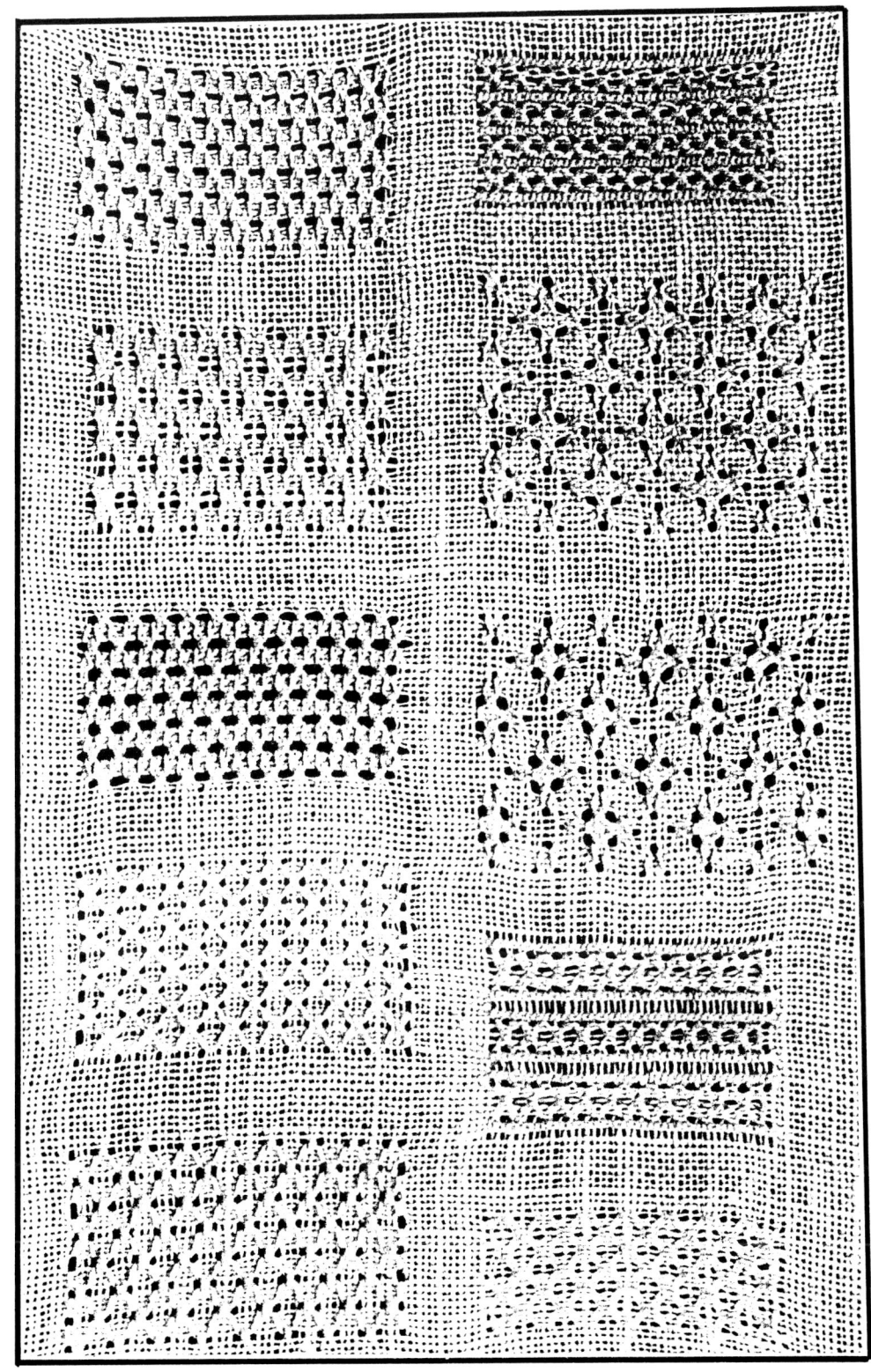

WAVE STITCH SAMPLER

E-1	E-6
E-2	E-7
E-3	E-8
E-4	E-9
E-5	E-10

IDENTIFICATION CHART

WAVE STITCH

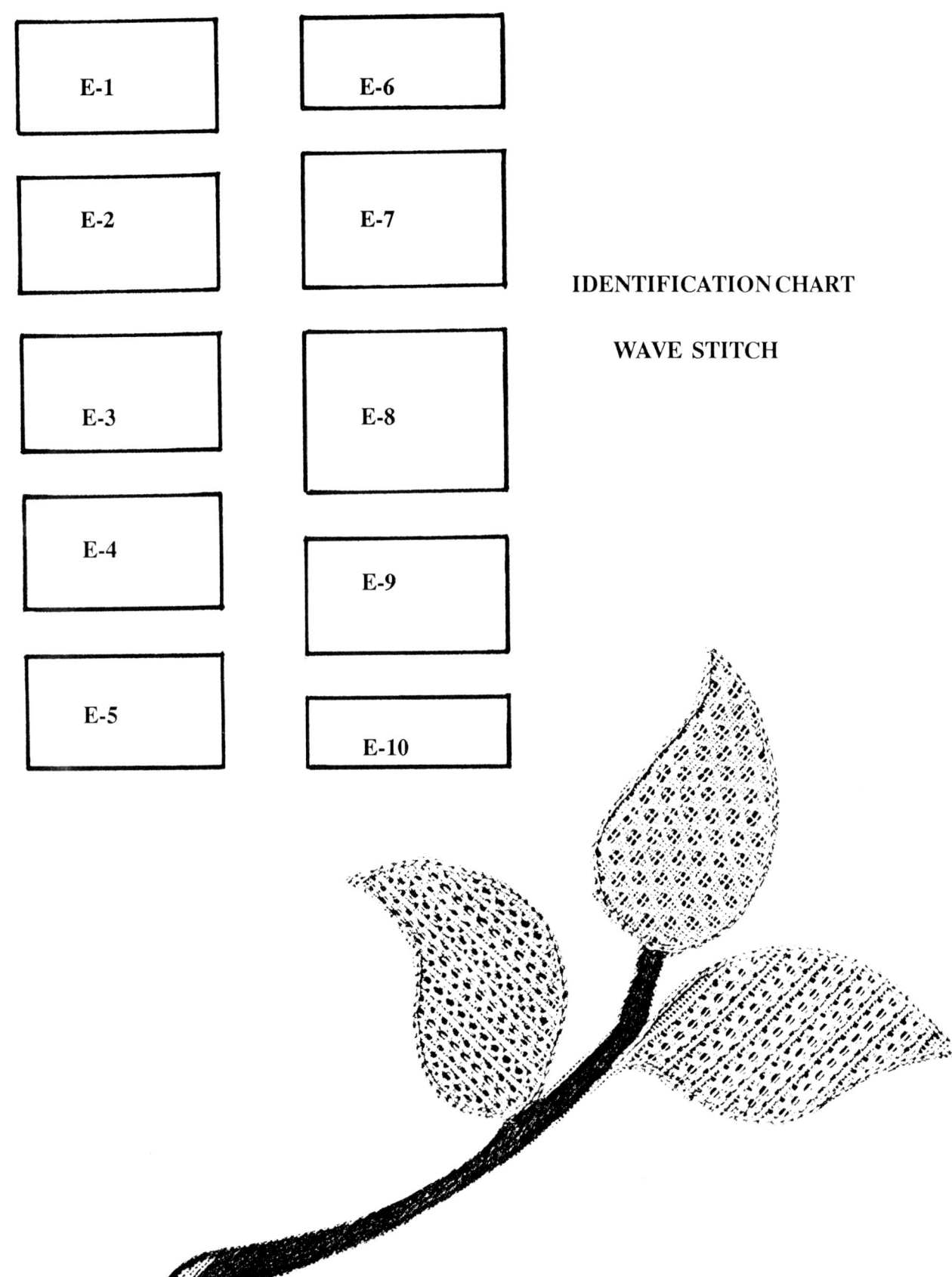

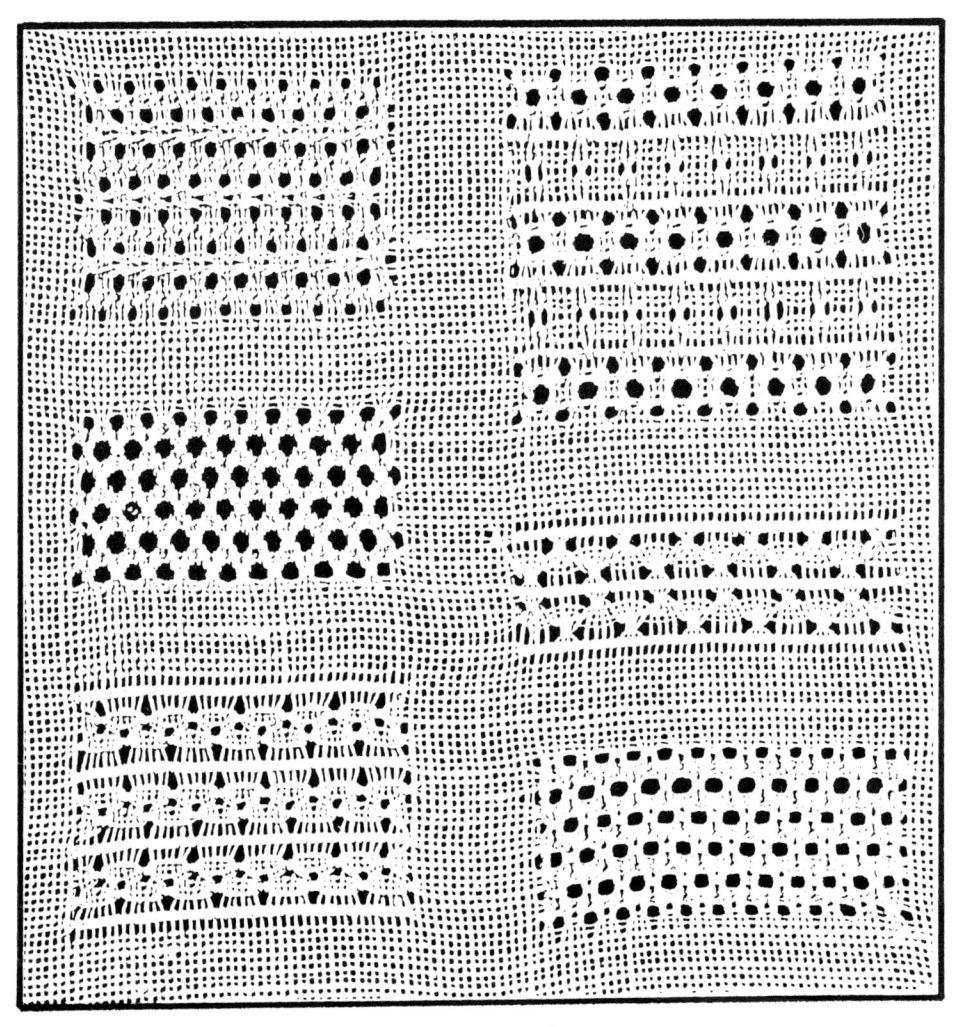

E-11	E-14
E-12	
	E-15
E-13	E-16

WAVE STITCH SAMPLER II

IDENTIFICATION CHART E

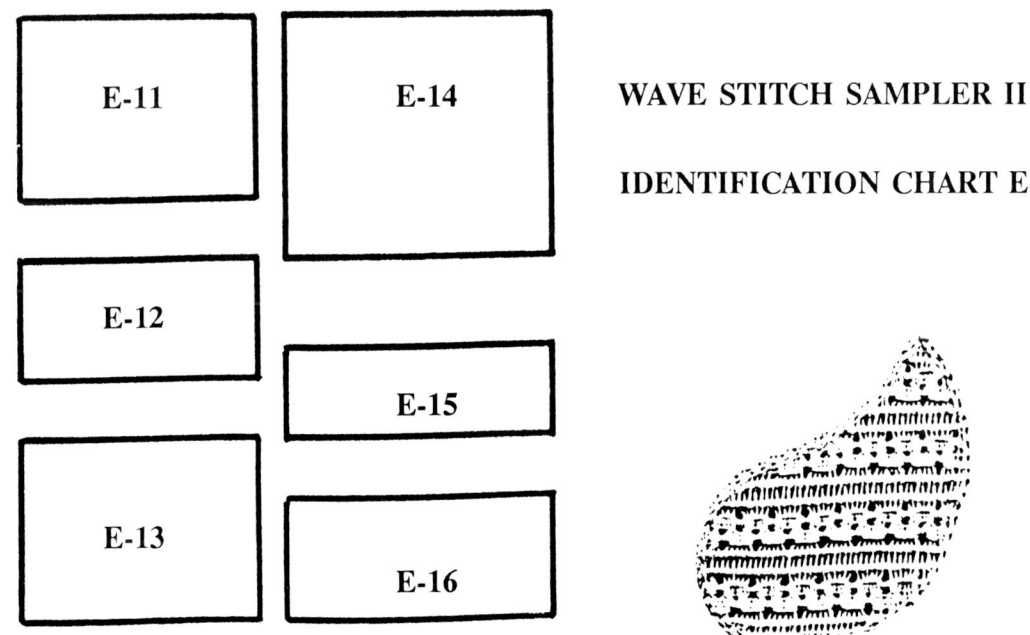

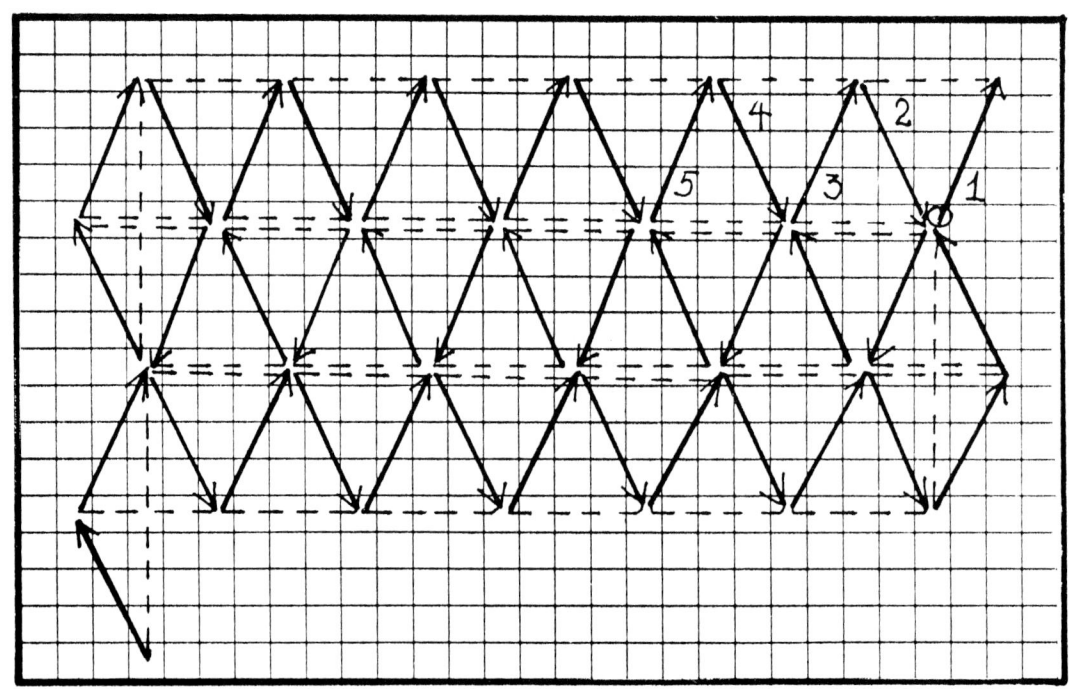

Pattern E-1 - Tight Pull

Needle comes up at arrow/stitch 1. Count up four threads and to the right two threads; needle goes down at this point. The slant has been established and no further "slant counting" is necessary. Needle picks up four threads to the left which is base of arrow 2 and is inserted sharing the position with arrow 1. Needle again picks up four threads to the left and the procedure is repeated.

After one row is completed, another will share its holes and open up new holes four threads below.

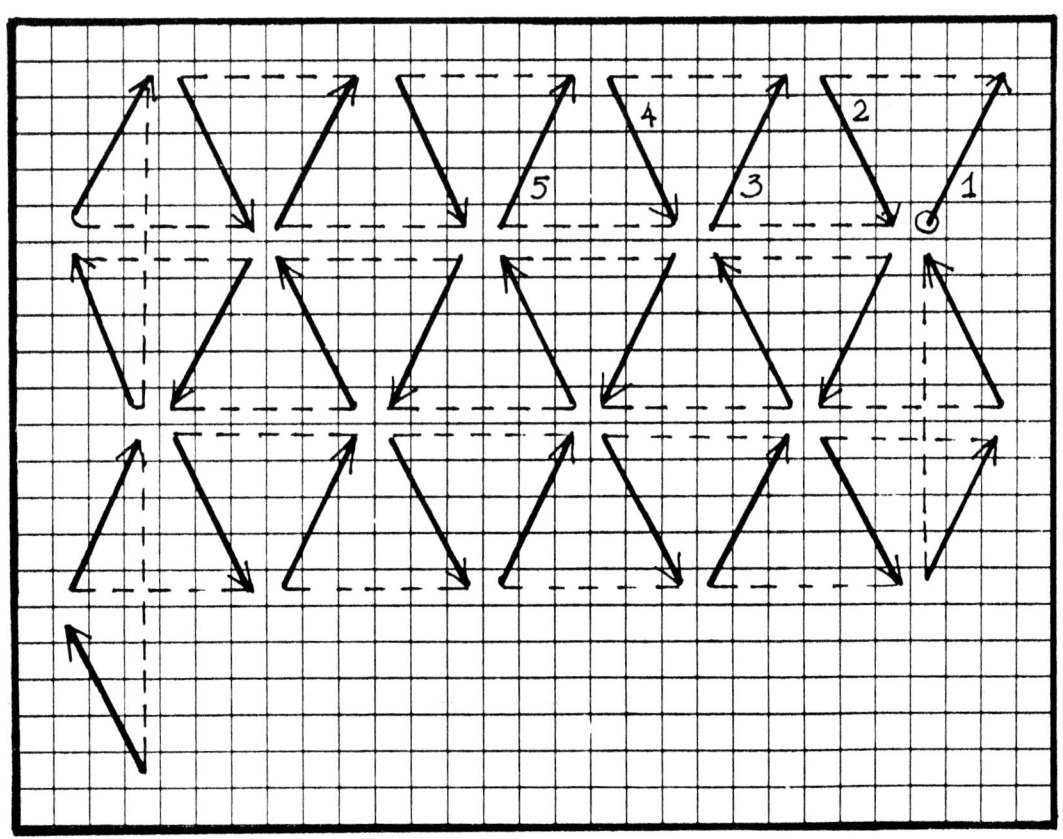

Pattern E-2 - Tight Pull

Come up at arrow 1 and go down as arrow indicates. Pick up five threads and work arrow 2. Do not share hole with arrow 1, but leave one thread between. Pick up five threads and repeat. Notice that one thread is always left between stitches.

When working the second and all subsequent rows, one fabric thread must be left between rows.

The horizontal and vertical fabric threads left unworked in this pattern form a cross in the pattern.

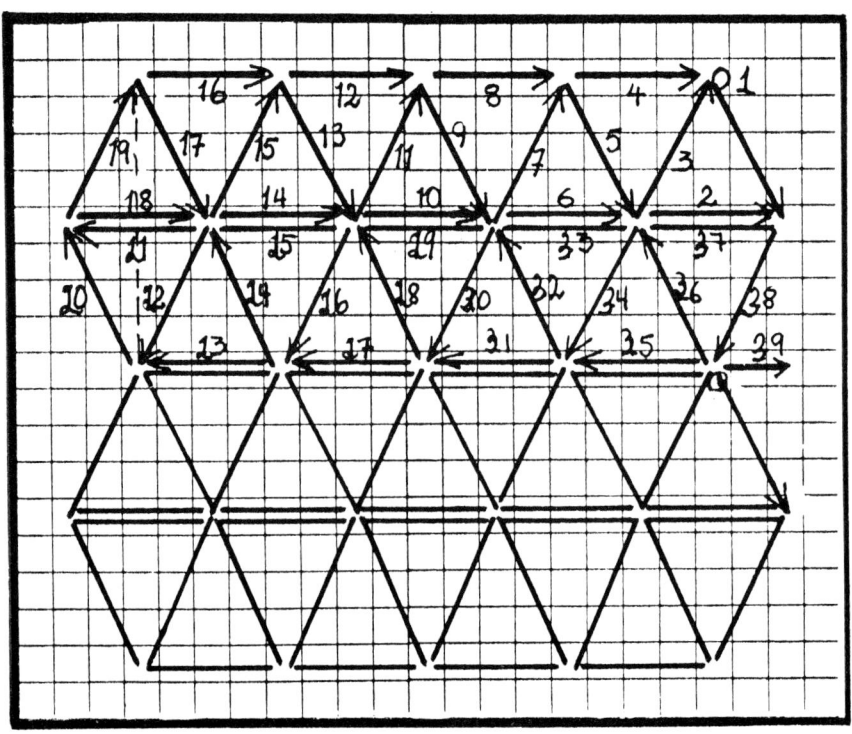

Pattern E-3 - Tight Pull

Come up at arrow 1 and work a slanted stitch as arrow indicates. Pick up four threads to the left. Work arrow/stitch 2 and come up at the base of arrow 3. Continue in this manner following numbered arrows 1-19.

The second and all subsequent rows are works in the same manner, arrows 20 through 39.

Notice that all horizontal stitches in the pattern are worked twice, that means that two working threads will show on top, while four working threads will show on the underside of the work.

Stitch 39 is a compensation stitch. It is graphed so you can see how a shape is squared when needed. This stitch will also serve as anchor as, without it, stitch 38 and stitch 40 could not be worked as shown unless otherwise anchored in back of the work.

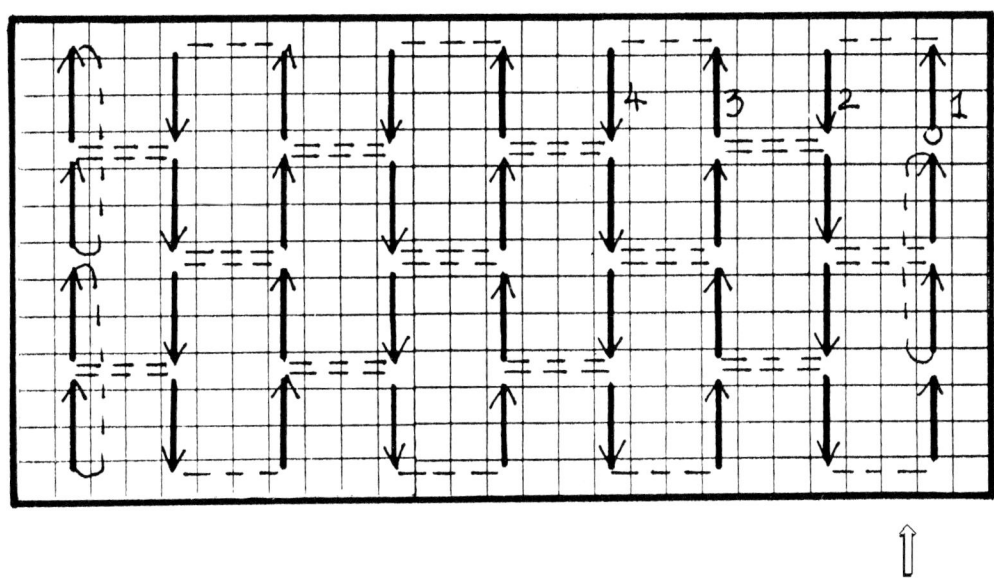

Pattern E-4 - Tight Pull

Come up at arrow 1, work up over three threads, insert and pick up three threads to the left. Come up at arrow 2, work down over three threads and again pick up three threads to the left. Repeat. If worked over more than three threads, a slightly heavier thread should be used.

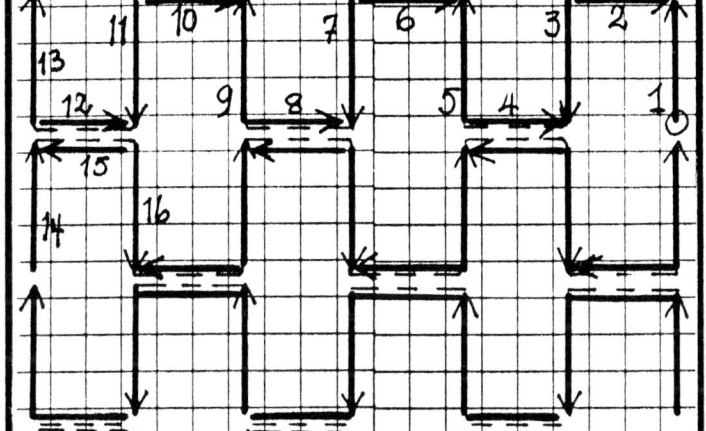

Pattern E-5 - Tight Pull

This pattern is called "honeycomb." It works in the same manner as Pattern E-4, only a horizontal stitch is added between vertical stitches. Follow numbered arrows working the stitches in the direction of the arrows point. This stitch will benefit if a slightly heavier thread is used.

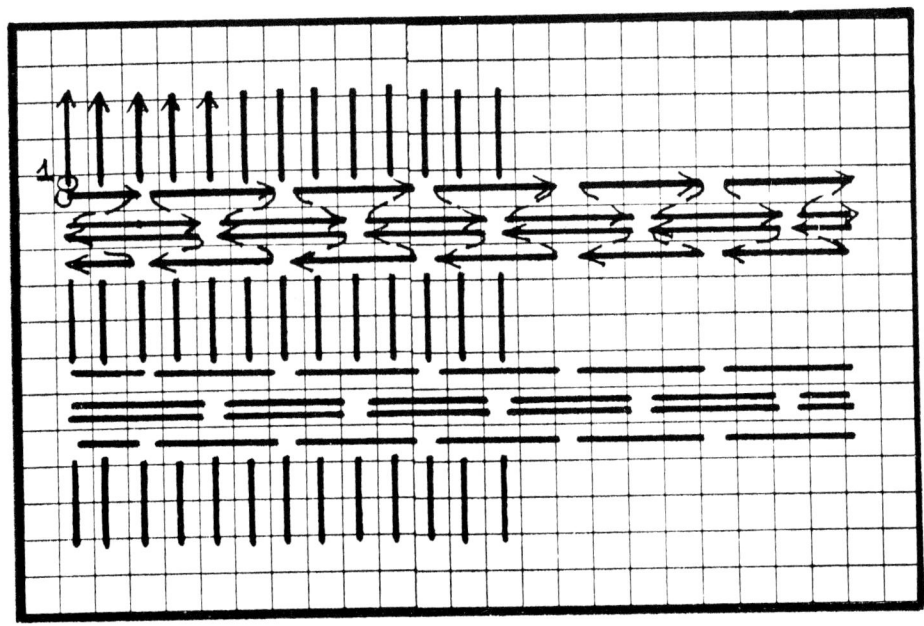

Pattern E-6 - Tight Pull

Fine thread is needed for this pattern. Work rows of tightly pulled straight (corded) stitches over three threads, skipping two threads between rows.

Work reverse wave stitch in between the cording. Come up at arrow 1. This stitch shares the hole with the first cording stitch. Work to the right going over two fabric threads. This small stitch is a compensation stitch as it is only half the length of all following stitches. Come up one thread below the hole where the first stitch came up through and work over four threads to the right. Bring the needle up sharing the position of the first stitch and insert four threads to the right.

Repeat these stitches, always sharing the preceding stitch, to the end of the row.

Work a companion row directly below, sharing holes as shown in the graph.

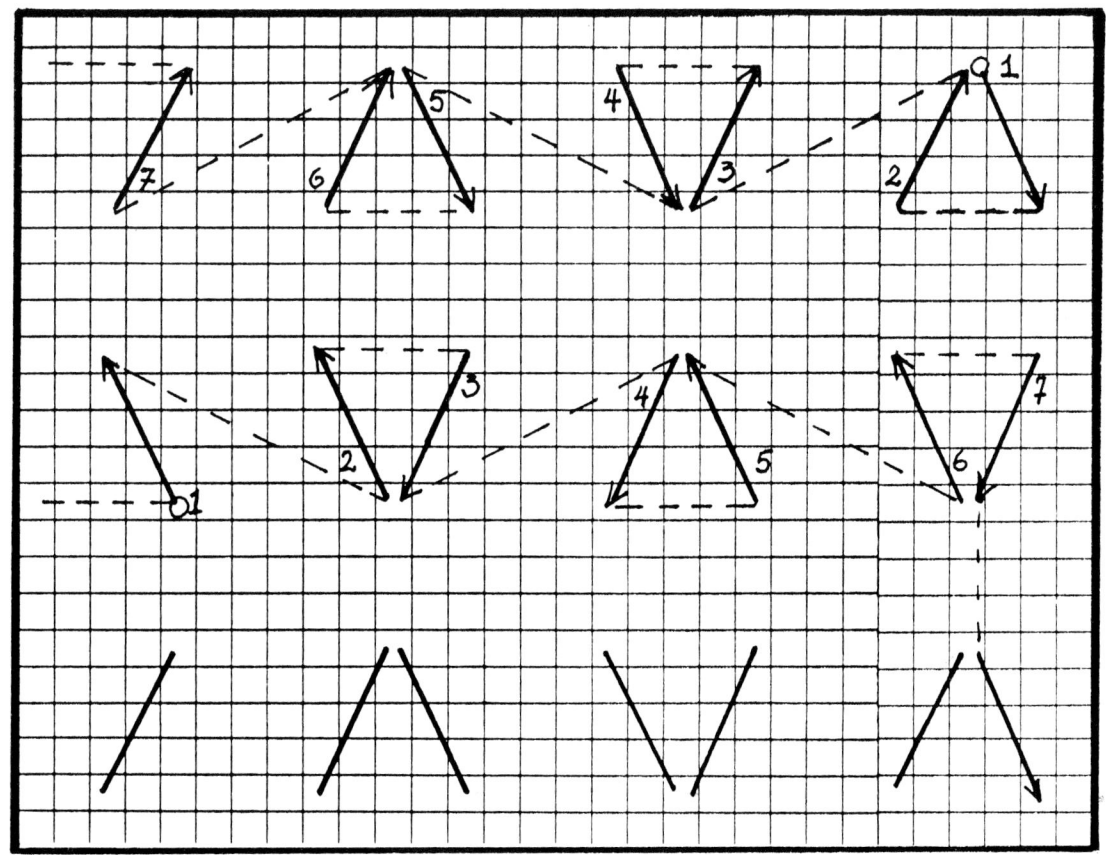

Diagram A

Pattern E-7 - Medium to Tight Pull

This pattern is very attractive as it forms little stars and should be worked with slightly heavier thread if the stars want to be seen.

Work alternated wave stitches in horizontal rows spaced by four threads. Follow Diagram A above. Work several rows.

Diagram B on the next page shows how to complete the pattern by working the same alternated wave stitches in vertical rows.

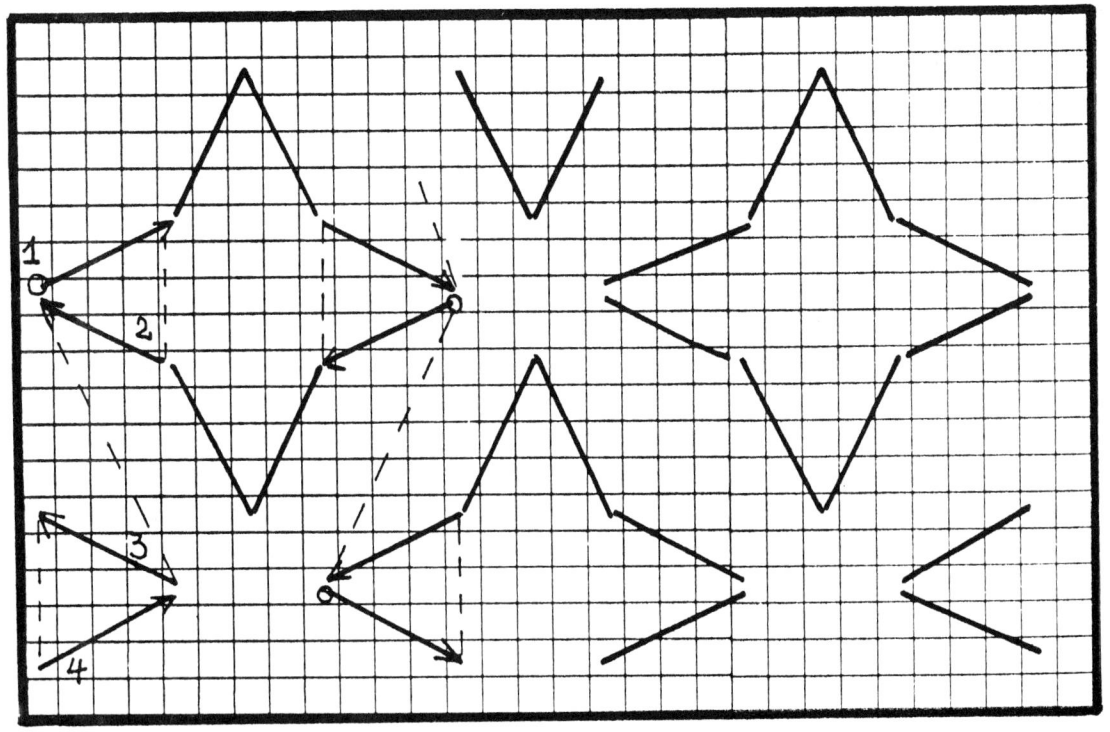

Diagram B

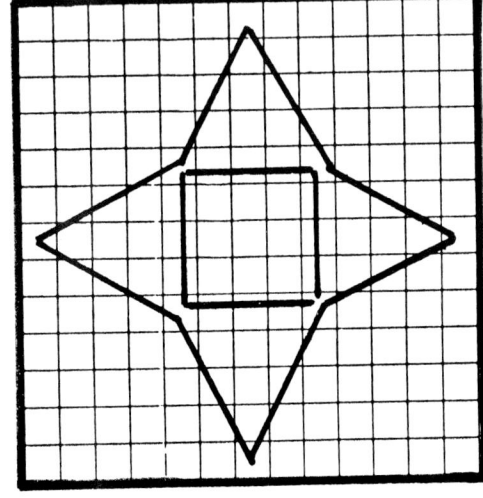

Pattern E-8

Work Pattern E-7. While working the vertical rows, insert a four-sided stitch in the center of each star-to-be. The four-sided stitches can also be added in a third step, but care must be taken not to obstruct any existing holes by carrying threads. The four-sided stitch is clearly diagramed in Pattern B-13 or in the chapter dedicated to this stitch.

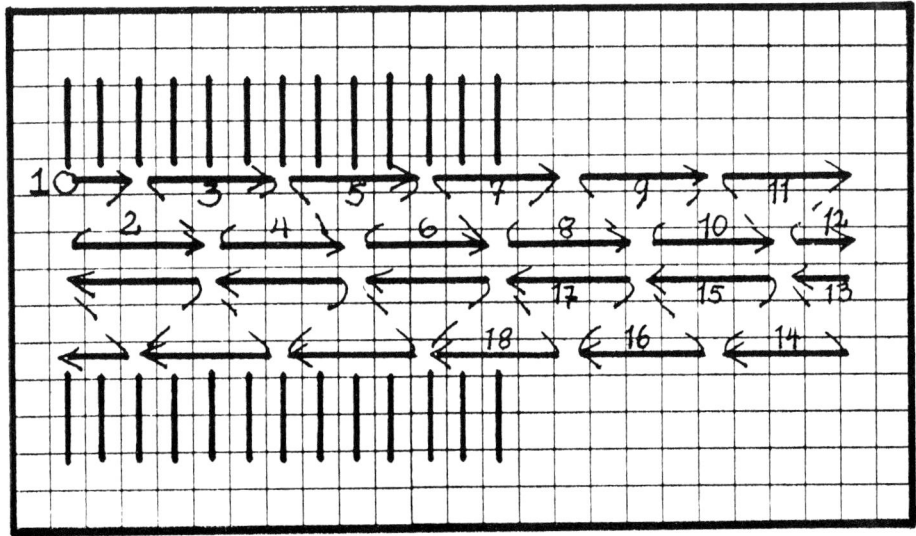

Diagram A

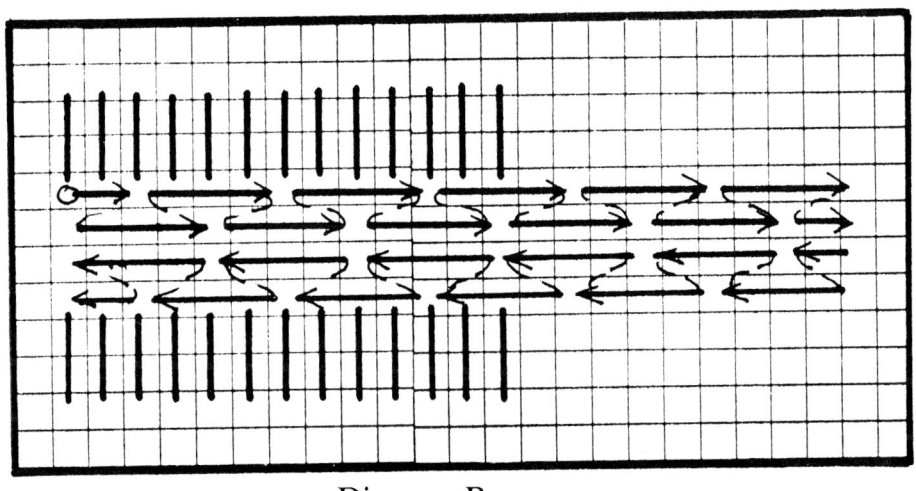

Diagram B

Pattern E-9 - Tight Pull

This pattern must be stitched with fine thread.

<u>Diagram A</u> - Work two rows of tightly pulled straight stitches, cording, over three threads spaced by five fabric threads. Work reverse wave stitch over the space between the rows as numbered arrows dictate. Diagram A.

<u>Diagram B</u> - Notice the different spacing count. To complete the pattern work diagrams A and B alternately.

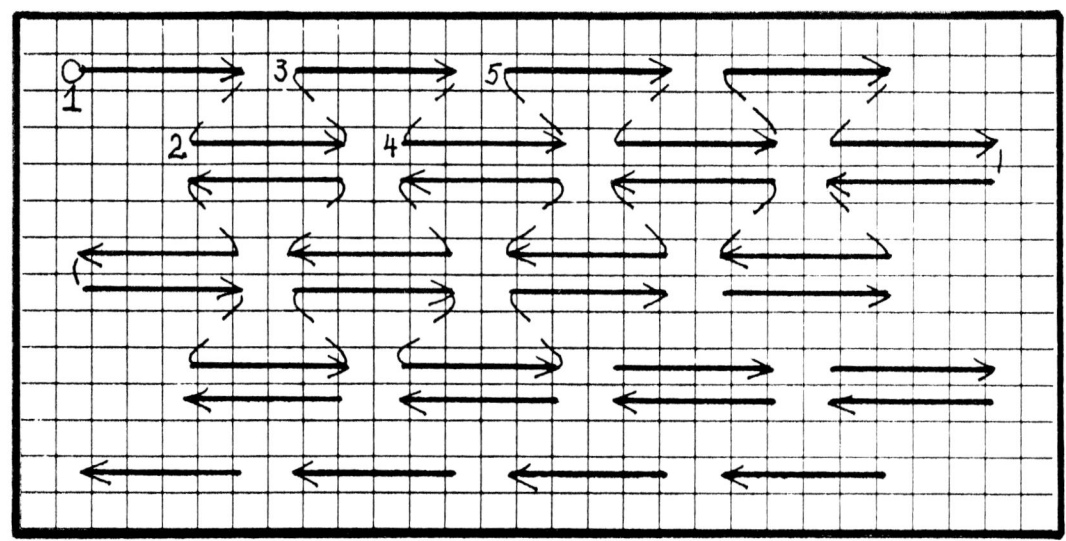

Pattern E-10 - Tight Pull

Work an overall pattern, spacing the reverse wave stitch as diagramed above. This is a rather dense pattern with an overall effect. Use it where a light value in a composition is wanted.

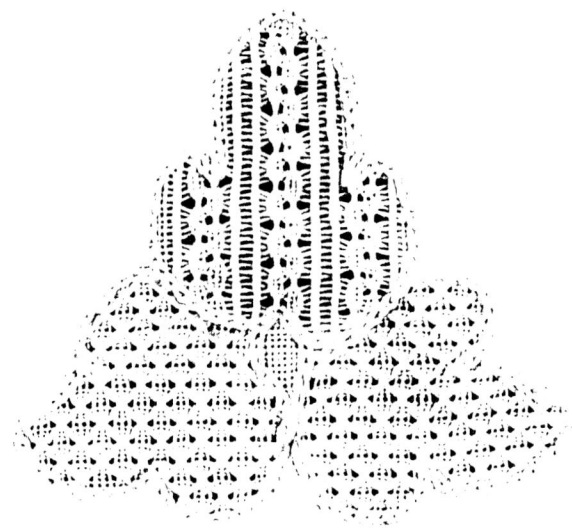

Patterns E-4 and E-13

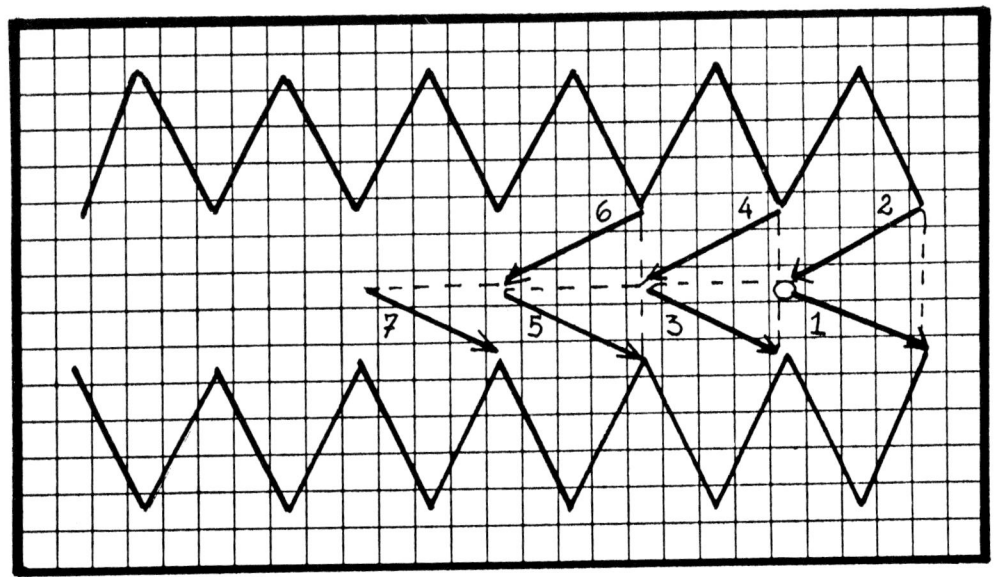

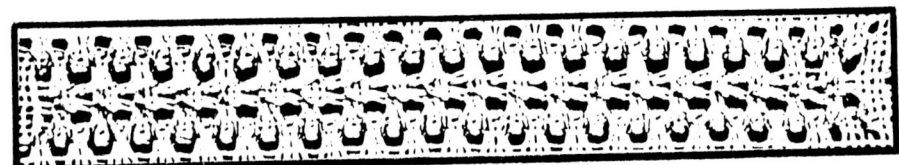

Pattern E-11 - Tight Pull

This is a very interesting pattern as the alternate directional pull gives a tridimensional effect. It looks great when used in a border and also if stitched with a thread slightly darker in value than the background fabric.

Work two rows of "facing" wave stitches as shown, spaced by four threads. Turn the work 90 degrees (this is important in order to obtain the correct directional pull) and work a row of stitches in between the two existing rows as follows: Come up at arrow 1, in the center hole between two peaks. Work a wave stitch by joining the two previously worked rows; insert the needle at the base of arrow 1 and bring it up four threads below, between the next set of peaks. Repeat.

Notice that the working thread will be slightly distorted or off-center which will not affect the charm of this pattern, but rather enhance its looks.

When using the pattern for a filling stitch or a wider border, add rows of wave stitches as before, but work the center row in the opposite direction.

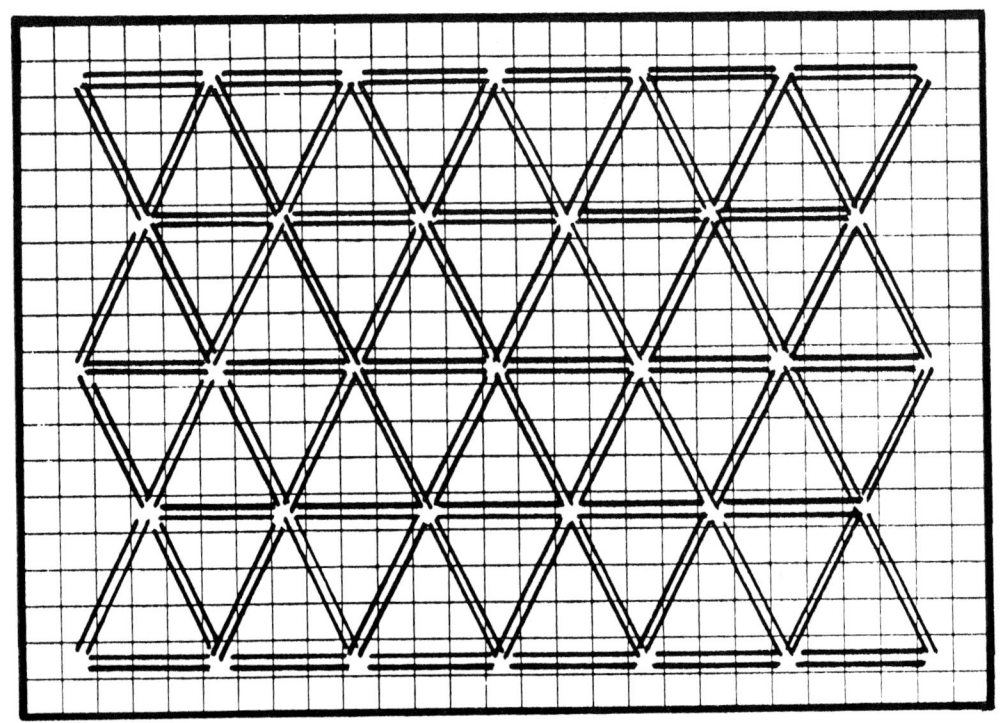

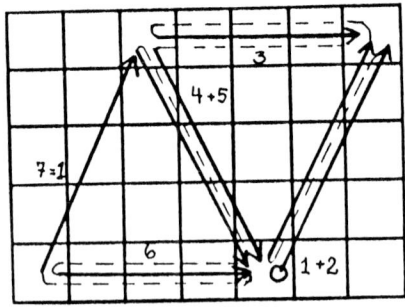

Pattern E-12 - Tight Pull

This pattern gives a very strong effect in that the holes are very pronounced.

Each diagonal stitch is worked twice, see arrows 1 and 2, in the enlarged diagram. Stitch 3 is only worked once since the next row will provide the other stitch, arrows 3 and 6. Follow arrows and dotted lines in the direction they are drawn, using the enlarged diagram.

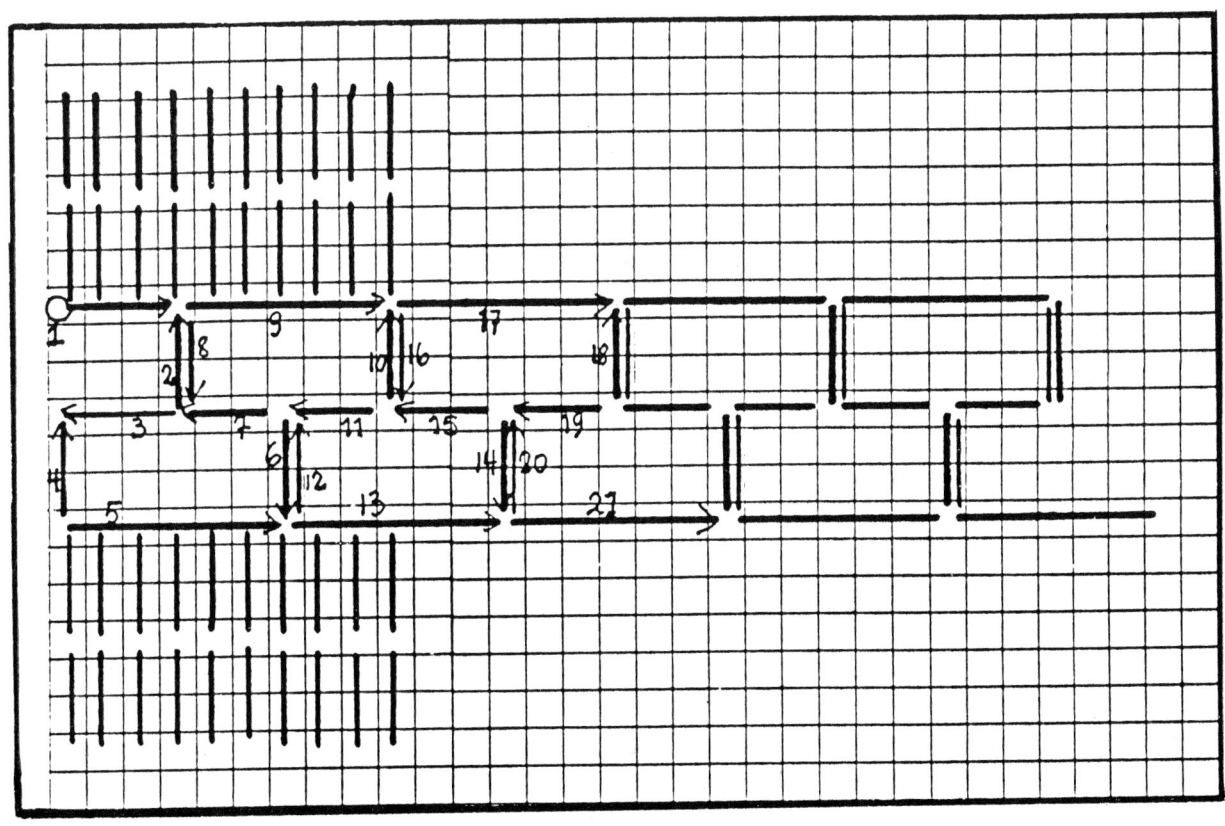

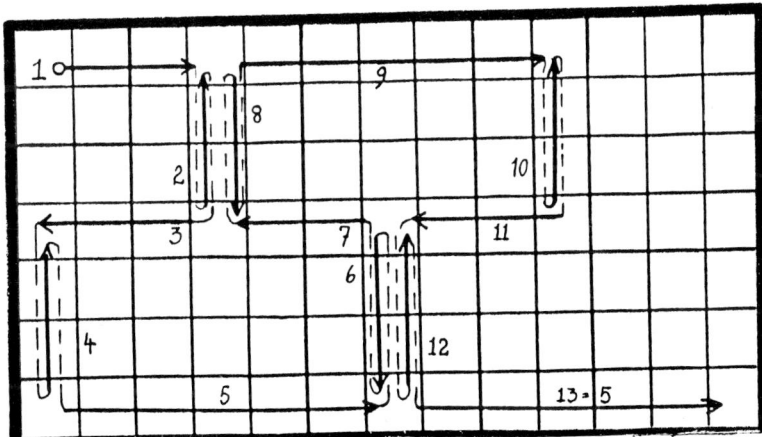

Pattern E-13 - Tight and Medium Pull

Two rows of straight stitches over three threads are pulled tightly into cording. Skip six threads and work another two rows of cording same as before.

Work "bricking" over the six empty threads as shown, also in the enlarged diagram. Use medium pull. Start at arrow 1. This stitch is a compensated stitch over three threads only. All other horizontal stitches are worked over three threads.

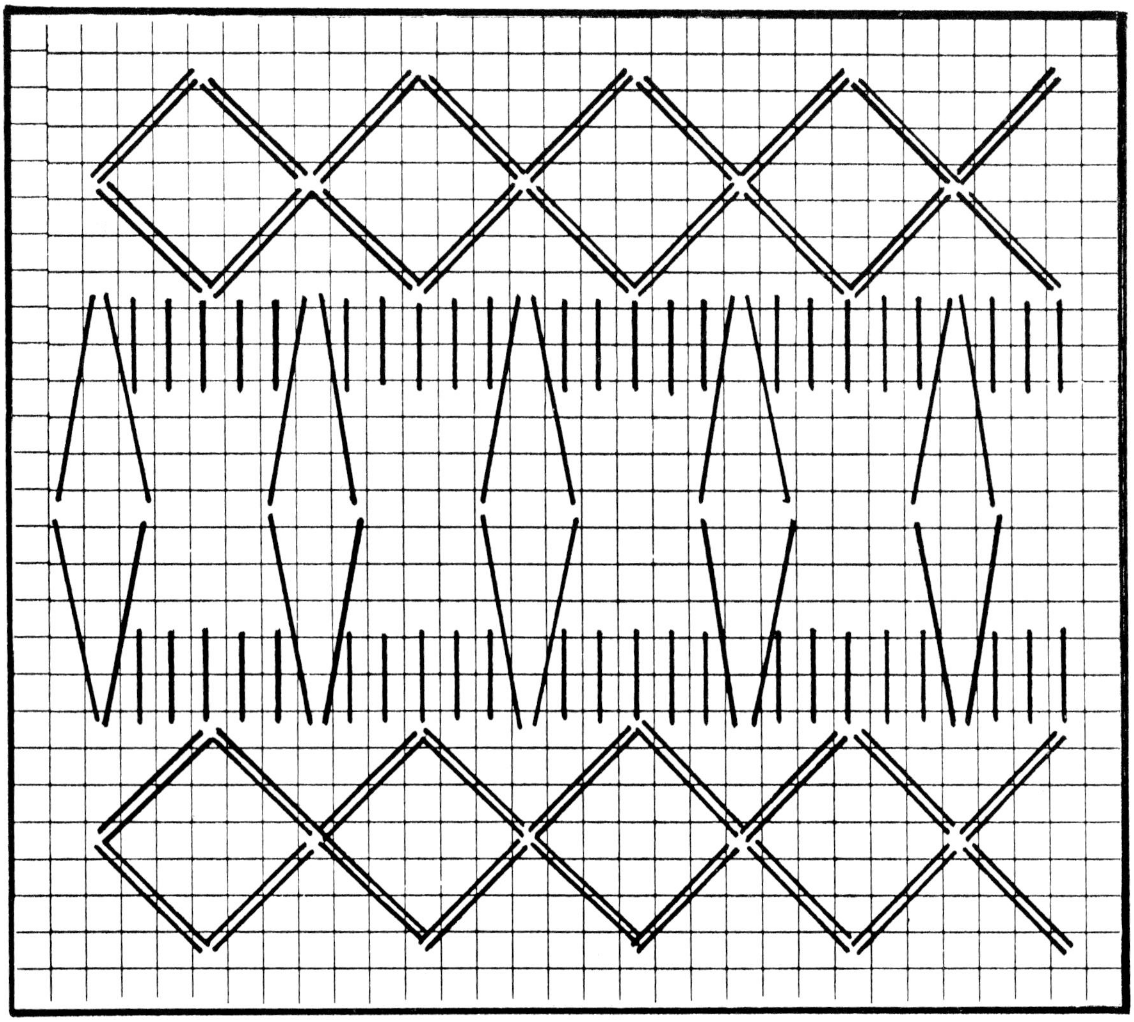

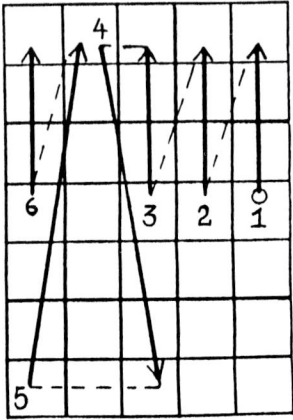

Pattern E-14 - Tight and Medium Pull

Work two rows of wave stitch, working each stitch twice. Se arrows on diagram. Tight pull.

Work straight stitches over three threads, tight pull. At the same time work a long wave stitch, medium pull, after every fifth straight stitch; check the position for this long stitch. The directions for working this step are shown on the enlarged diagram.

101

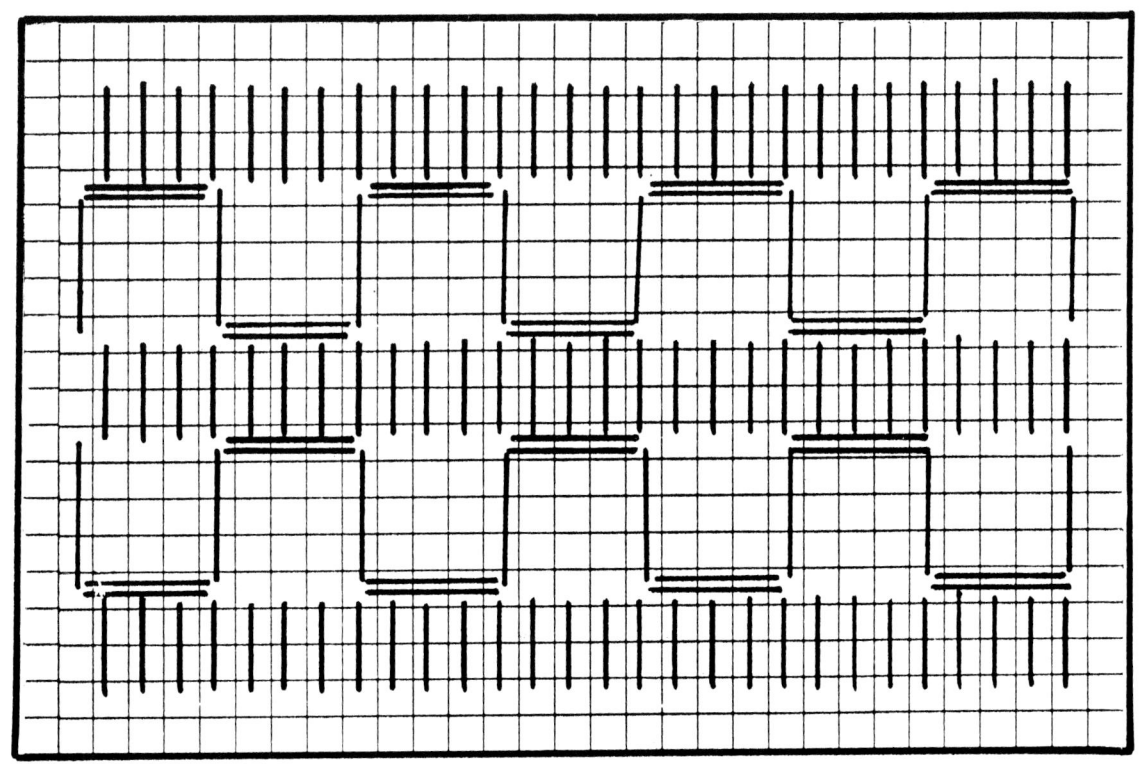

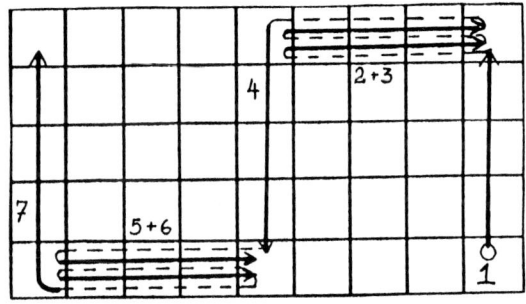

Pattern E-15 - Tight Pull

Work rows of straight stitches over three threads pulled into cording, spaced by four fabric threads.

Work honeycomb stitch. The horizontal stitches are worked twice as shown on the enlarged diagram.

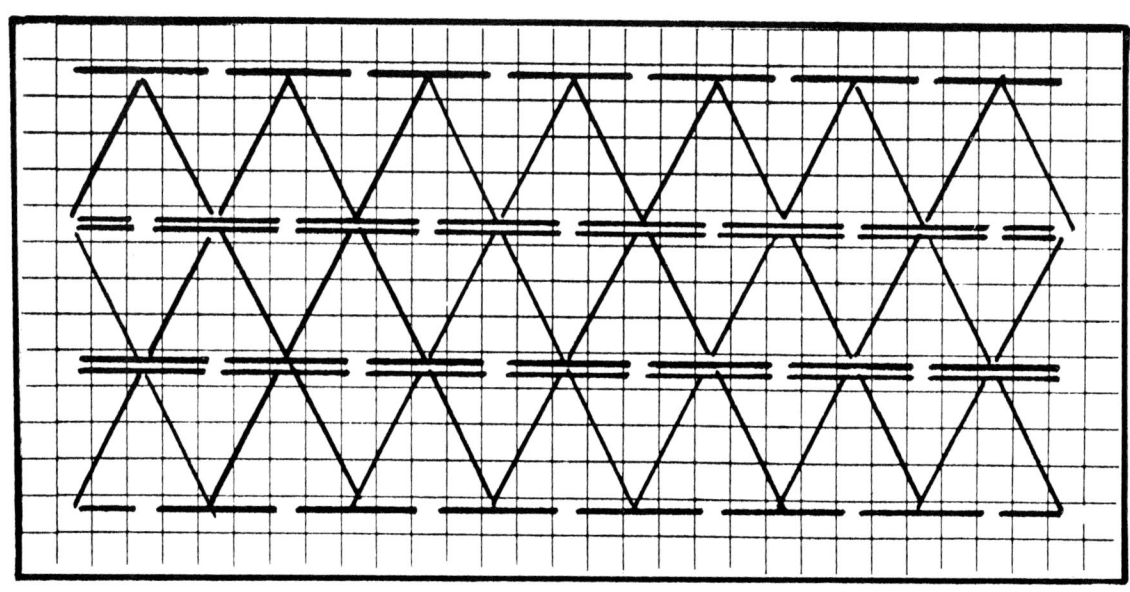

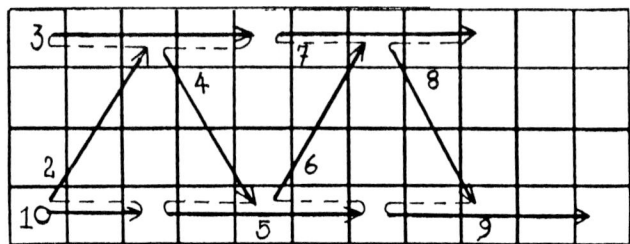

Pattern E-16 - Tight Pull

This stitch, although related to the wave stitch in it manner of working, is sometimes referred to as rick-rack stitch.

Using the enlarged diagram, come up at arrow 1. This stitch is a compensated stitch over two threads only. All other horizontal stitches are worked over four threads. Follow numbered arrows and dotted lines.

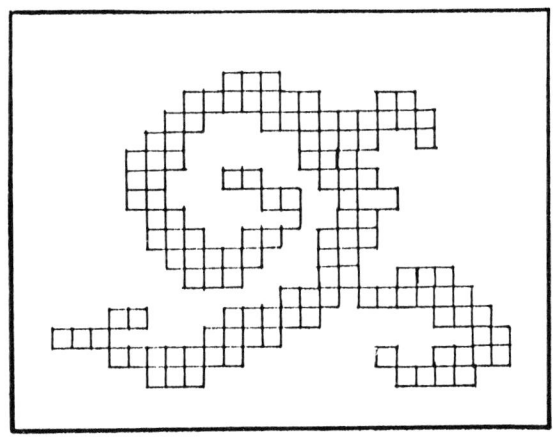

THE FOUR SIDED STITCH

This is probably the most popular stitch in pulled thread work. It is also widely used in Hardanger technique. It should be studied thoroughly as it appears over and over again, not only by itself but in composite patterns as well. The four-sided stitch aside from cross stitch may very well be the only stitch which is suitable to be used for whole designs and alphabets. In fact, any counted cross stitch pattern or border designed to be stitched in one color only, such as most ethnic patterns, can be successfully adapted for the pulled four-sided stitch. It has the added advantage that if worked over a different thread count one can easily reduce or enlarge a design up to a certain point. As an example, the above illustrated design could be worked in four-sided stitch over two, three, four or more threads, thus changing its overall dimensions.

The four-sided stitch can be worked in horizontal, vertical and diagonal rows. The stitch can also be placed on the bias of the material, see Patterns F-7 through F-10. The holes are far more pronounced when each single stitch is worked twice; this is especially recommended if a larger four-sided stitch, over six threads, is worked.

When row is placed upon row, the method of working dictates that the horizontal stitches be worked twice, that is, once for row one and then again for row two. See Pattern F-1. If you were to stitch all vertical stitches twice, but horizontal ones only once, a more uniform pattern would result. This choice is up to the stitcher as both methods are correct. If one wishes to work a design as illustrated on page 108, uniformity is desirable and working each stitch twice gives a more pronounced effect to the pattern. Furthermore, the stitching sequence is easier as one must only remember that where on individual stitch meets the other in subsequent rows, this individual stitch should be worked only once.

On the next page you will find a small sampler which I suggest you copy with needle and thread. It will give you the experience needed to work a more intricate pattern.

Place your initials instead of mine in the space provided. Any alphabet from a cross stitch book will aid you in selecting the suitable letters.

First border: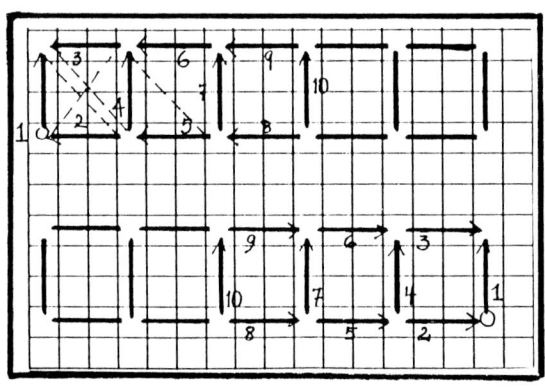

Second Border: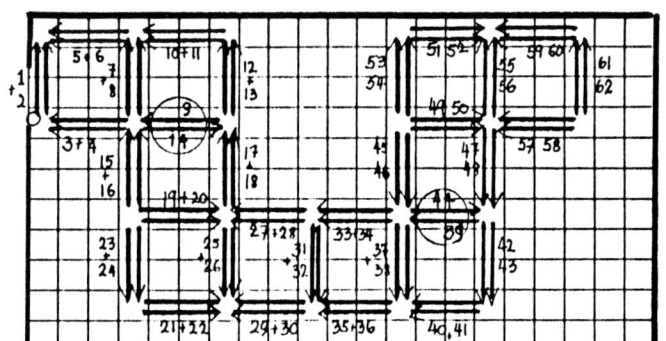

Third Border: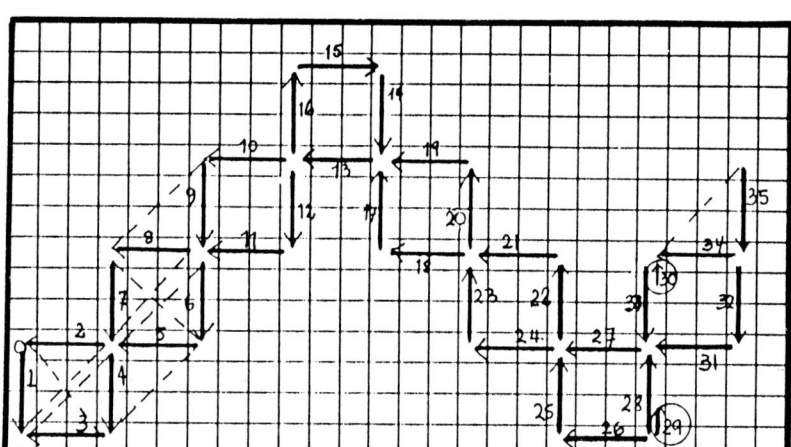

Initials:

Curved Motif: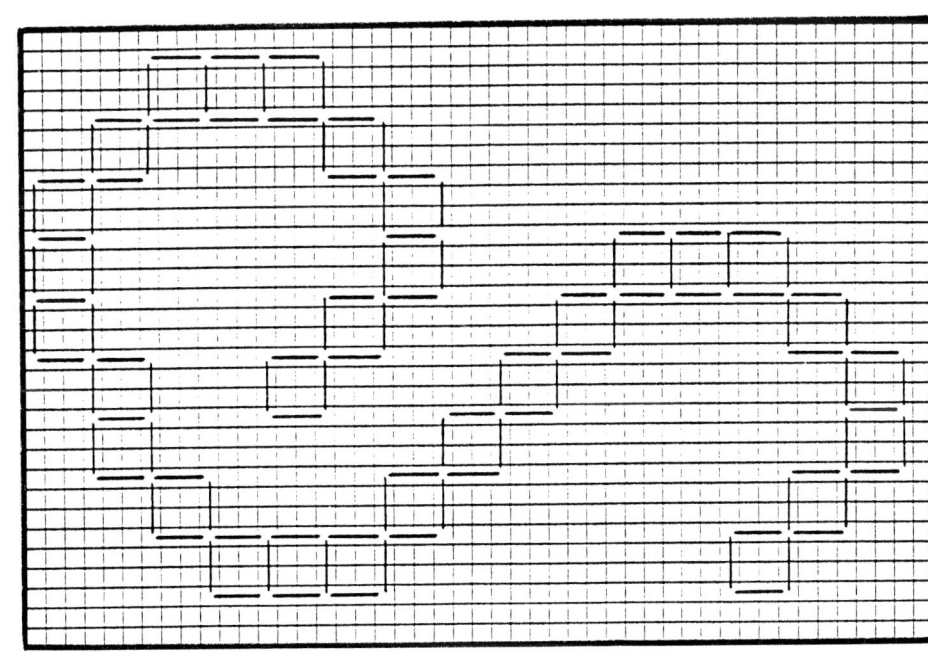

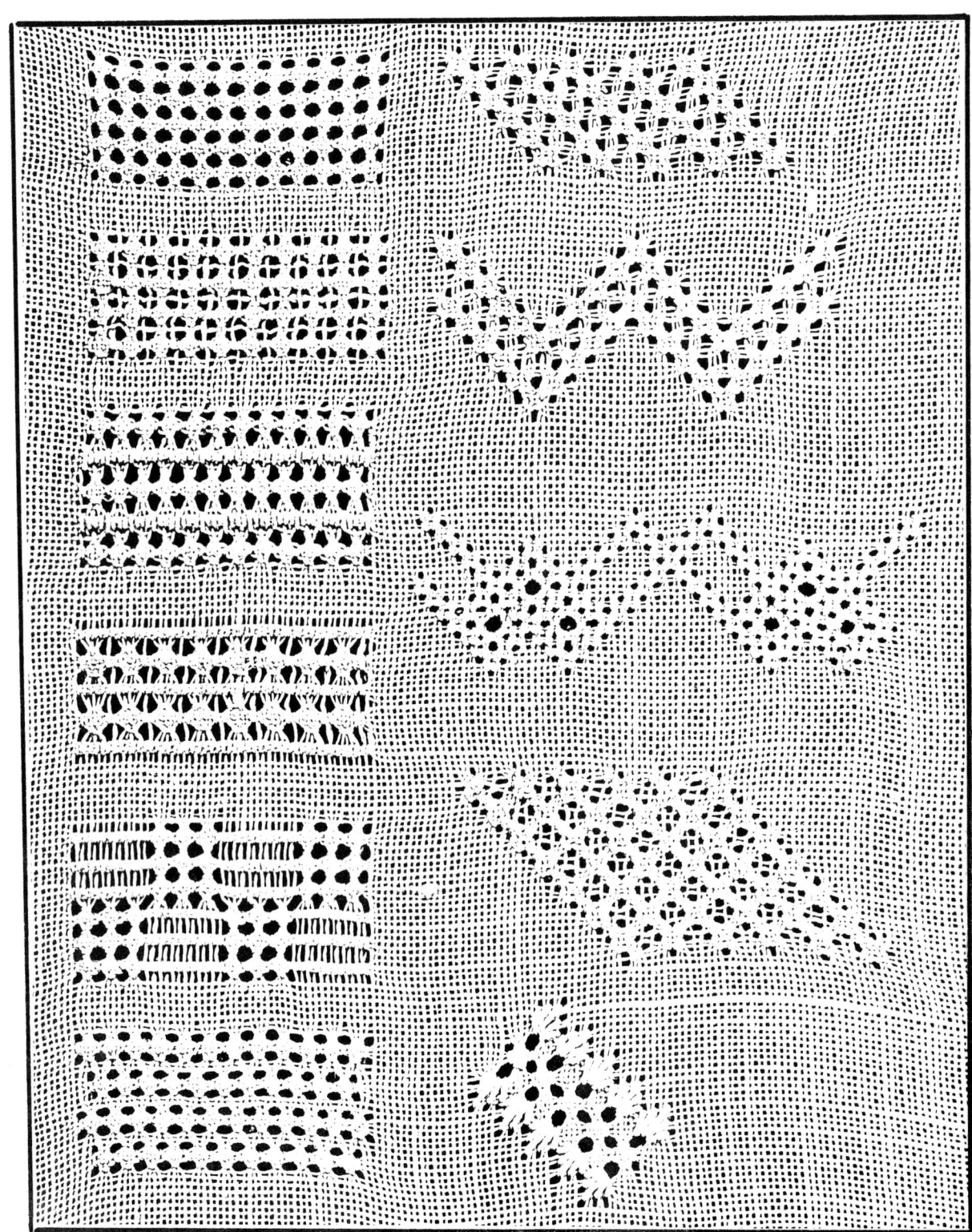

FOUR-SIDED STITCH SAMPLER

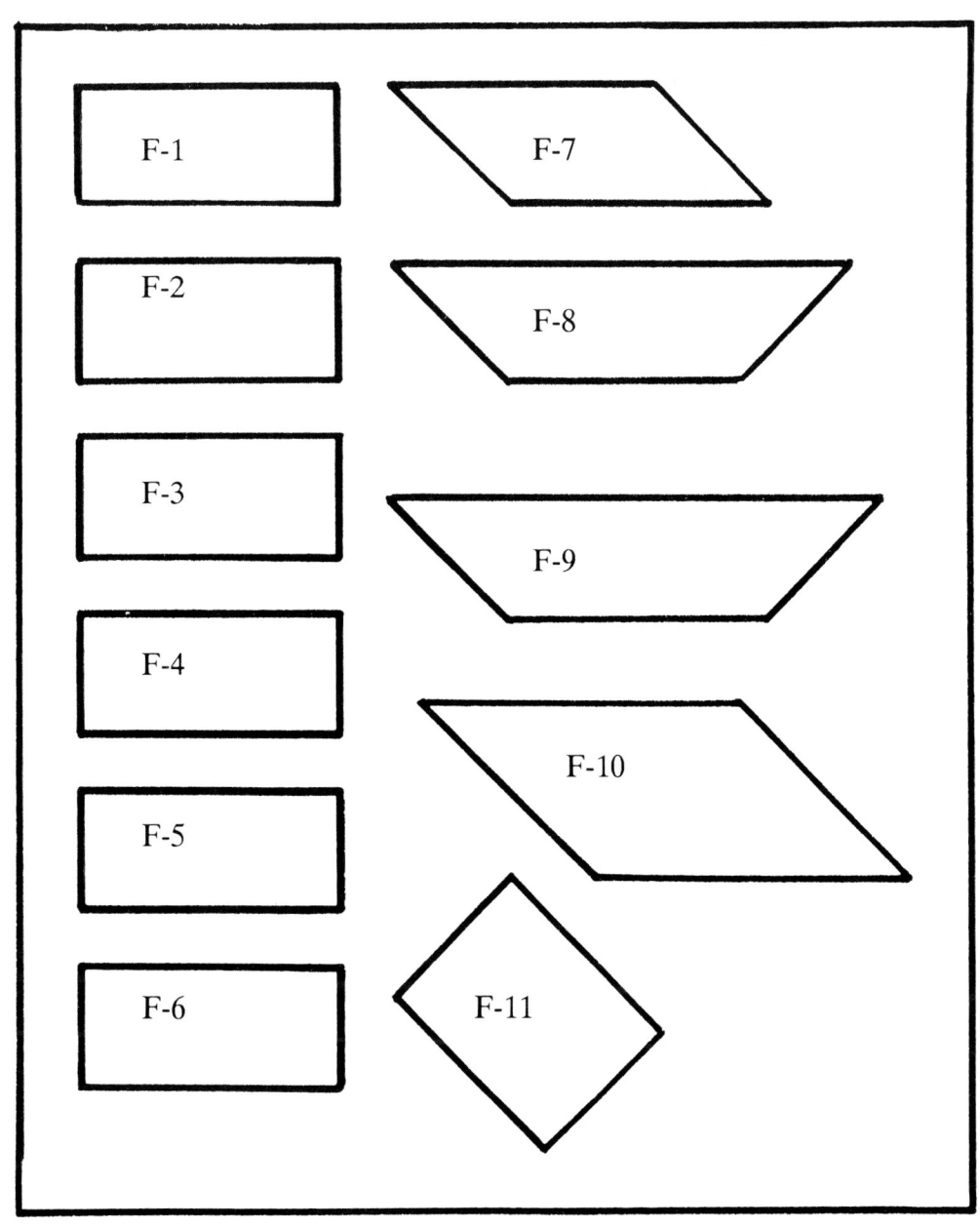

STITCH IDENTIFICATION CHART F - FOUR SIDED STITCH

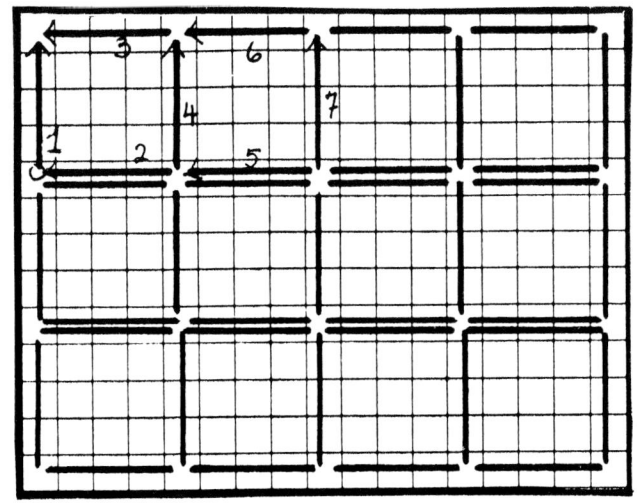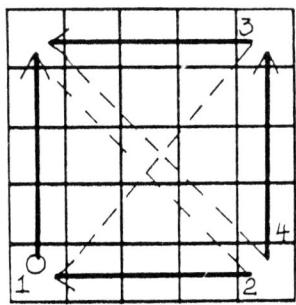

Pattern F-1 - Tight Pull

Work in horizontal rows. Here the stitch is graphed going over four threads. This number can be adjusted either way.

A clear working diagram is provided. Following it exactly will give the desired, correct effect. Notice that the back side shows only threads crossing on the diagonal. Use this diagram for all patterns in his chapter, except where other directions are given.

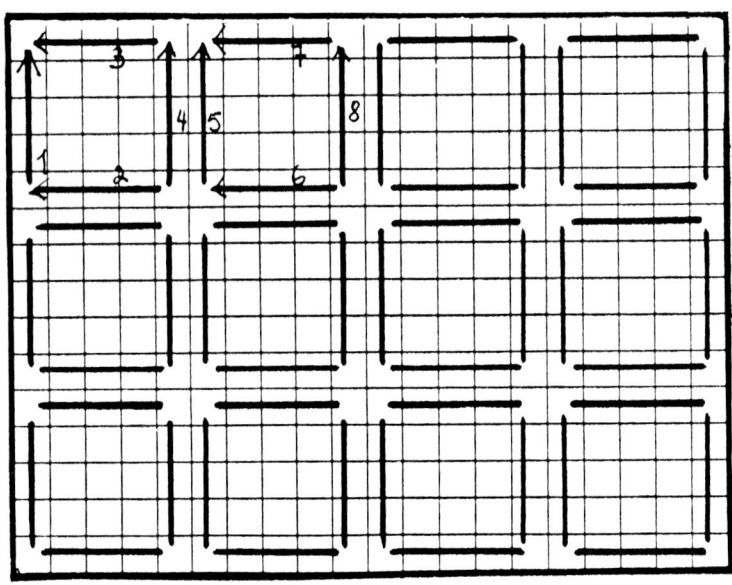

Pattern F-2 - Tight Pull

Work four-sided stitches spaced by one thread. Space rows by one thread.

109

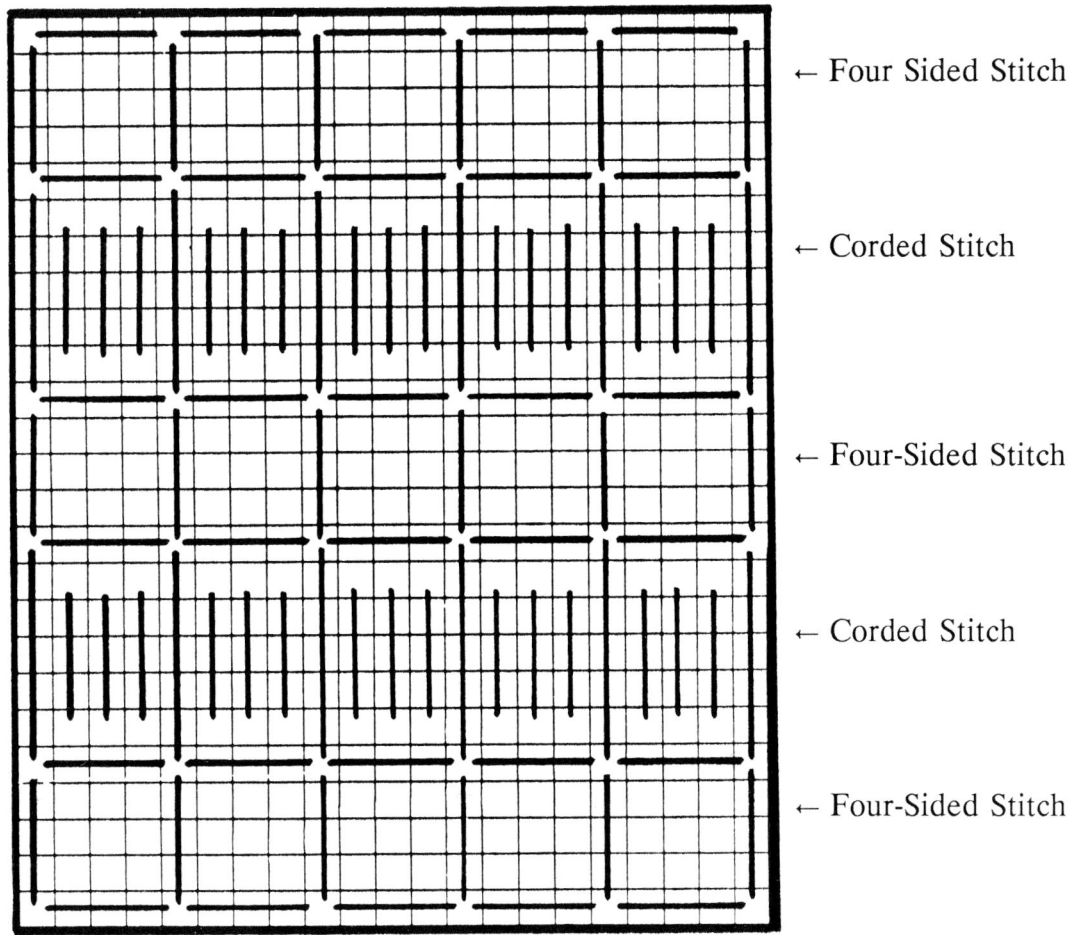

Pattern F-3 - Tight Pull

Work one row of four-sided stitch.

Work one row of tightly pulled vertical straight stitches (cording) as follows: work three stitches over four threads and one stitch over six thread. This longer stitch must be placed under the vertical stitch of the four-sides stitch of the previous row.

Note: If the four-sided stitch is worked over a different count, adjust the count of the straight stitches as well.

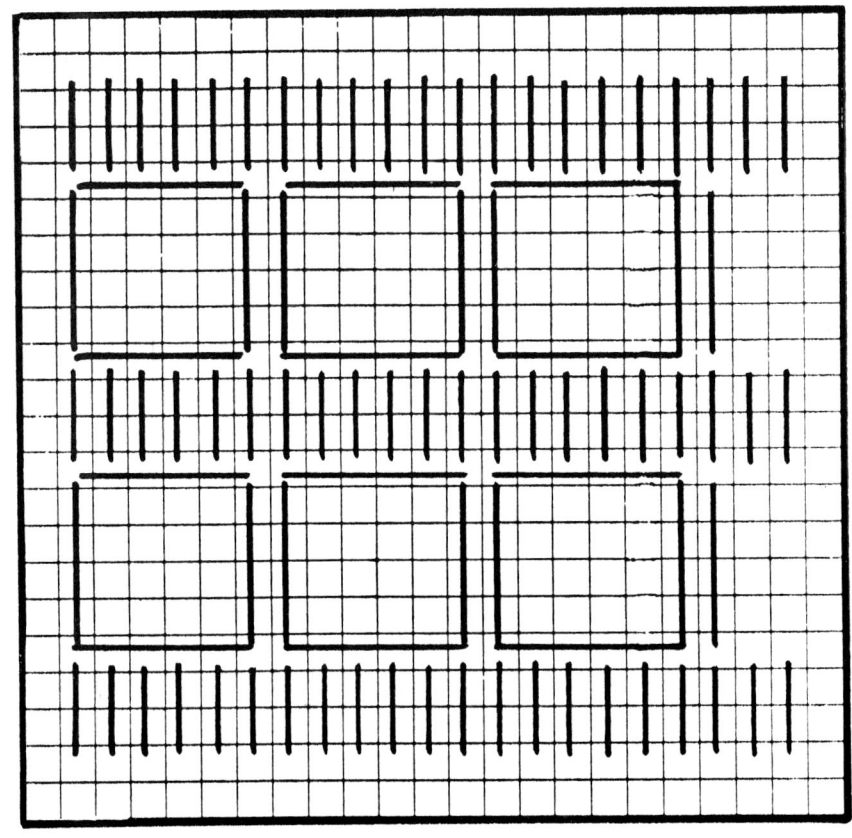

Pattern F-4 - Tight Pull

Work rows of tightly pulled straight stitches over three threads spaced by five threads.

Work four-sided stitch over five threads, spaced by one thread.

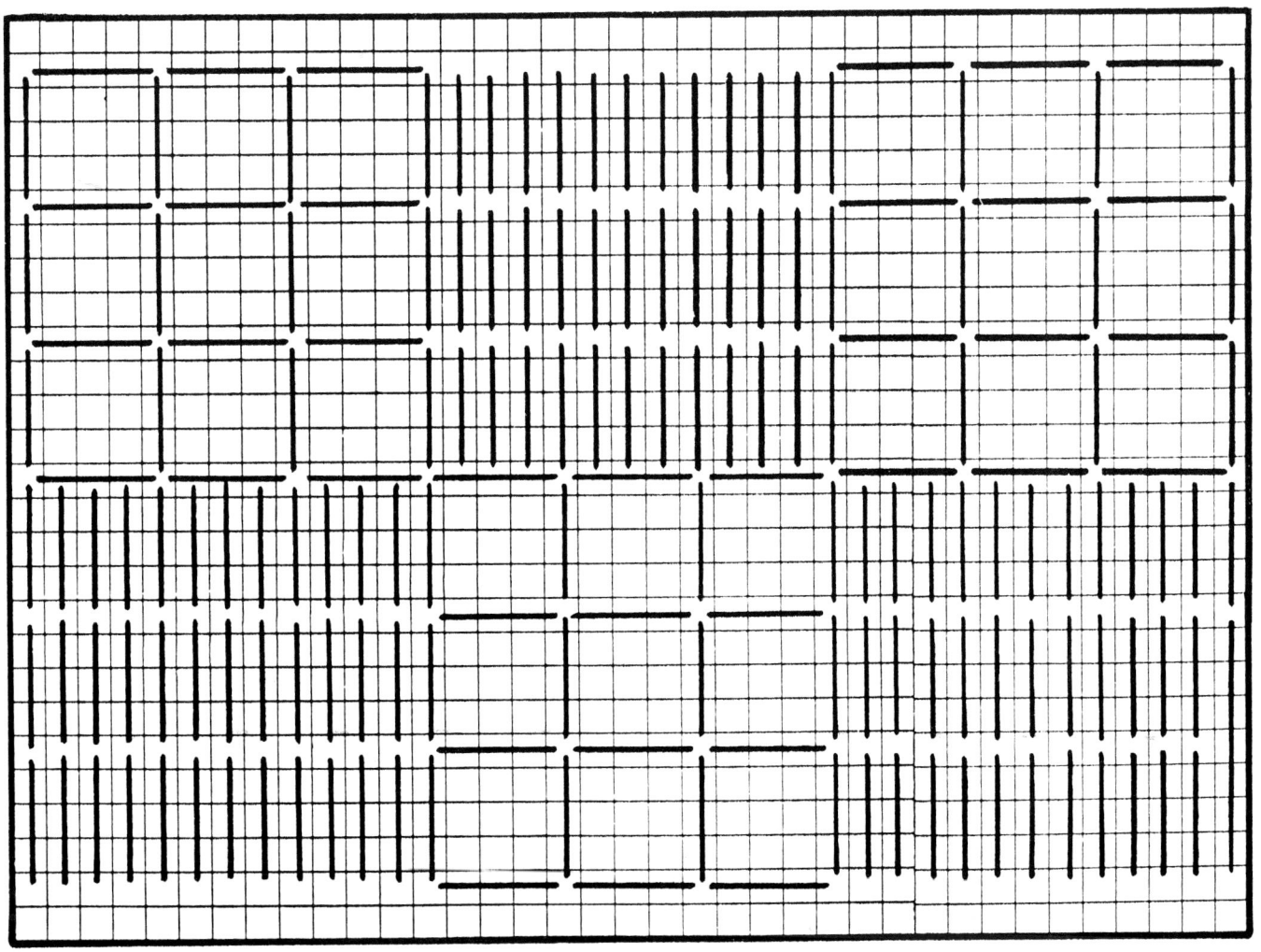

Pattern F-5 - Tight Pull

This very effective pattern works well as overall filling for a fairly large space. It also makes a lovely border.

Work three four-sided stitches over four threads spaced by eleven tightly pulled straight stitches over four threads. Work three identical rows.

Alternate the position of the four-sided stitches and the straight stitches every three rows.

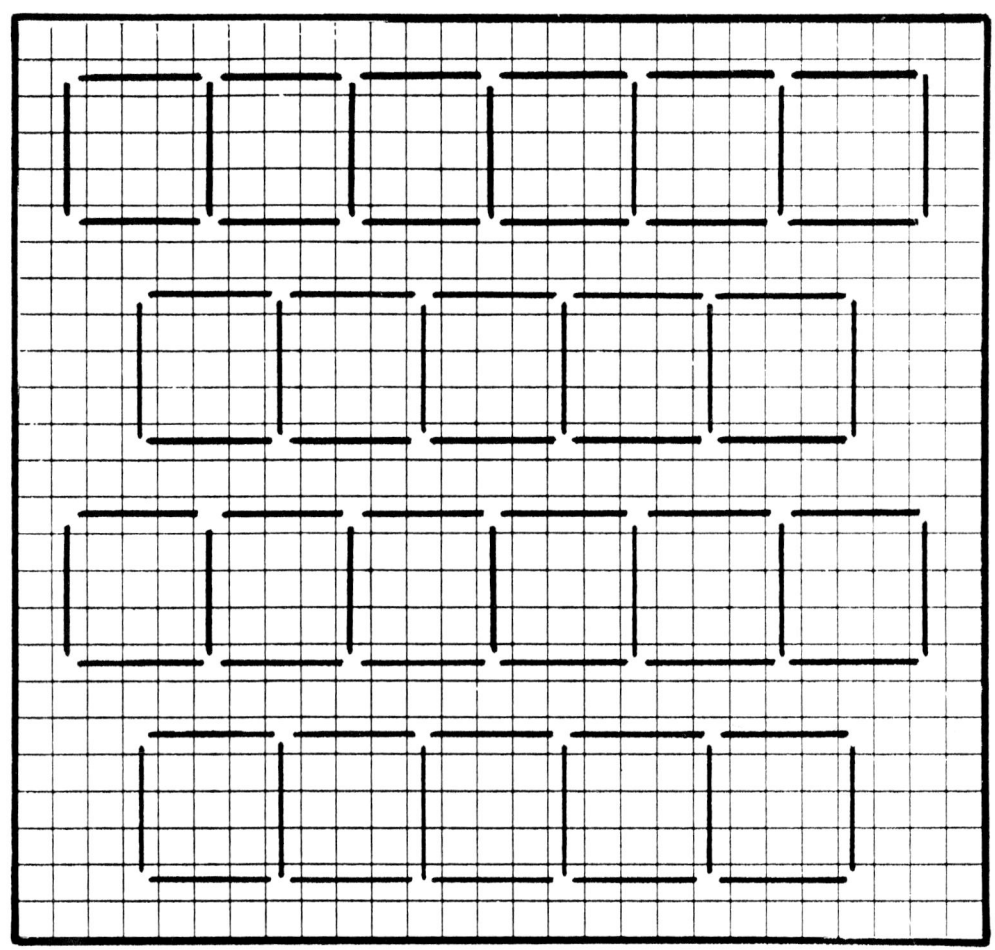

Pattern F-6 - Tight Pull

Work a row of four-sided stitches over four threads. Skip two threads.

Work a second row of four-sided stitches, but this time place them in a shifted position as shown on the graph.

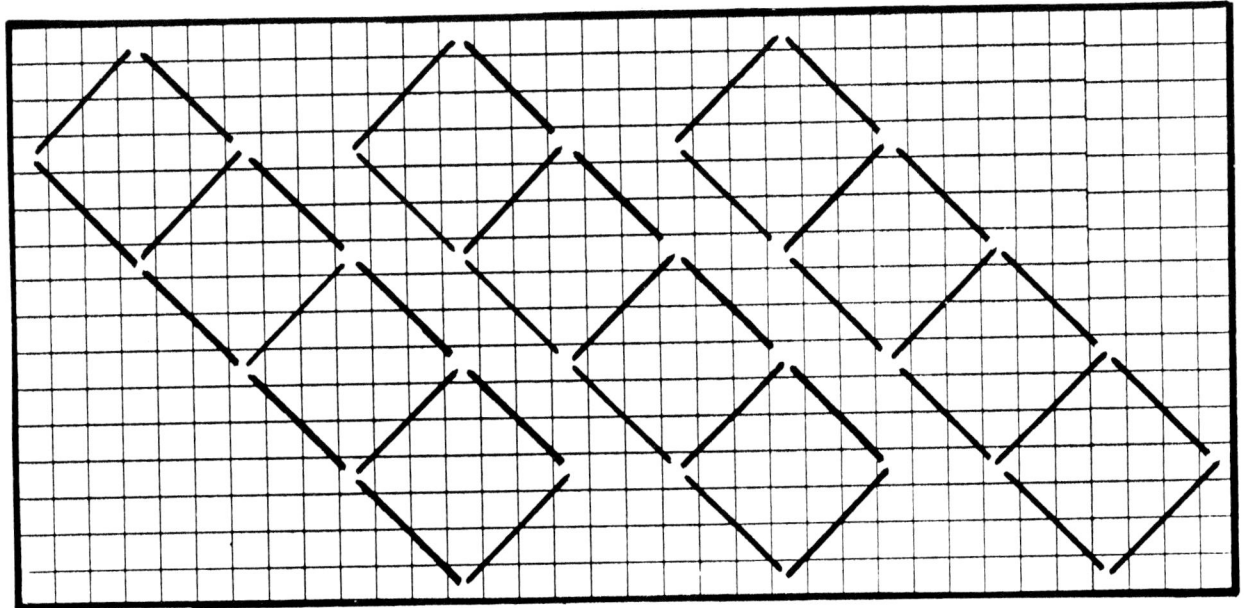

Pattern F-7 - Tight Pull

Here the four-sided stitch is placed on the diagonal or bias of the fabric. The principle of working the stitch is the same as before.

Work over three intersections. Work in diagonal rows as shown. Rows are spaced by three fabric threads. The stitches must be placed in the shifted position. This gives the desired zig-zag effect of the unworked fabric threads which divide the rows.

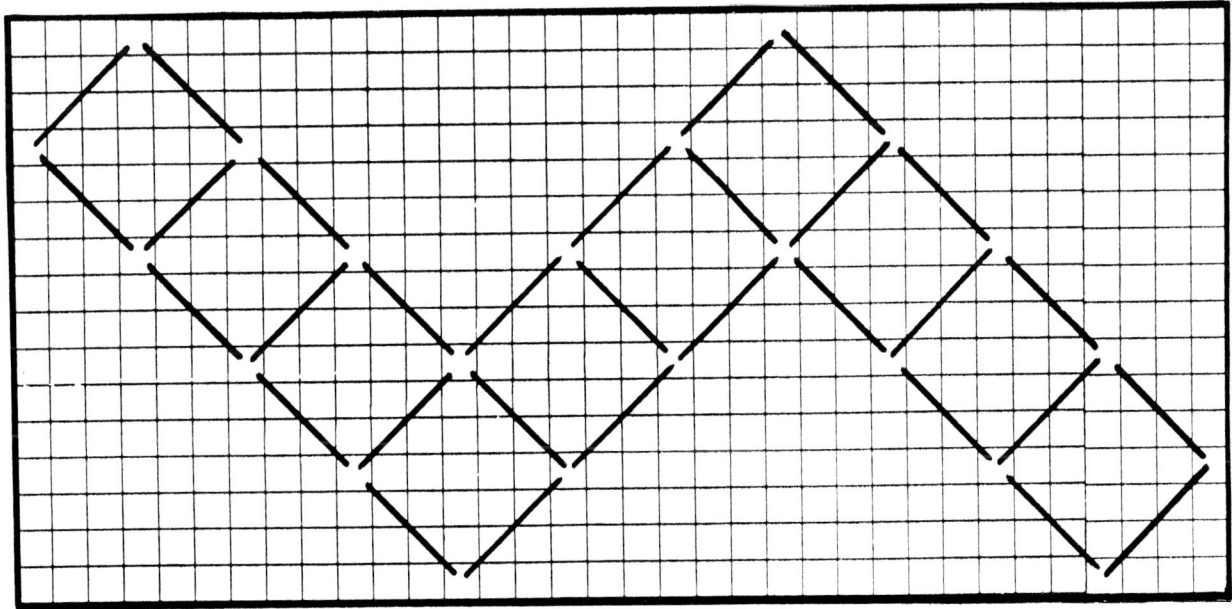

Pattern F-8 - Tight Pull

This pattern is similar to Pattern F-7. The four-sided stitches are arranged in a zig-zag fashion. This is especially nice for a border.

114

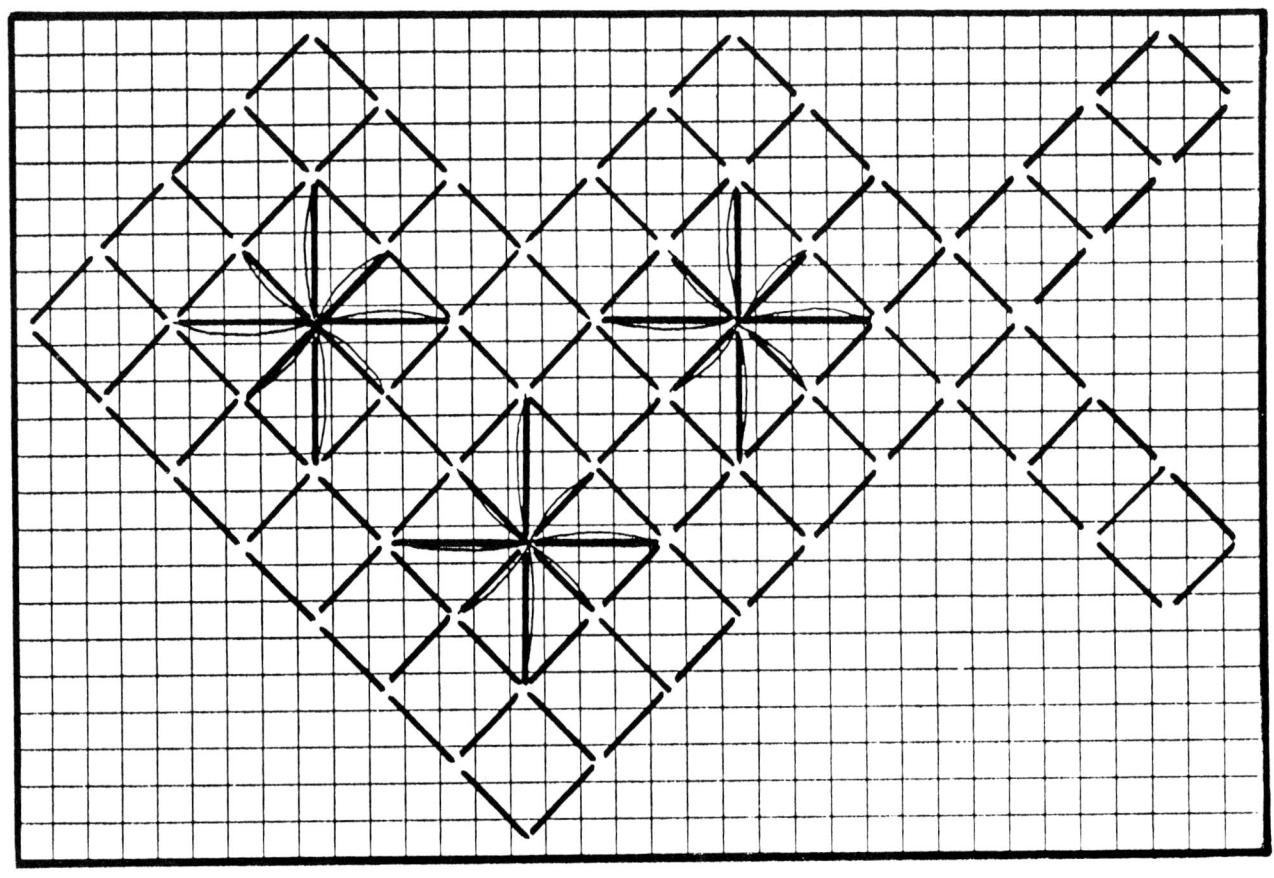

Pattern F-9 - Tight Pull

Work a grid of diagonal four-sided stitches. Fill the empty diamonds with an eyelet.

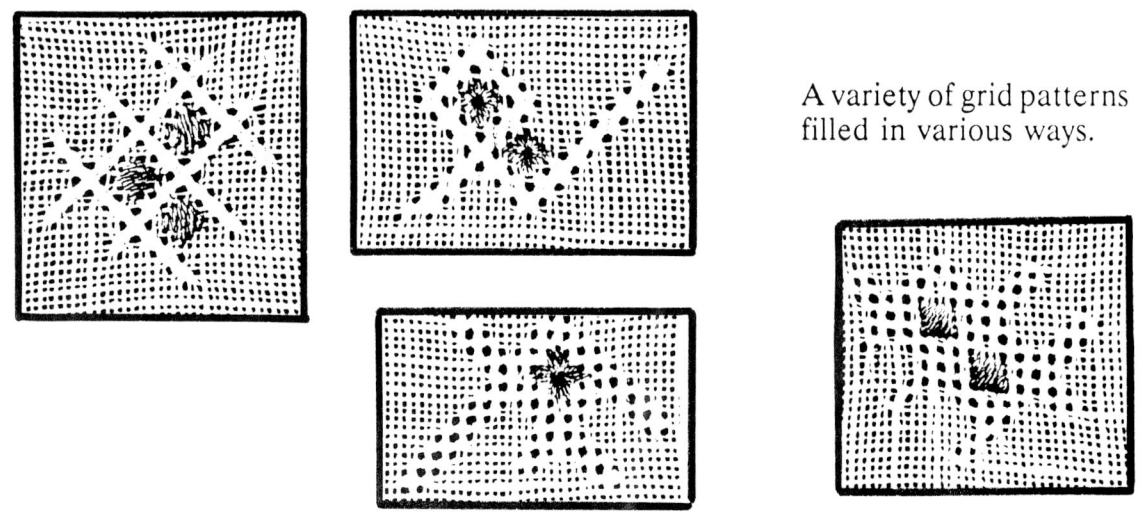

A variety of grid patterns filled in various ways.

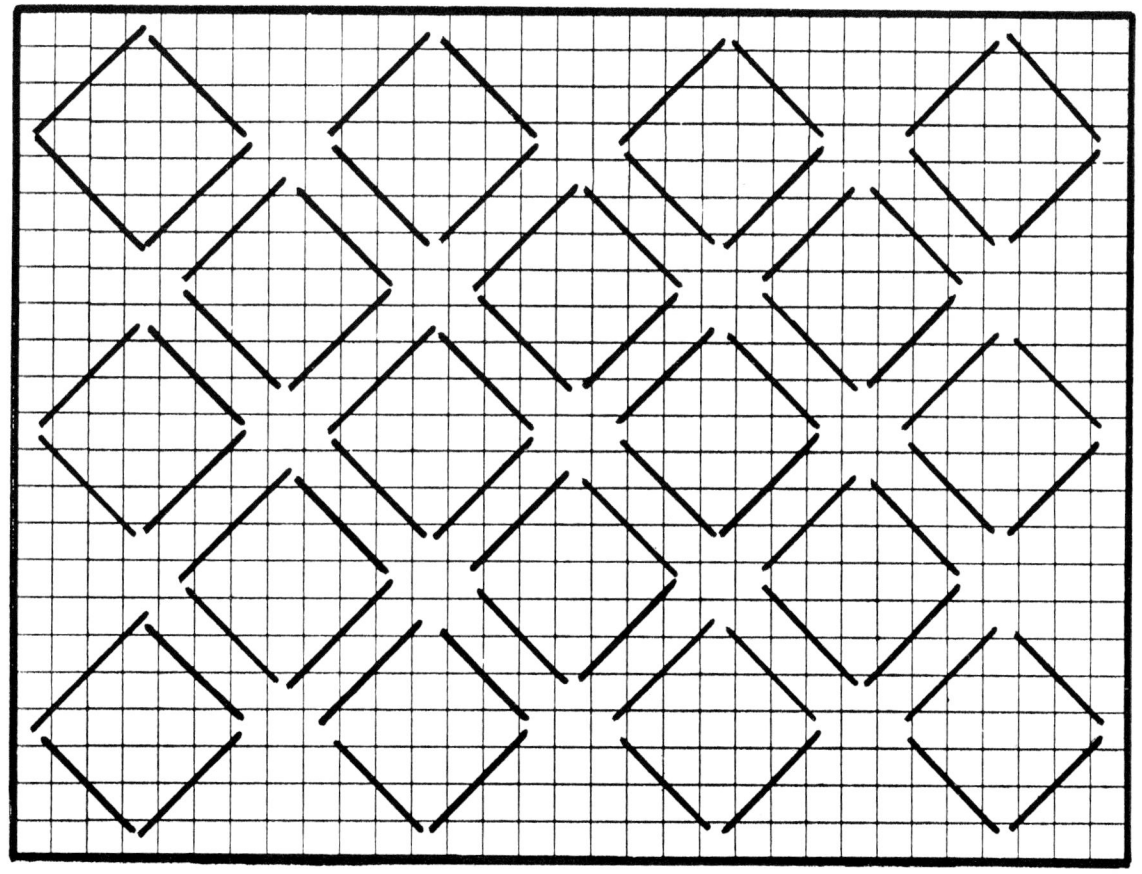

Pattern F-10 - Tight Pull

This pattern is especially nice as an overall pattern. It does not look at all like the graph seems to suggest.

Work diagonal four-sided stitch in diagonal rows, spaced as shown on the graph. The four fabric threads left between each set of four stitches (circled), make this pattern especially appealing.

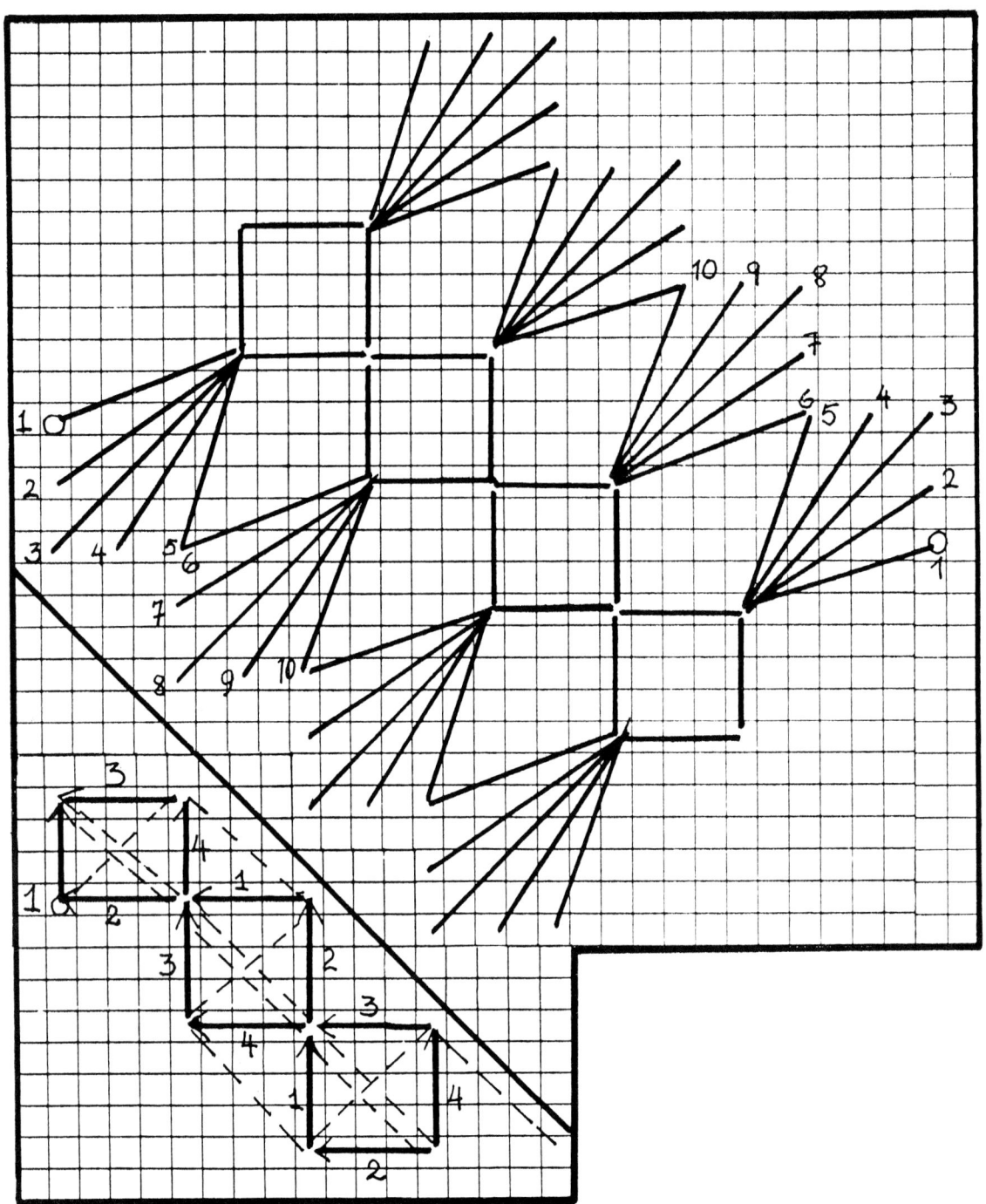

Pattern F-11 - Tight Pull

This pattern is ever so nice as its combination of stitches gives it a special effect. It works well in a diagonal border or in an overall pattern for which several rows must be placed close together as to share holes. The four-sided stitch must be worked over four threads.

PLAY A LITTLE!

What is a four-sided stitch? The answer would be: a square composed of four sides. This is correct, but is it not also correct that a rectangle, vertically or horizontally placed, also has four sides? What about a rhombus or diamond? Don't these also have four sides? Or a rhomboid or any other four-sided geometric figure? So why not stitch any of these four-sided figures using the principle and method or sequence of working as described in the preceding pages?

You will find that you can work lines, not only straight, but wavy and curved, with equal ease. As an example, I worked a small piece titled "Spring Meadow." Through it you can see the versatility of the ever important FOUR-SIDED STITCH!

Play a little! This is where fun and creativity and personal expression starts. There could not possibly be two "Spring Meadows" alike, in nature or in creative design!

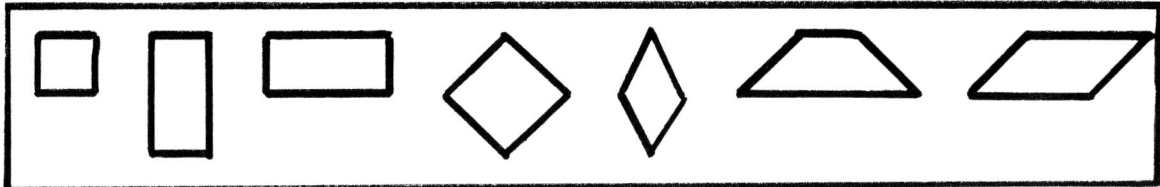

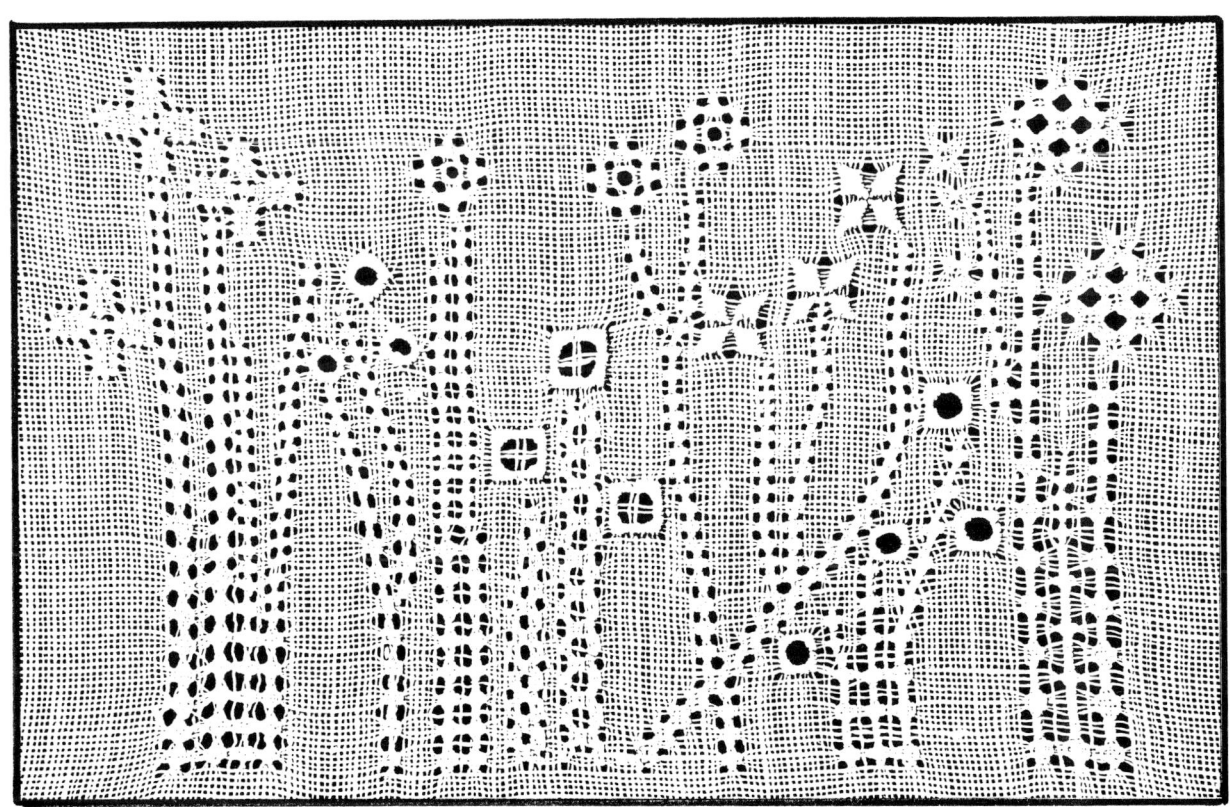

"SPRING MEADOW" Designed and worked by author

EYELETS AND RELATED STITCH PATTERNS

Eyelets hold a place of honor in Pulled Thread embroidery. While they are seldom used for a grounding patter, they more often than not are combined with other stitch patterns to form a composite. Anywhere in an embroidery where a vacant spot becomes apparent within a pattern, an eyelet can serve as filler as this little stitch is so adaptable in size and manner of stitching.

Basically, an eyelet is a hole, opened wide by the surrounding stitches. As a rule, one brings the needle up on the perimeter and inserts it in the hole which is to become the actual eyelet, pulling the thread outward. If this hole is shared many times as in most cases, it is suggested that you first distort the fabric threads in order to open the hole somewhat so that it can accommodate the many threads with ease, lying side by side, rather than being bunched up in a disorderly manner. To do this, insert the needle in the hole-to-be and move around and around in a circular motion. The hole should thus widen sufficiently.

Eyelets can be worked in a square, rectangular, diamond or round shape. They can have a "window cross" in their center or they can be worked in an irregular manner with the hole off-center. A few examples are shown on the sampler and are listed as Pattern G-1.

Eyelets can also be worked in half circles or even in partial circles or shapes. Several examples of patterns are shown and you will be able to create many, many more. The sampler only shows some of the possibilities.

Borders are especially nice and delicate when combined with eyelets or partial eyelets. When worked in fine thread, one can easily produce lacy bands comparable only to the finest needle made laces.

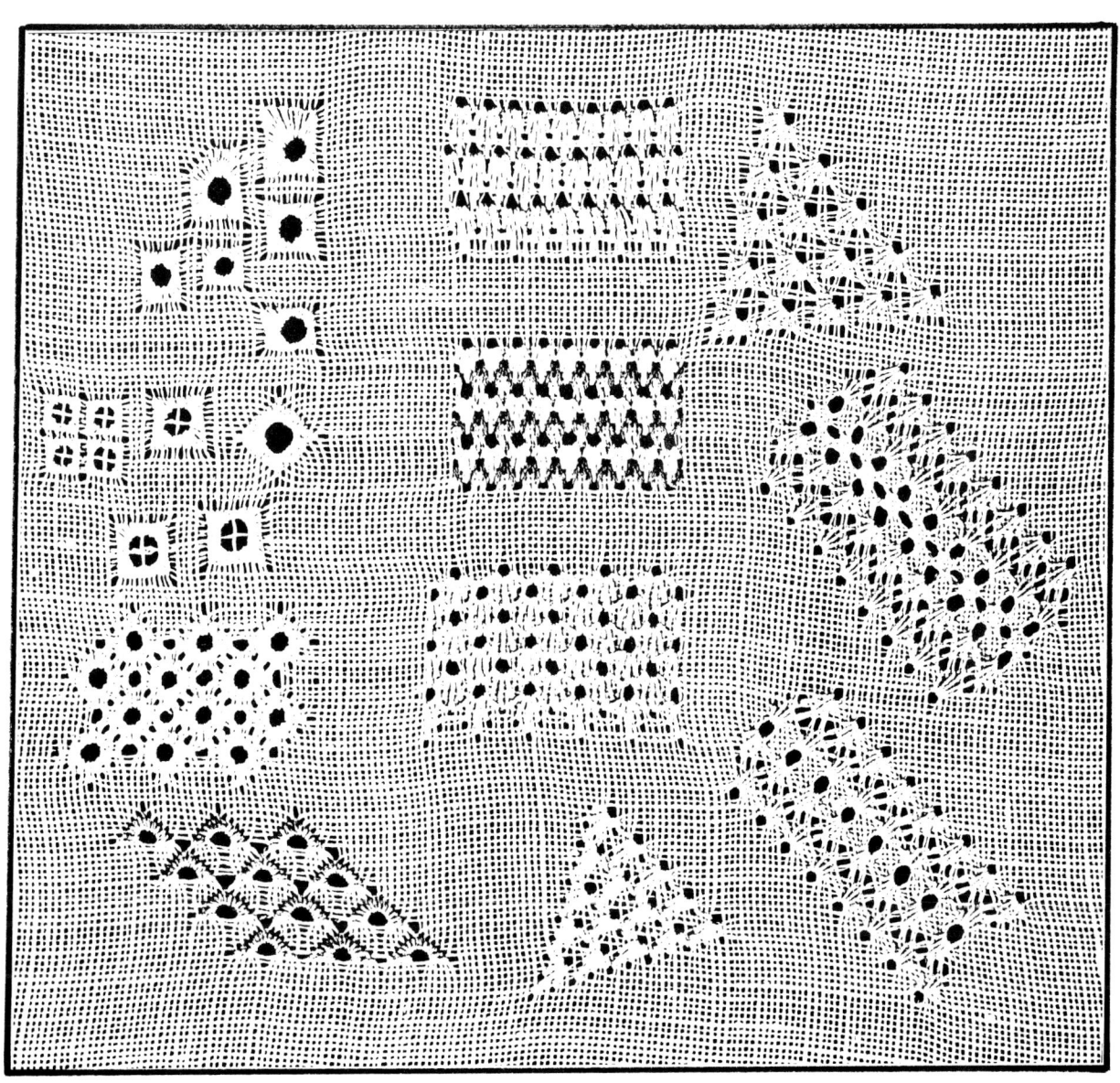

EYELET SAMPLER

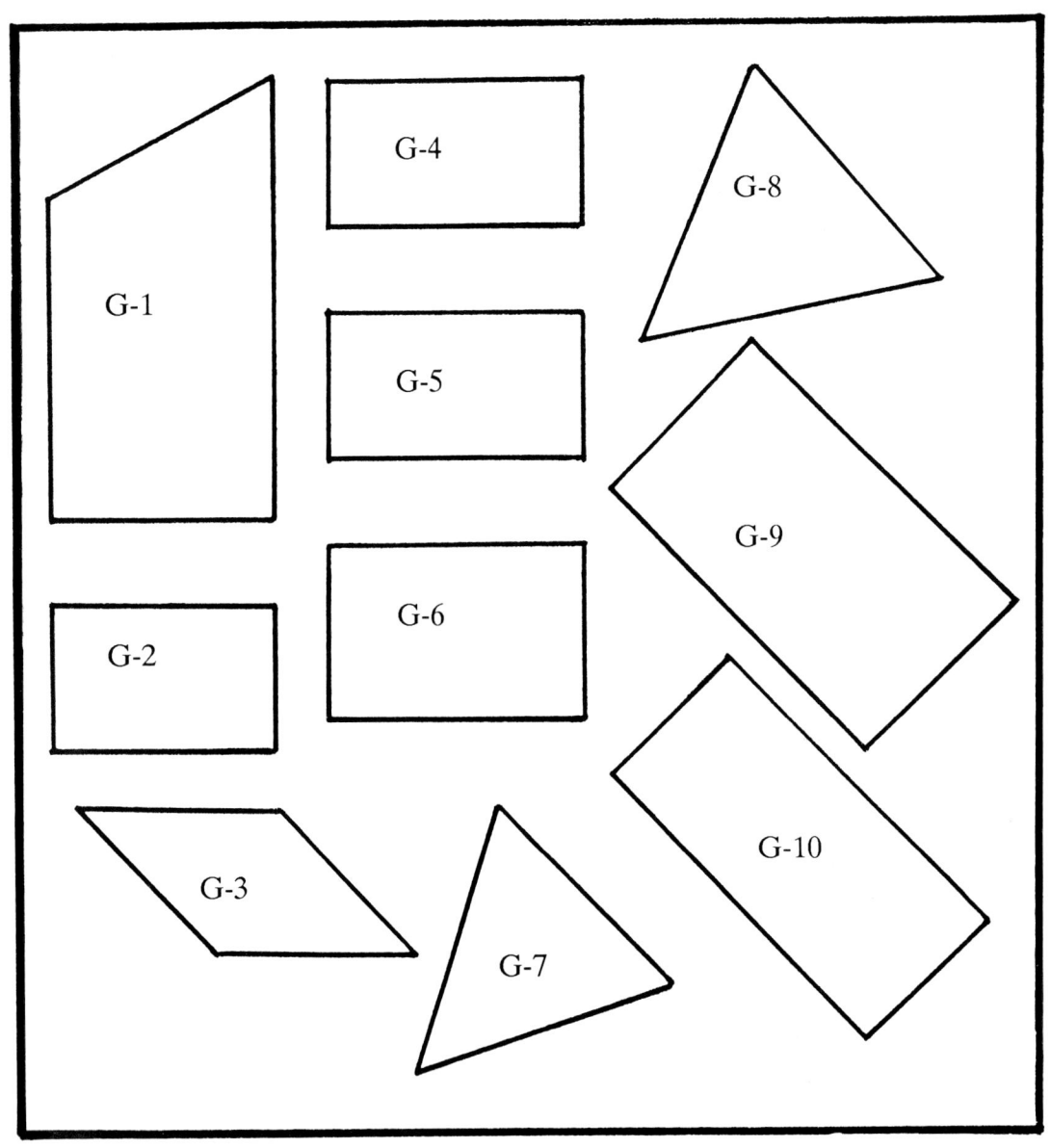

STITCH IDENTIFICATION CHART G - EYELET STITCHES

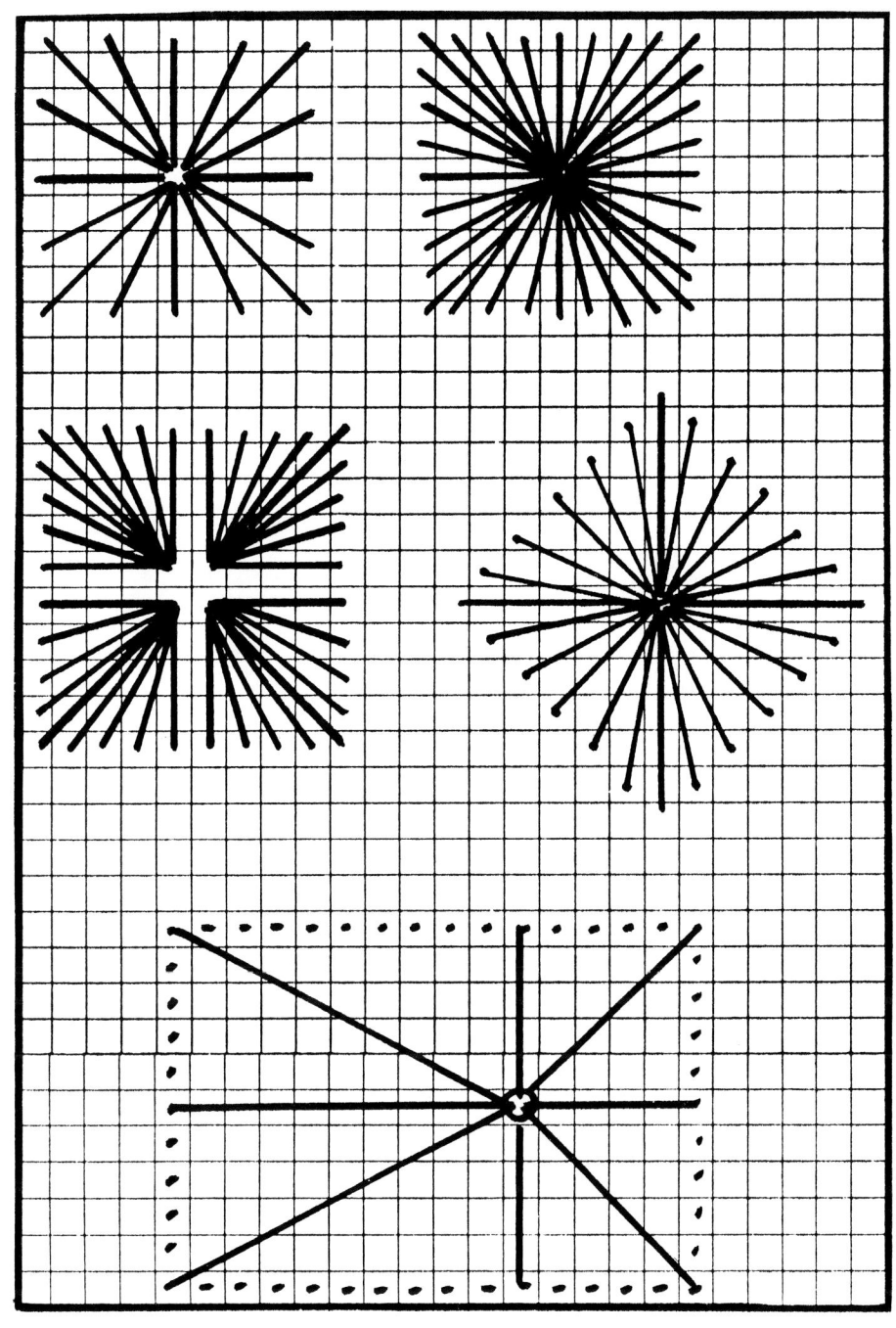

Pattern G-1 - Tight Pull

A variety of eyelets are shown. Always come up on the perimeter and insert the needle in the hole, with the directional pull outward, so that the hole opens up.

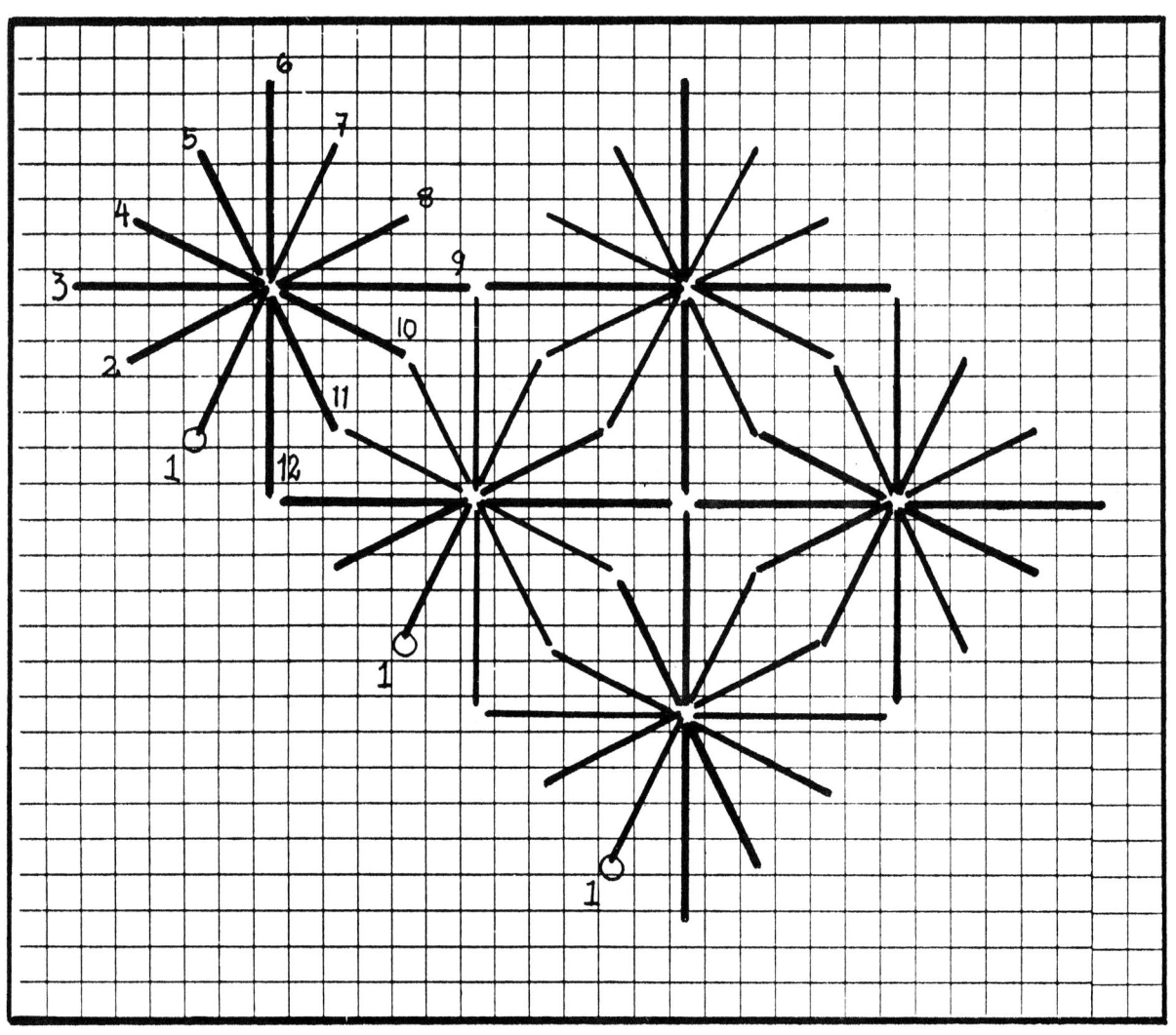

Pattern G-2 - Tight Pull

Eyelets as an overall pattern. Work in diagonal rows. In order that the first stitch pulls as neatly as the last, the sequence of stitching must be maintained.

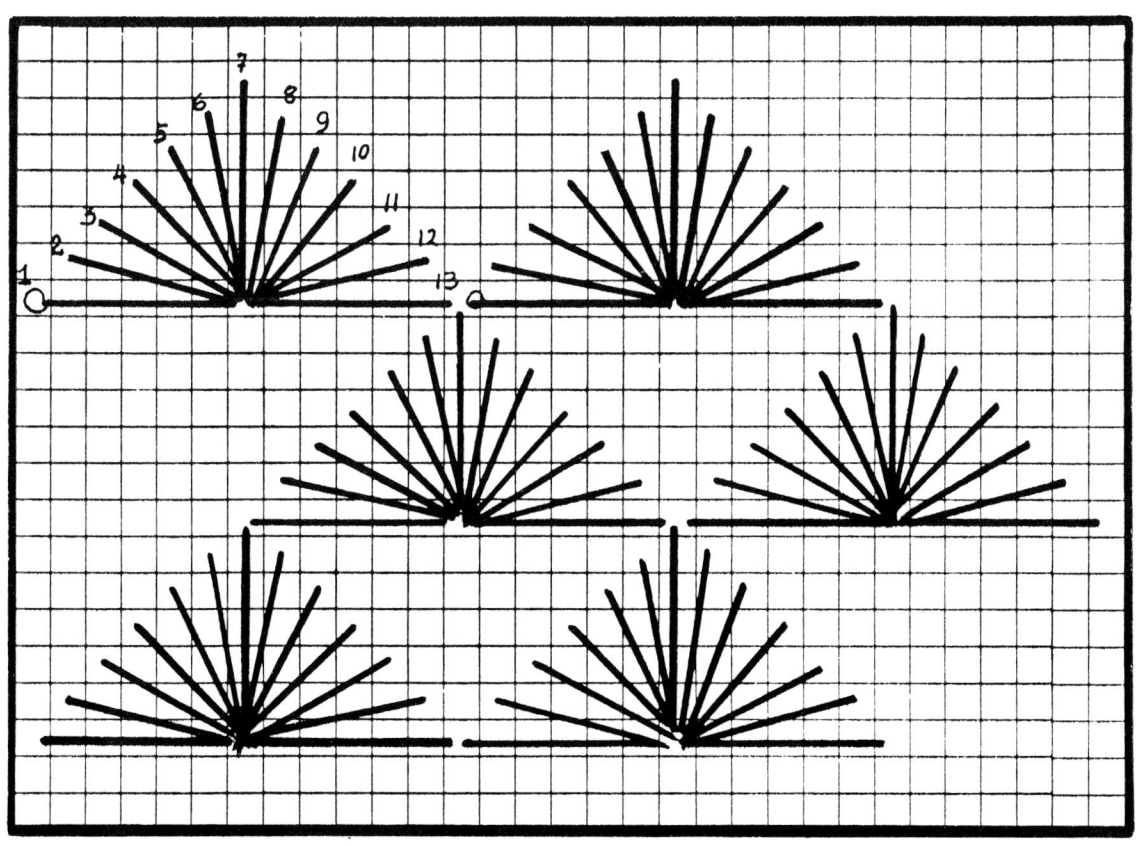

Pattern G-3 - Tight Pull

Half eyelets, work in diagonal rows. This pattern can also be worked in horizontal rows. When working the second unit, a carrying thread will become noticeable through the hole. This thread can then be caught by stitch 7 of the subsequent row, thus pulling it out of view.

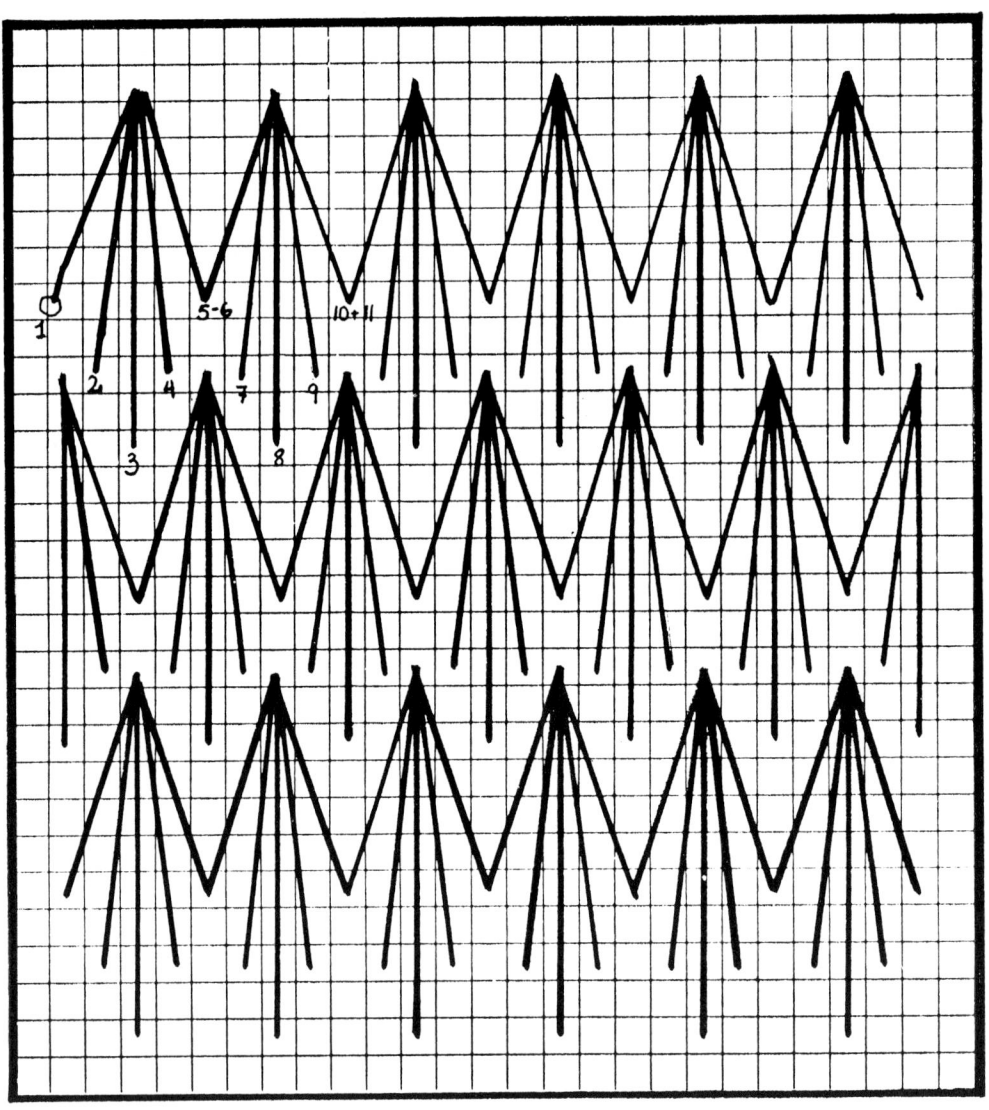

Pattern G-4 - Tight Pull

This pattern looks better when worked in a slightly heavier thread. It is ideal for a feathery look. I used it for the plumage of my swans.

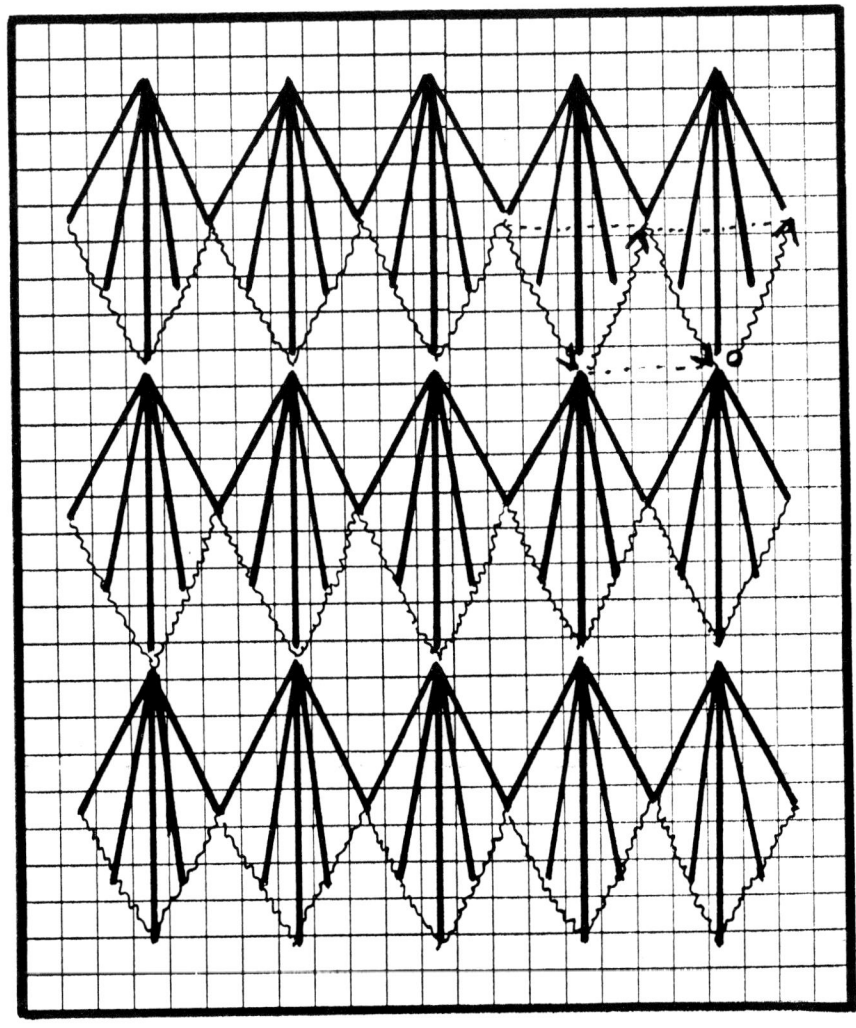

Pattern G-5 - Tight Pull

Use a slightly heavier thread for this pattern.

Work the partial eyelets first (heavy black lines). Then work a row of wave stitch in between the rows. I used gold thread (wavy lines) and thus worked my angel wings in this elegant manner.

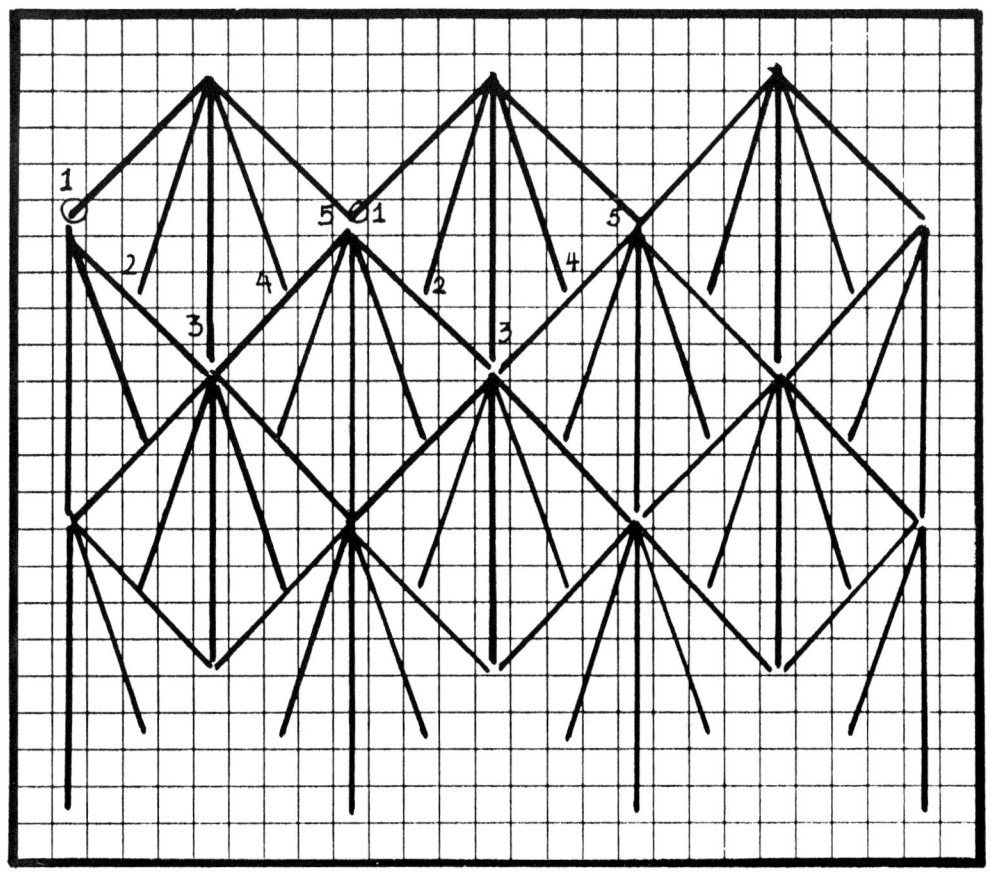

Pattern G-6 - Tight Pull

Use this pattern as a grounding as it fills an area nicely.

Work in horizontal rows. Notice that stitches share holes with previously worked row.

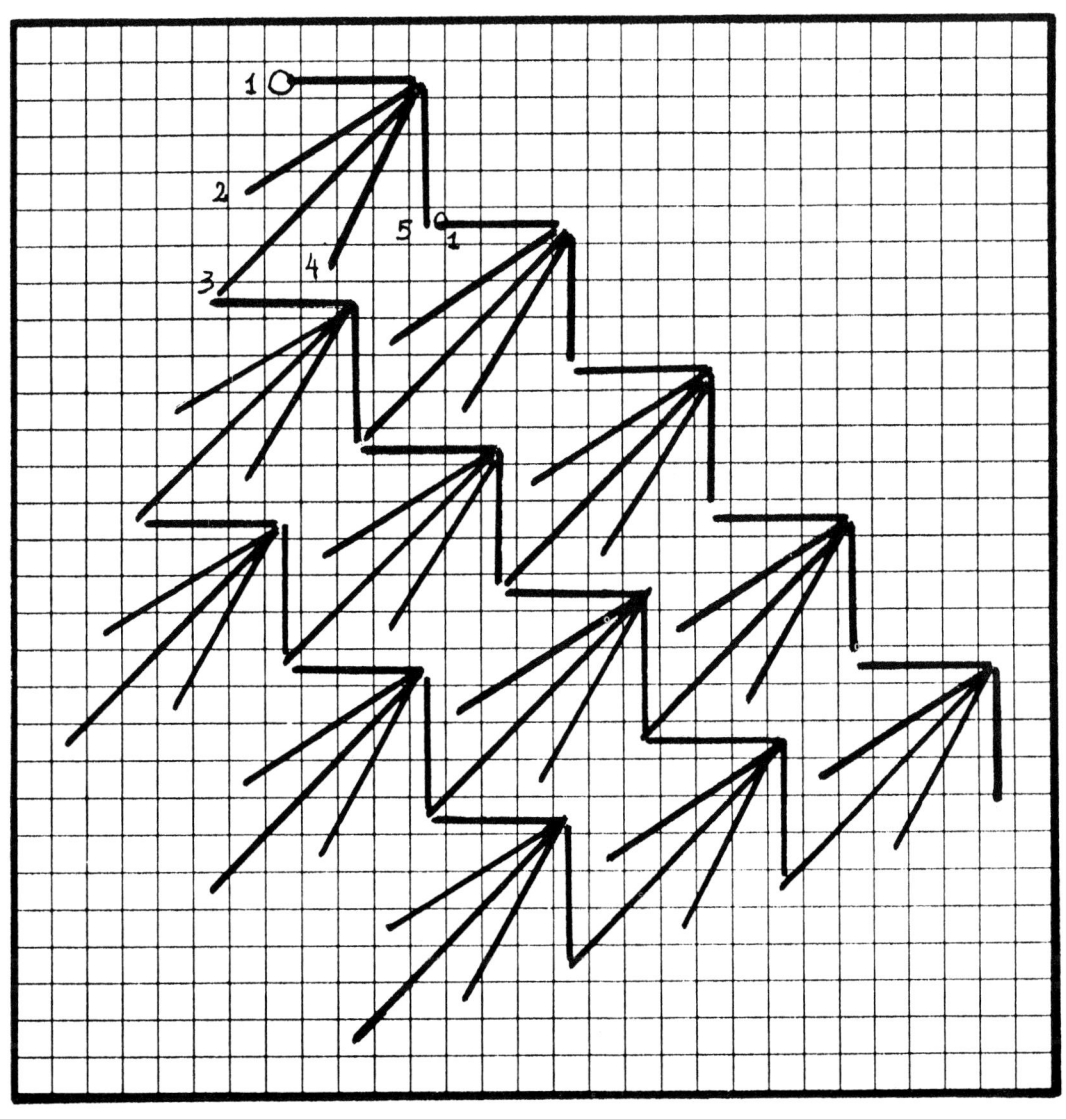

Pattern G-7 - Tight Pull

Work in diagonal rows as arrows indicate.

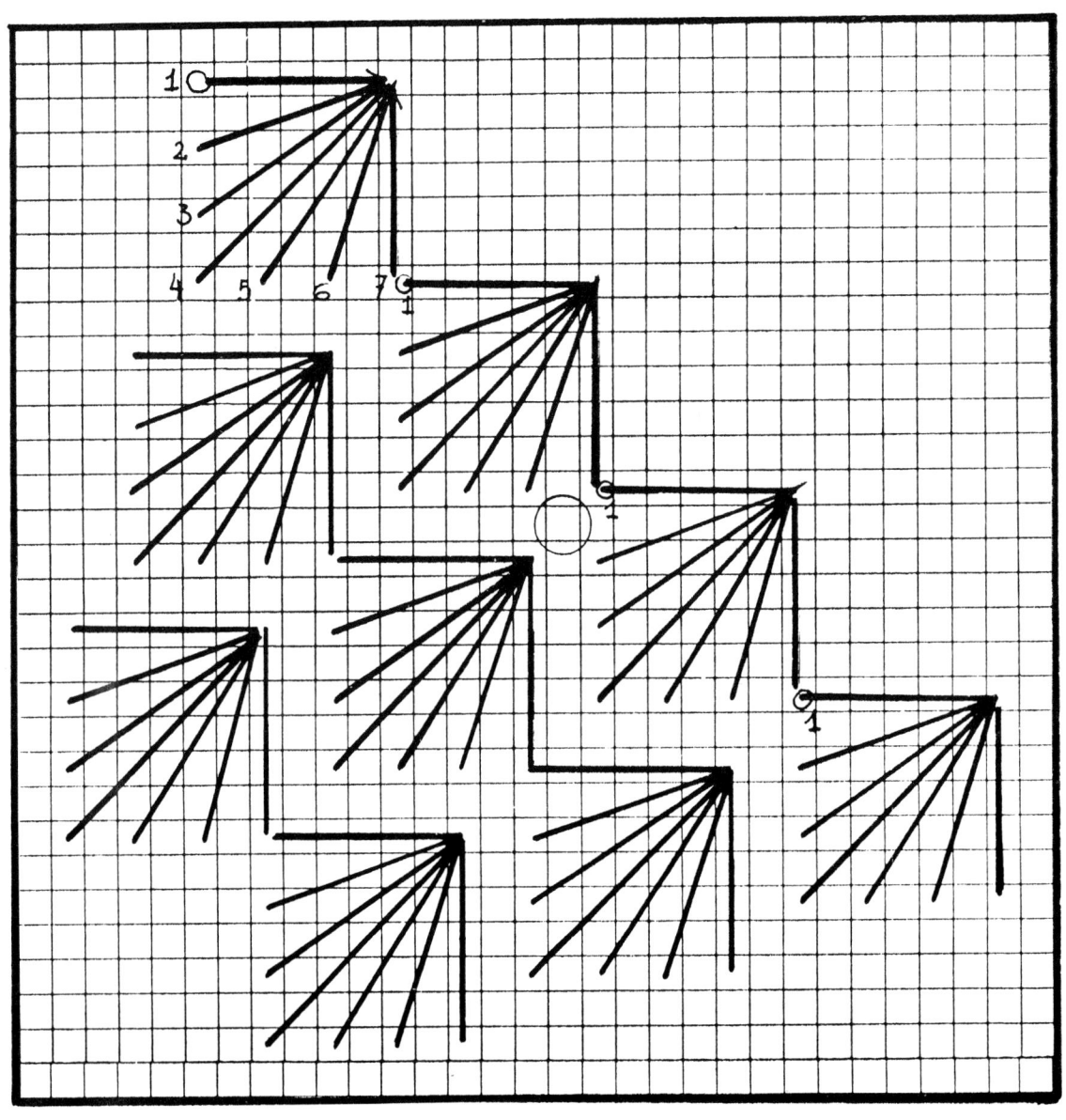

Pattern G-8 - Tight Pull

This pattern is placed on the diagonal and should be worked in diagonal rows. Space rows by two intersections as shown (see circle).

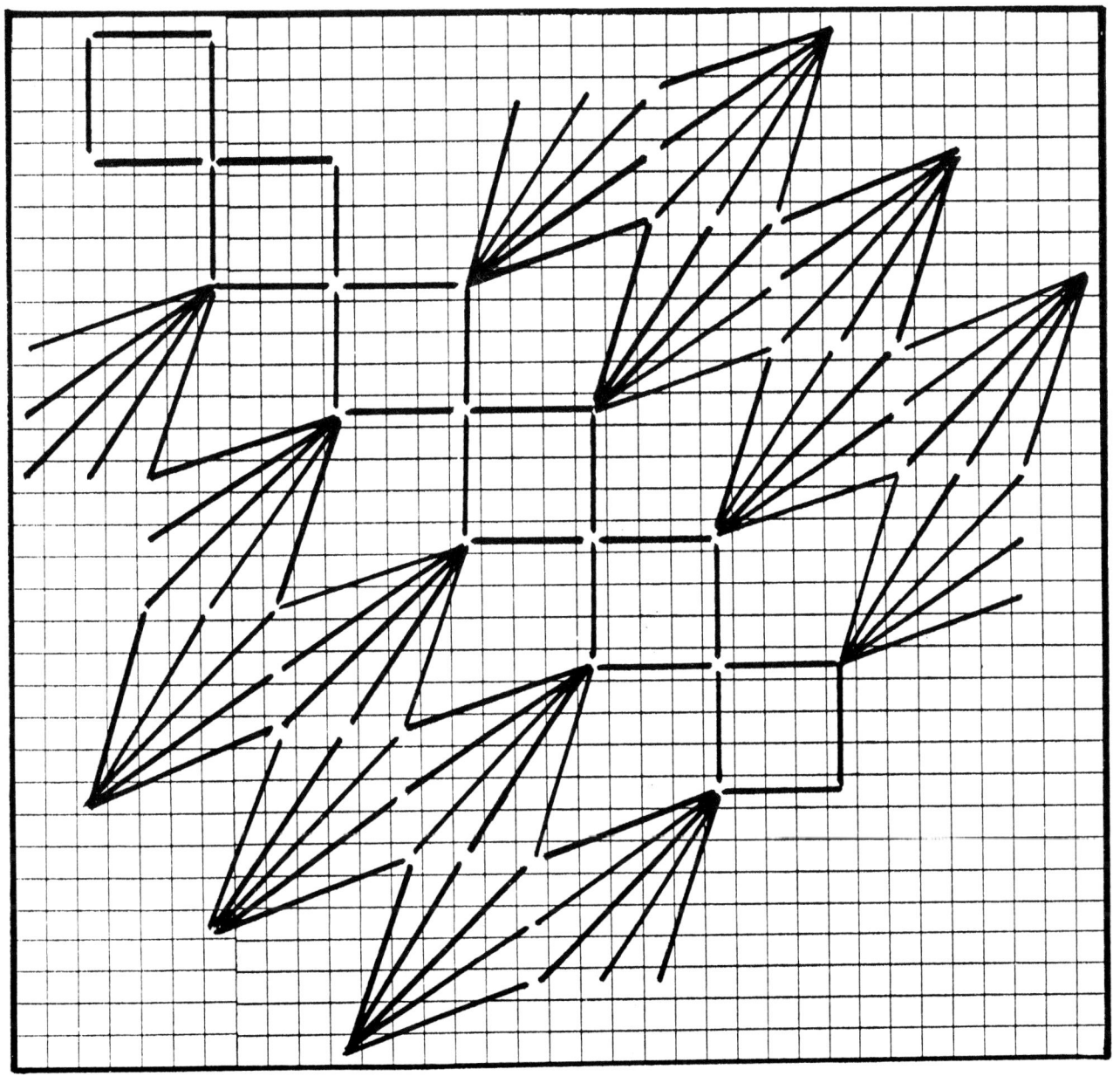

Pattern G-9 - Tight Pull

This pattern makes a beautiful diagonal border. It can also be used as a grounding pattern, but it requires a fairly large space to be appreciated.

Work a diagonal row of four-sided stitch. See Pattern F-11.

Work two rows of partial eyelets, their rays touching, i.e. sharing holes.

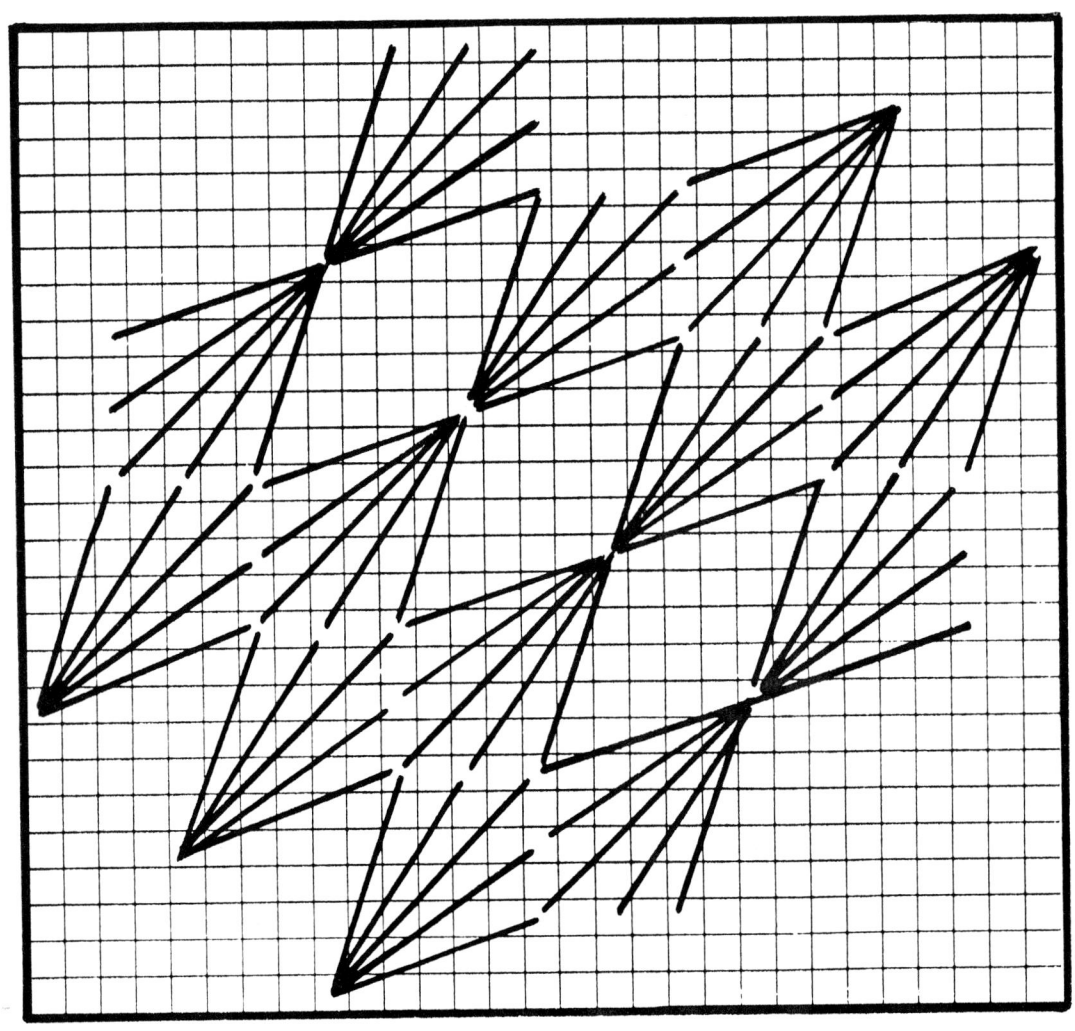

Pattern G-10 - Tight Pull

Work partial eyelets in diagonal rows, rays touching and sharing holes. This makes a lovely diagonal border as well as a good overall grounding pattern.

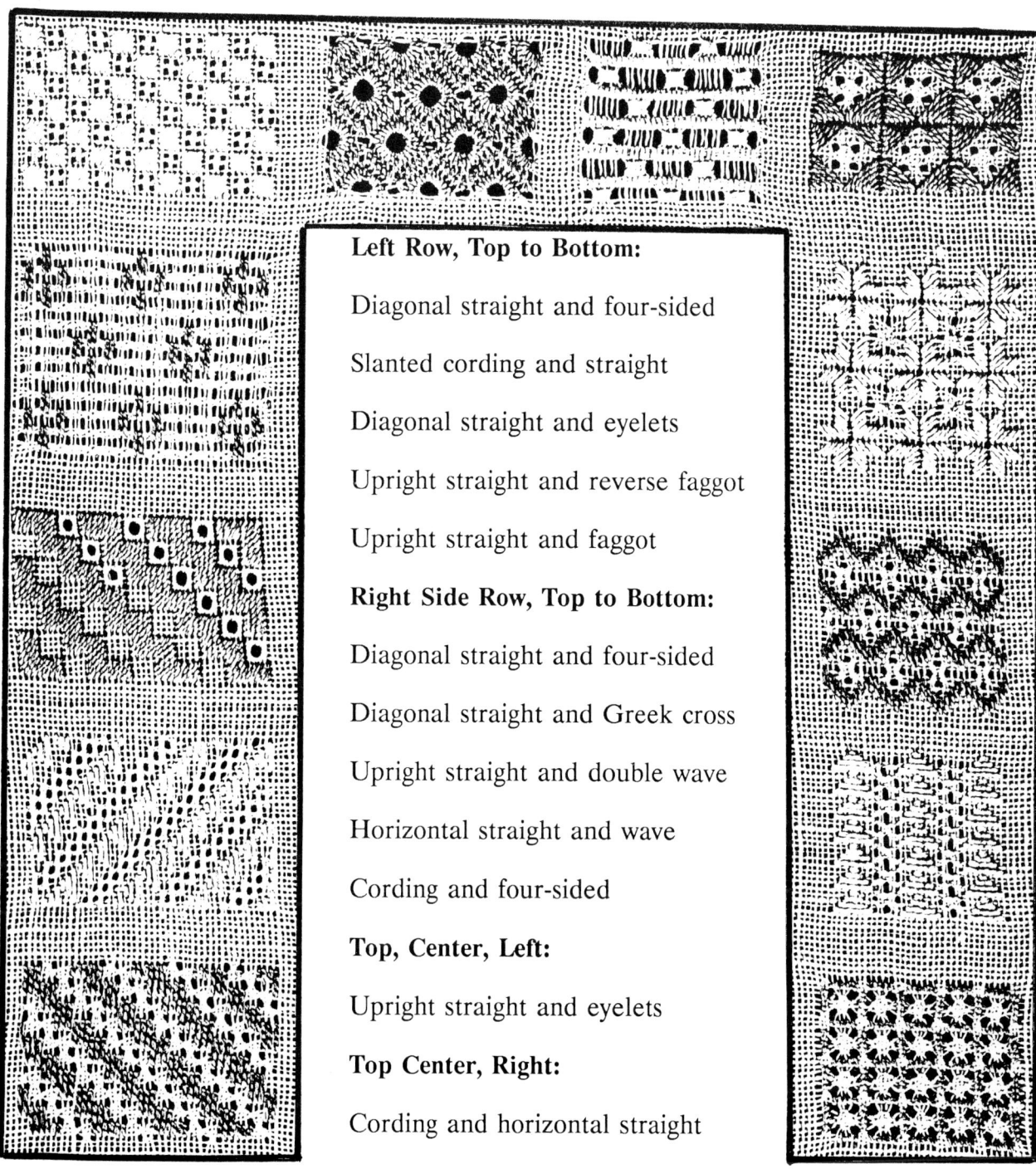

Left Row, Top to Bottom:

Diagonal straight and four-sided

Slanted cording and straight

Diagonal straight and eyelets

Upright straight and reverse faggot

Upright straight and faggot

Right Side Row, Top to Bottom:

Diagonal straight and four-sided

Diagonal straight and Greek cross

Upright straight and double wave

Horizontal straight and wave

Cording and four-sided

Top, Center, Left:

Upright straight and eyelets

Top Center, Right:

Cording and horizontal straight

AFTERTHOUGHT

These composite patterns will get you started in creating many more combinations of patterns from those diagrammed in this book. Play a little; it is easier than you think.

GOOD LUCK AND BEST WISHES!

REFERENCES

1. *Danish Pulled Thread Embroidery*, Fangel, et al, Dover Publications.

2. *Pulled Thread Workbook*, Mary Fry, self-published.

3. *Pulled Thread Embroidery*, Moyra McNeill, Unwin & Hyman.

4. *Embroider Now*, Hetsie van Wyk, Perskor Publisher.

5. *Sammentraeksmonstre*, Clara Weaver.

6. *Drawn Fabric Embroidery*, Edna Wark, Batsford.

The above list reflects only the books I am familiar with. I have probably left our other good references which does not mean they should not be pursued by Pulled Thread enthusiasts.

As a general reference on embroidery on linen, the following book is worth mentioning; *Overture and Finale to Linen Embroidery*, Ilse Altherr, self-published.